The Woman Citizen

The Woman Citizen

SOCIAL FEMINISM IN THE 1920s

J. Stanley Lemons

UNIVERSITY OF ILLINOIS PRESS
Urbana Chicago London

A version of Chapter Six, "The Sheppard-Towner
Act: Progressivism in the 1920s," appeared in the
Journal of American History, LV (Mar., 1969), 776–
786; permission to use the material therein is hereby
gratefully acknowledged.

Contents

Preface

The popular image of the twenties is simpleminded: the Jazz Age, the Golden Twenties, the Roaring Twenties—prohibition, bathtub gin, Fords, flappers, fanatics, Al Capone, Charlie Chaplin, Charles Lindbergh, Jack Dempsey, and Babe Ruth. It was America's last "happy time" before the Great Depression and hot and cold wars in unheard-of places. Until recent years historians contributed to the general stereotype, labeling it as the Age of Normalcy, "a deplorable interlude of reaction." [1] Now that era is being re-examined and revised, and the emerging picture is much more complex; even Calvin Coolidge seems more human, and the Harding administration might be considered a success. [2]

This study intends to be part of that revision. Its focus is on women, whose history is mostly unwritten, and it may be added to the growing list of books on women's history. [3] It has been argued that American feminism was a failure and that the 1920s was when it collapsed and died. I believe that the major current of American feminism, "social feminism," was slowed in the 1920s, but it neither failed nor was destroyed. If, indeed, feminism "failed," the tombstone will have to bear another date, perhaps the 1930s or 1940s.

I attempted to consider certain aspects of the feminist movement and the survival of progressivism in the 1920s. The point is that as various women and organizations worked for a broad reform movement to civilize, democratize, and humanize the

American system, as they worked for progressive reform, they advanced the status of American women. And as they fought for women's rights, they pushed progressivism along in a decade of waning reformist impact.

Gerda Lerner has noted that "feminism" is a broad term which embraces all aspects of women's emancipation—social, political, economic, self-perceptive. "Women's emancipation" in turn means the elimination of "oppressive restrictions imposed by sex." "Women's rights" is more narrowly concerned with the winning of legal rights, such as property rights, suffrage, office-holding, jury service.[4] In addition, O'Neill has made some very useful distinctions about feminism which I have borrowed. He noted that the feminist movement was divided into the "hard core" or extreme feminists and the "social feminists." The hard-core feminists put women's rights and women's emancipation above all other considerations. The social feminists also wanted emancipation but tended to subordinate this to social reform.[5]

Because historians are concerned with the elements of change and continuity, a historiographical debate has centered on the question of continuity between progressivism and New Deal liberalism. One line of thinking stresses discontinuity. Richard Hofstadter argued in *The Age of Reform* that the character, philosophy, and problems of the two movements were dissimilar, that the New Deal was fundamentally different. Carl Degler suggested a similar emphasis as he called the New Deal "the third American Revolution." Otis Graham's study, *An Encore for Reform*, buttressed the school of change by showing that 60 percent of his sample of surviving progressives in 1936 opposed the New Deal.[6] On the other hand, the current of scholarship from Arthur Schlesinger, Jr., Frank Freidel, Arthur Link, Richard Kirkendall, Eric Goldman, Clarke Chambers, and many others stresses continuity. Their studies show that progressivism continued and developed in the twenties, though with much less general support than in the previous decade.[7]

One of my principal contentions is that the social feminists constituted an important link in the chain from the progressive era to the New Deal. The Progressive Movement was a highly complex creature: the result of the union of many impulses for reform and order—a "movement of movements." One of these was the drive for women's rights. However, the Woman Movement of the late nineteenth century was more than rights for women; it took on the coloring of a crusade to save the nation from its sins. Even before the Progressive Movement had coalesced, great sprawling organizations of women had developed, such as the Women's Christian Temperance Union following Frances Willard's "Do Everything" motto. The women's club movement advanced from garden parties and literary studies to peace, purity, prohibition, pure food and drugs, clean milk, and conservation. At the end of the century the feminist movement became part of the agglomeration which is called the Progressive Movement; and the various elements cut across, reinforced, and promoted each other. Women saw a link between suffrage and temperance and other crusades, such as civil service reform, conservation, child labor laws, mothers' pensions, municipal improvements, educational reform, pure food and drug laws, industrial commissions, social justice, and peace. While feminism continued to have its own goals, it blended with the broader movement.[8] Moving with progressivism before World War I, the women's movement was accelerated by the war.

The complex character of progressivism contributed to its decline in the face of events after World War I. Some elements achieved their goals and were satisfied. Then the issues of war, peace, and revolution fragmented the movement; however, one segment continued to promote reform in the 1920s—the social feminists. These were the woman citizens of the 1920s, who wanted to use their newly won citizenship to advance the reform effort. They created new organizations and established new contacts to promote progressivism in the 1920s. They wanted the extension of government further into the areas of education, health, labor, and social welfare. The social-justice movement, led by the social workers, found its principal allies to be the social feminists. In supporting the "social progres-

sives," women's groups backed the most advanced element of
the Progressive Movement.[9] For example, when the Children's
Bureau revealed the shocking infant and maternal death rates,
women mobilized and eventually forced a reluctant Congress
to pass the Sheppard-Towner Act in 1921, the first federal
social security measure. The National Women's Trade Union
League and the National League of Women Voters advocated
national unemployment compensation, health insurance, hours
and wages legislation, and governmental control of production
and distribution throughout the 1920s. While the American
Federation of Labor sought advances by union action, the
NWTUL pushed for governmental intervention to remove the
threat and effects of unemployment. When most of the nation
would have surrendered Muscle Shoals to private interests, the
League of Women Voters was the only national citizens' organization to support George Norris's plans for the Tennessee
Valley. These and other women's groups fought for social justice after most had given up the struggle in the New Era.

The social feminists continued to work for women's emancipation, but their concern for broad reform brought them into
conflict with the hard-core feminists. The long fight for the
ballot had obscured the division, but it broke into the open
very soon and weakened the feminist movement in the decade.
Social feminists believed that the exploitation of working
women was a more immediate, greater evil than the assertion
that protective legislation for women impeded the emancipation
of all women by enhancing the view that women were unequal
and required protection. The extreme feminists rejected social
reform in favor of the pursuit of complete equality, which required the government to take a laissez-faire position on the
condition of women in industry. The hard-core feminists
argued that unless the government adopted laws to protect male
workers, then women should not have special laws. In the legal
climate of the 1920s, this meant no laws governing such things
as wages, dangerous trades, hours, and conditions.

While the social feminists played an important role in the

survival and development of progressivism, they have received
little notice.[10] The fact remains that social feminists held the
progressive faith longer than most. While many turned away,
women espoused progressivism as loudly during the presidencies
of Warren G. Harding, Calvin Coolidge, and Herbert Hoover
as they had during those of the previous three presidents. They
promoted progressive solutions because the objectives of that
movement had become closely identified with the century-old
women's movement. Having only won the vote nationally in
1920, they hoped to use the new tool to win their other goals.

Winthrop Jordan noted that he had begun his study, *White
over Black*, before the Montgomery bus boycott, before the
civil rights movement became the great cause, and before it
became fashionable to write a book on race relations. I want
to enter a similar plea. I began this investigation before I had
ever heard of Betty Freidan; in fact, I read the *Feminine Mys-
tique* after I had finished my work. My interest in women's
history was in no way stimulated by women's liberation, but
rather it grew out of an interest in the Progressive Movement.
The importance of women to this great reform era was shown
me by my mentor and friend, Professor Allen F. Davis, whose
special interest was the social-justice movement and most particularly Jane Addams. Even a cursory survey of the work on
women's history in 1964 revealed that almost nothing had been
written about feminism, women's emancipation, or women's
rights after women won the vote in 1920. So I originally set
out to explore the general question, "What happened after the
Nineteenth Amendment?" It turns out to be a question that
will require volumes to answer. I have focused on the social
feminists and their organized efforts, because they were most
clearly the heiresses of progressivism. Even at that, major issues,
all worthy of extended treatment, have been excluded. The
women's efforts to promote peace and to preserve prohibition
are book-length subjects in themselves. I have not dealt with
important topics such as birth control, marriage reform, women

in the arts, the flapper, the image of the woman in the movies, magazines, and the press, changes in the family, the role of the mother, or the impact of Freudianism.

Any study incurs its debts to people who aided its progress. I am very grateful to the staff of the Schlesinger Library at Radcliffe College, the Sophia Smith Collection at Smith College, the Ohio Historical Society, the Indiana State Library, the Historical Society of Pennsylvania, the Manuscript Division of the New York Public Library, the Library of Congress, and the libraries of the University of Missouri and Ohio State University. Allen F. Davis guided and encouraged this investigation from its inception. My father, L. C. Lemons, and my friend, Eugene P. Trani, have read the manuscript at various stages and given me valuable help. Finally, I owe much to my wife, Nancy, who contributed immeasurably in the course of the research, sifting through such things as rat droppings, swatches of cloth samples for draperies, and landscape designs in the uncataloged mass of the Cornelia Bryce Pinchot papers. Later she kept me from becoming grafted to the typewriter. Withal, none of these is to blame for the product; I gladly bear that responsibility.

NOTES

1. The changing perception of historians was ably discussed in Henry F. May, "Shifting Perspectives on the 1920's," *Mississippi Valley Historical Review*, XLIII (Dec., 1956), 411–417.

2. Donald R. McCoy, *Calvin Coolidge: The Quiet President* (New York: Macmillan, 1967); Robert K. Murray, *The Harding Era: Warren G. Harding and His Administration* (Minneapolis: University of Minnesota Press, 1969). Burl Noggle, "The Twenties: A New Historiographical Frontier," *Journal of American History*, LIII (Sept., 1966), 299–314, surveyed the literature about the period and noted an accelerated attention to the twenties in the last fifteen years. One even finds some historians revising themselves; for example, compare Paul A. Carter's *The Decline and Revival of the Social Gospel* (Ithaca: Cornell University Press, 1956) with his revisionist essay "The Fundamentalist Defense of the Faith," in *Change and Continuity in Twentieth-Century America: The 1920's*, ed. John Braeman, Robert H. Bremner, and David Brody (Columbus: Ohio State University Press, 1968), 179–214.

3. A partial list would include Eleanor Flexner, *Century of Struggle: The Woman's Rights Movement in the United States* (Cambridge, Mass.: Belknap Press, 1959); Andrew Sinclair, *The Better Half: The Emancipation of the*

American Woman (New York: Harper & Row, 1965); Robert Riegel, *American Feminists* (Lawrence: University of Kansas Press, 1963); Aileen Kraditor, *Ideas of the Woman Suffrage Movement, 1890–1920* (New York: Columbia University Press, 1965); William O'Neill, *Everyone Was Brave: The Rise and Fall of Feminism in America* (Chicago: Quadrangle Books, 1969); Anne F. Scott, *The Southern Lady: From Pedestal to Politics, 1830–1930* (Chicago: University of Chicago Press, 1970); Page Smith, *Daughters of the Promised Land: Women in American History* (Boston: Little, Brown, 1970).

4. Gerda Lerner, "Women's Rights and American Feminism," *American Scholar*, XL (Spring, 1971), 236–237.

5. William O'Neill, "Feminism as a Radical Ideology," in *Dissent: Explorations in the History of American Radicalism*, ed. Alfred F. Young (DeKalb: Northern Illinois University Press, 1968), 276.

6. Richard Hofstadter, *The Age of Reform: From Bryan to F.D.R.* (New York: Vintage Books, 1955), 272–328; Carl Degler, *Out of Our Past: The Forces That Shaped Modern America* (New York: Harper Colophon Books, 1957), 279–416; Otis L. Graham, Jr., *An Encore for Reform: The Old Progressives and the New Deal* (New York: Oxford University Press, 1967). Significantly, neither Hofstadter nor Degler spent much time considering the 1920s. Hofstadter's brief treatment focused almost entirely on Prohibition and the Ku Klux Klan, and Degler simply leaped over the period.

7. Arthur S. Link, "What Happened to the Progressive Movement in the 1920's?," *American Historical Review*, LXIV (July, 1959), 833–851, has an extensive listing of books and articles which treat the question from many angles. See also Richard S. Kirkendall, "The Great Depression: Another Watershed in American History?," in *Change and Continuity in Twentieth Century America*, ed. John Braemen, Robert H. Bremner, and Everett Walters (Columbus: Ohio State University Press, 1964), 145–189; Arthur M. Schlesinger, Jr., *The Crisis of the Old Order, 1919–1933* (vol. I, *The Age of Roosevelt*, Boston: Houghton Mifflin, 1957); Frank Freidel, *Franklin D. Roosevelt: The Ordeal* (Boston: Little, Brown, 1954); Eric Goldman, *Rendezvous with Destiny: A History of Modern American Reform* (New York: Vintage Books, 1956); Clarke Chambers, *Seedtime of Reform: American Social Service and Social Action, 1918–1933* (Minneapolis: University of Minnesota Press, 1963); Preston J. Hubbard, *Origins of the TVA: The Muscle Shoals Controversy, 1920–1932* (Nashville: Vanderbilt University Press, 1961); Howard Zinn, *LaGuardia in Congress* (Ithaca: Cornell University Press for the American Historical Association, 1959); Joseph Huthmacher, *Senator Robert F. Wagner and the Rise of Urban Liberalism* (New York: Atheneum, 1968).

8. Kraditor, *Ideas of the Woman Suffrage Movement*, 64–68.

9. Allen F. Davis, *Spearheads for Reform: Social Settlements and the Progressive Movement, 1890–1914* (New York: Oxford University Press, 1967); Irwin Yellowitz, *Labor and the Progressive Movement in New York State, 1897–1916* (Ithaca: Cornell University Press, 1965), 2–3.

10. Anne F. Scott, "After Suffrage: The Southern Woman in the Twenties," *Journal of Southern History*, XXX (Aug., 1964), 298–318. She has incorporated this material in her recent book, *The Southern Lady*. Most studies of feminism stop with the winning of suffrage or pass over the 1920s to deal with more recent periods, but at least two have assayed the New Era: Dorothy E. Johnson, "Organized Women and National Legislation, 1920–1941" (Ph.D. thesis, Western Reserve University, 1960); Valborg E. Fletty, "Public Services of Women's Organizations" (Ph.D. thesis, Syracuse University, 1952).

The Woman Citizen

ONE

World War I—"the first hour in history for the women of the world"

> The greatest thing that came out of
> the war was the emancipation of women,
> for which no man fought. War
> subjected women and war liberated them.[1]

The Woman Movement, the expansion of women's sphere and horizons, gathered momentum in the Good Years[2] before World War I. The feminist movement became part of the kaleidoscopic effort for reform and order of the progressive era. As women made gains in so many areas of concern, the division between militant and social feminists disappeared from view, only to resurface partially in the last stages of the suffrage struggle in differing tactics. From 1900 to 1917 increasing numbers of women were drawn into the effort to reform a wide range of the nation's political, social, and economic problems; but *the* crusade after 1910 was suffrage.[3] While some women had struggled to win the franchise since before the Civil War, not until the first decade of the twentieth century did it become a major issue to millions of women. The suffrage drive experienced a quantum jump about 1909–10 and another around 1913–14. New leaders, new tactics, new ideas, and new interest accounted for these leaps.[4] Suffrage leaders like Harriot Stanton

Blatch felt that the problems of all women were interdependent; therefore, she brought all segments together in the Women's Political Union.[5] Women in business offices displayed little interest in suffrage until about 1909–10; but then office girls, professional women, industrial women, society matrons, and club women marched in suffrage parades and joined the suffragists for the final assault.[6] The progressive mood infused the ranks, and suffrage rode forward as a progressive reform and as a means to further reform.

Then came the Great War. One of the illusions of the Good Years was that such a war was impossible. Anti-war sentiment, even pacifism, had become a significant element within social feminism. Leading social feminists, such as Jane Addams and Florence Kelley, were confirmed pacifists; and the major women's organizations had peace divisions which pressed peace as part of the women's movement. Many women's groups feared the effect of war.[7] They were dismayed at its outbreak and were reluctant to see the United States intervene. The suffrage organizations themselves had a strong pacifist sentiment in their leadership: in the National American Woman Suffrage Association were Jane Addams, Carrie Chapman Catt, Florence E. Allen; the National Woman's Party had Alice Paul, Harriot Stanton Blatch, Florence Kelley, Elizabeth Glendower Evans.

World War I acted as a catalyst to the feminist movement, just as it stimulated other reforms.[8] Progressives saw the war as a fulfillment of certain aims and applauded the social control exercised by the government over production, industry, agriculture, transportation, and prices. Many would look back on the war mobilization as a model for the New Deal.[9] The war allowed the prohibition crusade to win; though well advanced by 1917 with nearly two dozen dry states, it succeeded as a program to win the war.[10] Like prohibition, the suffrage movement had won many areas before the war, but the war accelerated the winning of the franchise by two years. The war experience demonstrated the need for new efforts in education and physical training and revealed a fundamental unfairness in American nationality laws as they pertained to women. The

Women's Bureau, an important element in the women's movement after the war, was a wartime product. In addition to reform, a new surge of organizational activity swept women, especially touching business and professional women. The National Federation of Business and Professional Women's Clubs was a direct outgrowth of the mobilization effort. Most important, the war greatly increased the confidence and self-image of American women. It demonstrated what they might do if given a chance.

Although horrified at the beginning of war, the women resolved to make the best of it. The *Woman's Medical Journal* argued: "It would be an act of cold calculating wisdom for the men of America, as they enter the Great War, to give the women of America equal part in the government of the nation. Women should be given here and now, the vote, not as a bribe —thank God, they need no such incentive to effort and sacrifice—but as an aid to enlarge usefulness." Cooperation, not subjection, would lay the foundation for the new democracy to emerge from the trial of arms.[11] The women's groups, even the militant National Woman's Party, tried to turn the national desire for unity to the advantage of the women's rights movement. The Woman's Party tactics were the most spectacular, but they harped on the fact that women were not full citizens, really not permitted to be a part of the nation because they were excluded from the franchise. Grant the vote and unity would prevail.

The tiny National Woman's Party, under the leadership of Alice Paul, attempted to apply the British practice of holding the party in power responsible. In addition to urging women in suffrage states to withhold support from all Democratic candidates, the NWP applied pressure directly on President Wilson. Many of the tactics which became famous and common in the civil rights struggles of the 1960s were first used by these women. They hectored and embarrassed President Wilson by picketing the White House, chaining themselves to the White House fence, blocking traffic on Pennsylvania Avenue by lying in the street, ceremoniously burning the President's

speeches, heckling him at gatherings, being arrested, and gener-
ating wide publicity by touring the country in prison garb on
the Prison Special.[12] The huge National American Woman
Suffrage Association disavowed such tactics but kept up quiet
pressure, offering a moderate, "reasonable" example to enlist
Wilson's support for the suffrage amendment. Instead, with
Maud Wood Park as their congressional organizer, the NAW-
SA perfected the art of pressuring and lobbying on Capitol
Hill.[13] Carrie Chapman Catt, who became president of
NAWSA in 1915 and who masterminded the suffrage victory,
dismissed the Woman's Party tactics as outdated and worse
than useless. Militancy would alienate the men, the only ones
able to grant suffrage. Suffrage needed the support of the Democratic party also.[14] Instead of harassing Wilson, NAWSA
pledged its support to the government and pressed suffrage as a
war measure.

The anti-suffragists denounced this suggestion as "Patriotism
—at a Price," and called the suffragists "conditional patriots." [15]
Catt replied that suffrage granted as a war measure would allow
America to escape "the charge that it has bargained with its
women—so much service, so much gain. . . . It is belittling
to the Government, not to the women of the country, to withhold grudgingly what it must ultimately give. . . . It must start
about setting the world right for democracy . . . for democracy's sake, not for the sake of benefits received at the
hands of women." [16] Suffragists repeated this line throughout
the war, and it proved to be an argument acceptable to Wilson
and members of Congress who had not supported suffrage in
the past.

Carrie Chapman Catt opposed American intervention in the
war partly because of her pacifism but mostly because she
feared the war would check the increased tempo of suffrage.
She engineered a resolution through the Executive Board of
NAWSA on the eve of American entry which pledged support
for the government in the war but put suffrage work first; and
she constantly urged the suffragists to put it ahead of war-service

work.[17] However, war work often crowded overt suffrage efforts aside.

The suffrage cause advanced despite reports from many states that war work predominated. The chairman of the New York State Suffrage Party, Mrs. Norman de R. Whitehouse, reported to the convention in August, 1917, that the war had greatly modified their efforts. "We knew when we made the offer of our services that we were the greatest organized body of women in all the country, trained in service and cooperation." While grudgingly received in some parts of the state, the suffragists had won out. Suffrage speakers spoke for the Liberty Loan and the Suffrage party sold over $4,000,000 worth of bonds. They organized Red Cross chapters where none existed, thirty-five in one county alone. They registered women for defense and canvassed for food-conservation pledges. "We have put government work first and suffrage work second." [18] Still, they won the vital suffrage referendum in November, 1917, finally cracking open the East.

In Cleveland the Suffrage party converted its club room into a Red Cross center; and their leading member, Belle Sherwin, served as chairman of the local Council of National Defense (CND). Most of the county chairmen of the Council of National Defense in Minnesota were suffragists, and others devoted much time to Red Cross work and knitting.[19] A Maryland leader reported: "Frankly, the Council of Defense has been using me and the other suffragists here so much for war we haven't had much time for suffrage. That is the condition throughout the state." She complained that she could not even get suffrage news and propaganda printed.[20] From Vermont the report was similar: "There is practically no suffrage work being done in Vermont. All organizations are aiding Red Cross and Navy Leagues. Helping with Liberty loan and Food Conservation." [21]

In Texas the women worked for the White Zone movement to eliminate prostitution and vice around the army mobilization camps, but they reported little success. Equally important was their drive to get rid of the governor of Texas, who was interfering with the University of Texas. Women in Nevada, Tennessee, New Hampshire, and Arkansas worked in the Liberty Loan drives and for the Red Cross. The Kentucky Equal Rights Association equipped the battleship *U.S.S. Kentucky* with 600 woolen outfits and purchased an ambulance for the Red Cross.[22] In Iowa five-sixths of the women in the food-conservation campaign were suffragists; in California the women did most of the war-service work, even in mixed organizations. The first vice-president of the Chicago Equal Suffrage Association served as chairman of the Women's Liberty Loan Committee. Assigned a quota of $780,000 worth of bonds, they sold over $7,000,000. The principals in the Council of National Defense in Chicago and Indiana were suffragists. In Indiana they campaigned for a woman factory inspector to safeguard women in industry, and they adopted the practice of knitting a bit of yellow into everything to dramatize suffragist war work.[23]

If war work came first, NAWSA made it benefit the suffrage movement. The work provided an opportunity for getting new recruits through contacts with other women's organizations, "an opportunity hitherto denied us as suffragists."[24] The NAWSA chairman of the Department for Elimination of Waste urged local chapters to secure newspaper coverage of their efforts: "Show how suffragists are demonstrating their love of country and home by willing co-operation with the Government, also emphasize that the first offer of service from them had to do with the home, thus laying forever that old bogey that wanting the vote takes women's interests from the home."[25]

NAWSA publicized the key roles taken by its leaders in the war effort, pointing out that the chairman of the Woman's Committee of the U.S. Council of National Defense, Anna Howard Shaw, was the past president of NAWSA. She was joined on the CND by Carrie Chapman Catt, the current president, Mrs. Stanley McCormick, second vice-president, and Antoinette Funk, NAWSA Congressional Committee. Mrs.

Henry Wade Rogers, treasurer of NAWSA, headed the Woman's Land Army of America.[26]

Carrie Chapman Catt ridiculed charges of disloyalty against Anna Howard Shaw and herself by noting that when the attacks were being made in New York, they were in Washington meeting with the Council of National Defense to formulate the women's part in the program. Finally she had to threaten libel suits when the charges persisted.[27] NAWSA answered the attacks of the anti-suffragists by emphasizing the role undertaken by NAWSA as an *organization* in the war effort. They chided the anti-suffrage groups for being paper organizations which had little worth to the war effort. The National Association Opposed to Woman Suffrage (NAOWS), the "Anti's," tried to reply to this barb,[28] but NAWSA paraded extensive evidence of the work of organized suffragists: the war-service census, canvassing for food conservation, Liberty Loan drives, Red Cross work, canteen service, knitting, protection of women in industry, Americanization of aliens, the leadership for most of the women's committees of the CND on federal, state, and local levels. At war's end two suffragists, Anna Howard Shaw and Hannah J. Patterson, were awarded the Distinguished Service Medal by the government, making them the first women in civilian life to be decorated for war duty.

NAWSA supported several hospitals in Europe called the American Women's Hospitals. This was a joint effort begun in June, 1917, with the Medical Women's National Association, which staffed the hospitals while NAWSA financed them. One of the units was disrupted temporarily by the abrupt departure of a doctor amid mutual name-calling. Carrie Chapman Catt sent Mrs. Raymond Brown to France to investigate and warned that NAWSA would replace every member in order to create a working unit that would win the gratitude of the French and bring credit to American women.[29] In both they succeeded. Nearly every member of the Women's Hospitals in France was decorated by the French and British governments, and money was raised in Paris to erect a monument to the American women.[30] The outstanding record of success made by the hospitals was a source of immense pride and satisfaction to the suffragists and the medical women. The Women's Hospitals remained overseas throughout the 1920s, ministering to disaster and war victims in the Balkans, Russia, Greece, Turkey, and Armenia.

While diverting the suffragists from their main task, the war work disarmed some critics and blunted the effect of the opponents' charges of disloyalty. The National Association Opposed to Woman Suffrage claimed that woman suffrage, socialism, and feminism were "three branches of the same tree of Social Revolution."[31] In 1916 the anti-suffragists had been vigorous preparedness advocates and equated opposition with a lack of patriotism, if not treason. War came and the National Woman's Party picketed the White House. This action greatly agitated the anti-suffragists, and they claimed that militancy proved the suffragists were unpatriotic.[32] Mabel Dodge, the Anti president, believed that the pickets discredited the movement; and she declared that the anti-suffrage cause was growing and could not fail. Mrs. James Wadsworth, wife of the New York senator, became the new president of NAOWS in mid-1917; and she hopefully declared that feminism and suffrage were faltering.[33]

The reverse was true. The militancy of the National Woman's Party only emphasized the reasonableness of NAWSA's position. Furthermore, the obvious war service of the suffragists contradicted NAOWS's allegations. The effect could be seen in South Dakota. In 1916 the suffragists got 48 percent of the vote in a referendum; in 1918, despite the fact that their total vote declined by 4,000, the opposition melted away by nearly 30,000, and the referendum carried by a healthy 64 percent majority. In New York in 1915 they lost by nearly 200,000 votes, but won by more than 100,000 in 1917. In Michigan they lost by 100,000 in 1913 and carried the state by nearly 25,000 in the 1918 referendum. The mood of the war enhanced chances, and 1917 alone saw an impressive string of victories.

While New York voted full suffrage, North Dakota, Indiana, Nebraska, Michigan, and Rhode Island granted presidential suffrage. Trying days lay ahead for the movement, but the suffragists rejoiced: "The New York State victory is the beginning of the end." [34]

Friend and foe saw the New York success as a major landmark in the suffrage struggle. Carrie Chapman Catt had believed that suffrage was inevitable before; now the opponents felt it. They responded with a frenzy of activity and claimed ever more loudly that socialism was behind suffrage. The Anti's hoped to capitalize on the middle-class fear of industrial strife and class warfare by associating the women's movement with revolution. They declared that the idea of woman suffrage was an integral part of Marxism. "Socialism, the parent of woman suffrage, twin born with Anarchy . . . has a strange and peculiar character and history." They charged that the New York victory was a triumph of disloyal groups. [35]

Feeling the pressure of suffrage momentum, Everett P. Wheeler, chairman of the Man Suffrage Association Opposed to Political Suffrage for Women, called for coordination and cooperation among the anti-suffrage organizations. [36] The NAOWS, which had existed for years without a national meeting, called its first convention for December, 1917. Mrs. Wadsworth set the new tone for the organization: "The keynote of our campaign now is the determination to protect America from the enemies within her borders." They would combat radicalism and subversion. She took hope from the New York suffrage victory, saying that it openly revealed the connection between suffrage and socialism, thereby making the defeat of both easier. [37] The change from anti-suffrage to shrill anti-radicalism was reflected in the decision to change their magazine from the *Woman's Protest* to the *Woman Patriot*. They hoped "to express the ideas of the *majority* of American women and afford them an opportunity to get the latest information of what the average woman can do and is doing to help her country." [38] The journal became increasingly irresponsible in 1918, reflecting the frustration of failure. The remnant of the NAOWS became the Woman Patriot Corporation after 1920 and lived on as a red-baiting assailant of social feminism.

The Man Suffrage Association converted itself into the American Constitutional League that same December in order to attract more support. From being strictly an anti-suffrage organization, the ACL adopted a platform of defending states' rights on all issues, including prohibition and suffrage. Wheeler, the chairman, asserted that imposing political suffrage for women on states that objected to it was undemocratic. "Compelling another State to adopt your own ideals is the essence of the German Kulture which is bringing woe to the world. It would be particularly unjust to impose it upon the Southern States involving, as it would, the votes of negro women." [39] The Women Voters' Anti-Suffrage Party (formerly the New York State branch of NAOWS) echoed the states' rights line: "No issue before the people today compares with the Federal Suffrage Amendment in its far-reaching consequences to them and its destruction of their liberties." It was states' rights or "Federal centralized despotism." [40]

As it became apparent that nothing could stop enfranchisement, both parties sought to take credit for the reform. Senator Warren G. Harding's stance paralleled that of other uncommitted members of Congress. He evaded an endorsement before the war by saying that his party had not taken a position. [41] When suffrage became popular in Ohio, he voted for the amendment in the Senate; even then he avoided any mention of the issue. Not until mid-June, 1920, did he publicly endorse the reform; and by that time ratification centered on Tennessee, the thirty-sixth state! Republican women urged the presidential candidate to pressure the Republican governor of Connecticut or New Hampshire into calling a special session so that a Republican state would give final ratification. Unwilling to antagonize anti-suffrage voters or embarrass any state organization, Harding declined, pleading states' rights. [42] On the other hand, campaign literature to women stressed that most of the senators, congressmen, and states ratifying the amendment were Republican.

Woodrow Wilson, after years of opposition, finally supported the suffrage amendment in January, 1918, endorsing it as a war measure. He privately urged his party members to support the amendment, and enough complied to carry the House of Representatives by the necessary two-thirds the very next day. In June he wrote that the war could not have been prosecuted without the women, and the nation's debt of gratitude could be paid by granting suffrage. He felt that women must participate in the post-war reconstruction.[43] He went before the Senate in September to urge the passage.

The anti-suffragists were dismayed and felt betrayed. They did not understand how Wilson could capitulate to suffragists who had besieged and insulted him and betray those who had always supported him. They had believed him to be opposed to suffrage, or at least a defender of the states' rights position. They noted that his first wife once considered becoming the president of the New Jersey anti-suffrage association.[44]

The bitter obstinacy of the opponents delayed the end. The amendment failed in the Senate in October, 1918, by only two votes and again in the lame-duck session in February, 1919, by a single vote. One negative vote was Senator James Wadsworth, who refused to favor the amendment despite the fact that his state had granted full suffrage and the rest of the New York delegation voted for the amendment. The women threatened his political life. "If the Republican Party in New York should be so foolish as to renominate Senator Wadsworth in 1920, the women will elect his Democratic opponent—that's all there is to that." [45] The Anti's hoped to stall the amendment long enough to prevent women from voting in 1920. If they held back until 1919, the only way to be ratified in time would be for most of the states to call a special session of the legislature. The Sixty-sixth Congress approved the Nineteenth Amendment in June, 1919, and twenty-nine states responded with special sessions to speed ratification within fourteen months.

The Anti's sought to stop the amendment finally in the courts. In April, 1920, the field secretary of the American Constitutional League sent an urgent call to eleven anti-suffrage

organizations to flood the courts with suits. He warned that
the plan must be "strictly confidential until we are . . . ready
to GO INTO COURT." [46] When Tennessee voted to complete the
ratification, the ACL tried to enjoin the secretary of state from
issuing the ratification proclamation, but he ignored them. Next,
the president of the ACL, Charles S. Fairchild, filed a suit
against the amendment, hoping to tie it up in litigation at least
until after the November elections, but the U.S. Court of
Appeals dismissed the suit as "frivolous and taken for delay." [47]
The Maryland League for State Defense then challenged the
validity of the amendment and the 1920 elections by bringing
suit against the registration of two Baltimore women. The petition argued that Maryland had been deprived of equal representation in the Senate because the electors of her senators
were dictated by thirty-six other states. They had determined
who could vote in Maryland over her objection, thereby attacking the very basis of the state government and destroying its
autonomy. Because Maryland had not consented, the amendment was invalid in that state. Furthermore, they argued, the
Nineteenth Amendment was illegal because it went beyond the
power of amendment of the U.S. Constitution. The league dismissed the Fifteenth Amendment, which is almost identical, as
being a dead letter and a product of revolution and military
force, "when civil war overrode all constitutional guarantees." [48]

These fine arguments were wasted as the Baltimore Court of
Common Pleas viewed the suit as a farce and dismissed it. The
Maryland Court of Appeals upheld the lower court. Finally,
Fairchild filed another suit with the U.S. Supreme Court in
1921, only to see it thrown out too. The American Constitutional League found the climate of the 1920s congenial and persisted through the period as an opponent of social feminism and
progressive reform.

II

World War I was not just a boon to suffrage; the entire feminist movement received a boost. Women felt the effect and

wanted to do their part. They were exhilarated by the chance to serve the nation, to aid in the national defense.[49] They harried government officials for something to do. This eagerness to join the war effort caused one commentator to observe later: "During the wartime period the women of this country were happier, probably, than at any other time in this twentieth century. . . . It was a great war, and the women in this country had a fine time; it is this joy of women in war time which must be taken into account in any scheme for universal peace, for women will not cease to run to the bugle's calling until something more interesting appears in their lives."[50]

Harriot Stanton Blatch exemplified this excitement, declaring: "War!—it does make the blood course through the veins."[51] She believed the war was liberating women from old molds and stereotypes, providing new opportunities, and making them economically independent. "American women have begun to go over the top. They are going up the scaling-ladder and out into All Man's Land."[52] She expected the virtual emancipation of women to be achieved if the country fully mobilized them. Agreeing with Theodore Roosevelt's notion that the vigorous life produced a healthy and virile race, she declared: "War compels women to work. That is one of its merits. . . . Active mothers ensure a virile race. . . . The rapidly increasing employment of women to-day, then, is the usual, and happy accompaniment of war."[53] She noted that women in all walks of life were finding a new sense of purpose, a greater cause: "She radiates the atmosphere, 'I am needed!' "[54] The response of women's groups, especially specialized professional organizations, substantiated Blatch's impression. Furthermore, the government's use of women, although ambiguous in intent, revealed a recognition that women could and would play a role in the war effort. The full effect of women's activities for war service never received a proper test; the war ended too soon. However, the importance of maintaining home-front support and enthusiasm for the cause certainly made the massive volunteer effort of women more than harmless, meaningless, utterly trivial.[55]

The government created the Woman's Committee of the U.S. Council of National Defense to organize and coordinate woman power. The committee had suffragists and anti-suffragists; however, only two of the eleven members were clearly opponents. Anna Howard Shaw, the chairman, fought against the secondary stature of the Woman's Committee and sometimes complained about men running everything.[56] Having only advisory powers and little money, it still did its work rather well by taking advantage of the extensive women's organizations and their willing spirit. It registered women all over the country for war service and canvassed them to inspire food conservation. The Food Administration under Herbert Hoover had the task of stimulating new production and conserving food. The CND coordinated women's efforts for the Food Administration. Badges were offered to homemakers who pledged to follow government instructions, and within two months the chairman of NAWSA's Department of Elimination of Waste requested 10,000 badges from Hoover.[57] The CND cooperated with the Children's Bureau in the Children's Year Campaign and helped save the lives of thousands of infants. From this latter effort grew the tremendous organization support among women for a maternity- and infancy-protection bill. The Committee on Women in Industry of the CND investigated conditions of women workers in war industries, found them bad, and stimulated additional pressure to establish federal working standards and a Women's Bureau.

While some of these activities might be dismissed as "utterly trivial," they had the positive effect of promoting the position of women. At least the government had to recognize them, new pressures for reform were created, and the opponents could not sustain their assertions of disloyalty in view of the extensive activity in behalf of the war effort—trivial or otherwise. The activities of women in the war showed surprising variety and gave evidence of how far women had come in a century. Gentlewomen rolled bandages and knitted, but women manned the war arsenals too. College girls worked on farms, women lawyers on exemption boards, women draftsmen in the Navy Department, and women physicians in hospitals in France. It all seemed so new that one magazine declared: "In a few short months since war was declared you have completely remade your lives." [58]

An unusual facet of the war effort was the appearance of volunteers for agricultural service.[59] The Woman's Land Army of America attempted to increase food production by mobilizing female labor to replace men gone to war. The idea had its first trial in the spring of 1917 in New York, when a serious shortage of farm labor threatened. The mayor of New York appointed a Committee on Women in Agriculture, and a camp was established at Bedford after the model of the English Land Army. An unoccupied house was secured and equipped, a supervisor named, women recruited from college and seasonal trades, and standard wages, working, and living conditions adopted. The women lived in the house and worked by day on the neighboring farms. The state's Bureau of Employment sent out additional units to pick fruit and perform parttime jobs.

The idea was so successful that the Woman's Committee of the CND asked the Woman's National Farm and Garden Association to call a conference of organizations concerned about the labor shortage and the need for increased food production. The conference met in New York on December 21, 1917, and created the Woman's Land Army, which began forming state branches. The following year forty states were organized and 15,000 women joined. Most were assembled into units and worked in camps like that at Bedford; the rest were used piecemeal as emergency groups. The eight-hour day was rigidly maintained to prevent any exploitation. In Illinois the Land Army established "Liberty Farms" to train women for farm work. The impact of this work on the suffrage movement was suggested by a magazine which felt that farm work helped swing the vote to women in New York. After the war, the remnants of the Land Army flowed into the Woman's National Farm and Garden Association.[60]

Business and professional women gained status in the war as they took and made openings to prove their equality. By mid-

1918, 11,742 registered nurses had volunteered and had been assigned to military duty. They comprised one-fifth of the nation's 66,000 nurses. So many went that a serious shortage developed for civilian needs. New enterprises and the removal of nearly 3,000,000 men into the military made additional business opportunities for women. Special classes were arranged for them to prepare for civil service exams, teach them bookkeeping, typing, and stenography. The federal government urgently needed women to fill civil service jobs to relieve men of non-military duties. The Secretary of the Navy opened his department to women, including the skilled position of draftsman. War demands brought women into their own in civil service. Before the war between 5 and 10 percent were women, but the proportion leaped to 20 percent during the war. At this time women also received 75 percent of the appointments in Washington and 50 percent of those elsewhere.[61]

The small, vocal Women Lawyers' Association leaped at the chance. One member offered to form a cavalry regiment of women. Her offer, like that of Theodore Roosevelt, was rejected. The association urged women lawyers to volunteer their skills in order to speed the mobilization effort. Their special training meant they owed the country "just so much more than women of lesser degree of expertness." [62] As the war continued the *Women Lawyers' Journal* declared that women lawyers now "had greater opportunities of aiding their country than ever before and have worked side by side with men lawyers, proving their equal ability." Their expertise put them on exemption boards, legal advisory committees, occupational boards, and preparedness committees. It was no longer necessary to wait for equality of numbers to bring equal opportunity. "Women lawyers know the opportunity has come." [63]

Women physicians felt the same; the war would be a chance to prove their claims of equality. "This is surely the day of opportunity for medical women. . . . Medical women are coming into their own." The *Woman's Medical Journal* argued that even if women were not accepted into the Army Medical Corps, the gaps caused by departing men would force more and more hospitals to turn to medical women in the emergency. Schools and hospitals previously closed began to admit women, and the U.S. Public Health Service opened to women physicians.[64]

The Medical Women's National Association attempted to gain equal recognition for its physicians throughout the war. In June, 1917, they enthusiastically endorsed a resolution urging the Secretary of War to utilize women physicians to the fullest and asked that they be given opportunities equal to men "both as members of the staffs of base hospitals and otherwise; and that women so serving be given the same rank, title and pay given to men." [65] The Illinois CND endorsed this proposal with a unanimous resolution. Numerous women applied for commissions in the Army Medical Corps but were rejected because of their sex. Army regulations stipulated that army physicians had to be men. The medical women agreed to accept anything the government would offer, just to have the chance to serve. "We should free ourselves from every vestige of ambitious pride and respond with generous disinterestedness." [66] The women urged President Wilson to appoint women by executive order until legislation could eliminate the word "male" from the regulations. General William C. Gorgas told the American Medical Association convention in June, 1918, that he saw no reason why women physicians should not be given equal recognition, and the AMA adopted a resolution calling for equality for medical women in the Army Medical Corps.[67]

The CND created a Volunteer Medical Corps in January, 1918, and reorganized it in August to include all qualified physicians who did not hold commissions. The *Woman's Medical Journal* urged women physicians to enlist since it was the only chance to be enrolled for military service under existing conditions. They would demonstrate their willingness as well as provide a list in case of need.[68] This gesture, coupled with the American Women's Hospitals, would promote the status of medical women. Because the government would not accept them in the Army Medical Corps, the Medical Women's National Association organized the American Women's Hospitals in Europe and induced NAWSA to undertake the major burden of support. In the early 1920s Congress voted military ranks to nurses, but ignored women physicians—a fact which rankled them for years.[69] This eagerness of medical women vexed Anna Howard Shaw, a physician herself. She blamed them for their own problems. "Women doctors should stand together and offer their services exactly as men offer theirs, and refuse to accept any other position. But the difficulty is that women are so willing to be door mats that they fail to stand together." [70]

Women in industry also viewed the war as an avenue of advance. Mrs. Raymond Robins, president of the National Women's Trade Union League, addressed the 1917 biennial convention, saying that the war was a final test of three great principles: democracy, the worth of labor, and women's rights. "Wonderful as this hour is for democracy and labor—it is the first hour in history for the women of the world. This is the woman's age! At last after centuries of disabilities and discriminations, women are coming into the labor and festival of life on equal terms with men." In the industrial and economic field the war would mark the most far-reaching changes in the condition of women. "From casual to permanent, from unskilled and unimportant to trained and essential factors in the economic life of the world, this will be the effect of the war in the condition of the working women of the western nations." She concluded that the NWTUL must give loyal support to the government in the war, defend constitutional rights, maintain the standards for women in the face of mounting efforts to undermine them in the emergency, and demand full enfranchisement of women. "We shall continue to be discriminated against in securing and enforcing protective legislation until we are fully enfranchised." [71]

Industrial women were not new, for they had worked since the inception of the factory system. In 1831 in Massachusetts 80 percent of the textile-mill operatives were women, and the 1910 U.S. census revealed more than 3,000,000 women working in manufacturing and trade.[72] However, most were exploited in unskilled, low-paying jobs. As the war drew large numbers of men into the military service, women filled their places. Surveys showed that women came from other industries into the war industries, not from the ranks of the unemployed. One study found that 65 percent had come from other factories, 25 percent from domestic service and restaurant work, and 5 percent from laundries; only 5 percent had never worked before.[73]

Pre-war prejudice held that women simply could not do some kinds of work, but the war proved otherwise. They were originally employed as a "war emergency": they would at least keep the machinery running until the men returned. Then they were admitted to skilled and technical crafts from which women had been previously barred. The war was a splendid test: if the women failed, men would be justified in confining them to certain industries. But they did not fail; they did as well as or even better than men. At least 77 percent of the firms reported satisfaction with the results of experimenting with female labor. Now they worked as streetcar conductors, trainmen, and ticket sellers, elevator operators, typesetters, linotype operators, electric linemen, blacksmiths, painters, mechanics, car washers, bricklayers, lathe operators, telegraphers, and many more. Equally surprising and important for the status of women was the fact that they learned skills in a few weeks for positions for which a training period of many months had been required formerly. "Women can beat [men] at nearly every line of work," boasted one observer.[74]

While post-war reconversion, depression, male union pressure, and reversion to traditional industrial patterns eroded some of the gains, women held on to many positions. Those lost included streetcar conductors, yardmen, switchmen, motormen, railroad engine hostlers and boiler washers, baggage and freight handlers. By 1930 virtually no women retained these occupations.[75] On the other hand, the war opened up the iron and steel mills, sheet-metal plants, lumber mills and wood fabricators, and the automobile, aircraft, electrical, and chemical industries.[76] The percentage increase in female factory workers was much higher in the war decade than between 1920 and

1930. From 1910 to 1920 the increase was 28.6 percent while the increase in the 1920s was 8.6 percent.[77] The U.S. Women's Bureau investigations indicated that most of the gains for women between 1910 and 1920 occurred in the war emergency. Reconversion reduced the figures from their wartime highs, but the peacetime levels were significantly higher than the pre-war situation.[78]

Now women demanded equal opportunity for jobs, training, and equal pay. They occupied jobs thought to be for men only and did them as well, and they were determined to stay. There arose the issue of jobs for returning soldiers versus the right of women to earn a living. Women labor leaders maintained that the essential issue was not jobs, but equal pay. Women received inferior wages in the traditional "women's industries," and the new positions offered an escape. If they were paid less and excluded from the unions, they would undercut men and work as scabs.[79] Women raised the issue of equal pay ever more insistently, since they felt more justified in their claims to equality. Congress acted first in 1918 by requiring equal pay for equal work with respect to railroad workers, and Michigan and Montana passed general equal-pay laws in 1919.[80]

These advances encountered resistance from the men's labor unions. Particularly blatant examples of male prejudice in the labor movement were the generally successful actions taken by the street-railway unions to eliminate women who were employed during the war.[81] The issue of women in "men's" jobs was at the heart of the attempts by the streetcar unions in Cleveland and Detroit to force dismissal of women. They had been hired because of the manpower shortage but were refused admission to the union, though willing to join. In Cleveland the Amalgamated Association of Street and Electric Railway Workers struck to force a return to the union shop. The transparency of this demand was the fact that only the union itself stood in the way of the union shop. The mayor of Cleveland appealed to the National War Labor Board (NWLB) to rule on the question. On December 3, 1918, the NWLB ordered that the 150 women conductors be dismissed, effective March 1, 1919. In the meantime the company itself had settled the strike by agreeing to the union's demand. The National Women's Trade Union League denounced the decision, saying it was "an amazing infringement of fundamental rights, since the women conductors were employed at the same pay and under the same conditions as the men and . . . would have been members of the union but for the fact that the men refused to admit them." The decision was "unjust, undemocratic, and un-American." [82]

The Detroit local of the Amalgamated Association also petitioned the NWLB to dismiss women conductors. Their contract said that women and Negroes could be employed only in an emergency, and the emergency was over. During the war 395 women had been hired, of whom 260 were still with the company. The union had a closed-shop contract and threatened to strike unless the women were fired by January 1. The NWTUL issued a warning: "This raises the fundamental issue of women's rights to equal industrial opportunity with men . . . [and] puts it squarely up to the Amalgamated Association once more to choose, on the one hand, between giving the women conductors a square deal by taking them into the union, and, on the other hand, forcing them to be scabs or starve." [83] The Equal Suffrage Association of Wayne County, the State Suffrage Association of Michigan, and the NWTUL hired an attorney to represent the women conductors. The War Labor Board ruled that the women should not be removed upon the demand of the men. Furthermore, fifteen women trainees to whom the union had refused work permits were ordered employed. This left the issue clearly up to the union, as the NWTUL had said, either to admit the women or see them work as scabs.[84]

Encouraged by the Detroit decision, the NWTUL engaged Frank P. Walsh, former chairman of the War Labor Board, as counsel and demanded a reconsideration of the Cleveland decision. Walsh argued that women had the same rights as men to work. He put several women on the stand to testify about the case and for the general right of women to equal opportunity. Dr. Anna Howard Shaw finished the testimony with an eloquent plea: "Gentlemen, it is time that justice decided such questions as this. Let women be judged by their ability. If we fail, let us fail not by the behest of men, but by our own acts. We have fought a great war to secure liberty and justice—not for men, but for people. . . . If one group of workers may say another group of workers shall not have certain work just because they are women, then we have neither liberty nor justice." [85] On March 18, 1919, the War Labor Board reversed the December ruling and recommended the reinstatement of the women conductors.

While both cases were decided for women, they were not complete victories. The Detroit ruling ordered the present women retained, but recommended that no additional ones be hired. In Cleveland the company decided to abide by its strike-settling agreement and ignored the War Labor Board's recommendation.

In Brooklyn union men had help from the Brooklyn Rapid Transit Company in eliminating women, and the company used the new night-work law passed in 1919 by the legislature as its pretext for dismissing them. The onus was shifted to advocates of social justice and protective legislation for women instead of to the true culprits. The firings were unnecessary, as was demonstrated in other cities with similar conditions. In Chicago, for example, women were employed on the day shift only, with equal pay and on eight-hour shifts. The B.R.T. simply dismissed all women without any attempt at adjustment and blamed the law for the deed. One company official had said that law or no law the B.R.T. would not employ women once the war ended. Out of this episode emerged the Equal Opportunity League, composed of female ex-employees of the B.R.T. in addition to women from business and the professions. This league battled the advocates of protective legislation in New York throughout the 1920s. The B.R.T. had hoped to discredit industrial legislation; the least that it did was cause the creation of a women's organization militantly and vociferously opposed to protective legislation for women.

The spectacle of union men trying to deny work to women caused William Howard Taft, a War Labor Board member, to reconsider his opposition to suffrage. He rebuked the unions for interfering with the rights of women and said that women should be admitted to the unions and given equal pay. He confessed that he was among those who had felt that the longer woman suffrage could be delayed, the better prepared women would be to exercise it. "But if organized labor is to oppose the right of women to do any lawful work by which they seek to earn a living, then they should be given the ballot at once, for this presents an issue which they can and should win by their votes." [86] Such problems persisted in the 1920s and helped account for the fragileness of the union movement among women. Many unions barred women, and the AFL made only halfhearted efforts to organize women. Although the 1920s was a difficult time for the trade union movement in general, the numbers of unionized women declined almost 30 percent.[87] Facing exploitation, discrimination, and exclusion from management and men's unions, women required special protective laws to boost their bargaining position. One of the leading promoters of such legislation was the Women's Bureau of the U.S. Department of Labor.

The advance of women in industry was an important part of the feminist movement.[88] Harriot Stanton Blatch expressed its meaning when she declared that a woman's "pay envelope may become her contract securing the right of self-determination." [89] In her view the equation was that the employment of women would lead to equal pay which would lead to independence. The creation of the Women's Bureau was a tactic in this larger scheme; hence support for the bureau came from varied organizations including the Women's Trade Union League, National American Woman Suffrage Association, National League of Women Voters, General Federation of Women's Clubs, YWCA, Women's Christian Temperance Union, and Daughters of the American Revolution. The bureau was used as an agency to promote the goals of equal pay, equal opportunity to jobs, promotion, and training, and equal dignity.[90]

The progressive answer to many problems was the establishment of commissions and bureaus. It was believed that facts and statistics, when properly collected and published, would mobilize the public to reform. The bureaus and commissions were to be staffed by experts who would bring knowledge and honesty to the solution of pressing problems, and the progressive era saw the multiplication and sophistication of agencies to deal with labor problems.

The demand for a bureau to concern itself with women in industry resulted from a series of studies conducted by the U.S. Department of Commerce and Labor from 1907 to 1909 at the insistence of women's organizations.[91] Late in 1905 the Chicago branch of the Women's Trade Union League urged the NWTUL to press for federal investigations into the conditions of women in industry. The president of the NWTUL, Mrs. Charles Henrotin, a former president of the General Federation of Women's Clubs, secured a hearing for a committee of three from the NWTUL at the 1906 biennial convention of the huge GFWC. The committee won GFWC's support and then earned the backing of President Theodore Roosevelt and his Commissioner of Labor, Charles P. Neill. A bill introduced in March, 1906, and passed in January, 1907, authorized the Secretary of Commerce and Labor to investigate and report on the conditions of women and children wage earners. At first the authorization carried no appropriation, and opponents argued that the federal government had no right to make such an investigation. Pressure exerted by the AFL, the railroad brotherhoods, and women's organizations, such as NWTUL, WCTU, DAR, GFWC, and Colonial Dames, secured an appropriation of $300,000—twice the original request. This special investigation took two years and piled up nineteen volumes of reports.

The conditions revealed were worse than imagined, and the experiment showed a need for continuing investigations. A

Women's Division of the Bureau of Labor Statistics was formed as a result, but it disintegrated rather quickly. Consequently, the GFWC, NWTUL, YWCA, and the National Consumers' League demanded a permanent women's bureau. The creation and success of the Children's Bureau fortified this demand. Opponents of a separate bureau argued that the Bureau of Labor Statistics could collect all the statistics that were needed because the conditions women faced in industry were the same as those faced by men. Proponents replied that the problems were not the same. Furthermore, women did not want an agency just to collect statistics about industrial women; they wanted a special counsel in government and continuous attention to the needs of wage-earning women. They wanted an open channel to present the problems of women, to give the women's point of view.[92]

The situation in the Bureau of Labor Statistics was so unsatisfactory that the Women's Division ceased to exist. All the women resigned and no one could be induced to take an appointment. The women's salaries were extremely low; its budget was subject to change by majority vote by the division chiefs or by superiors with the result that its funds were frequently diverted to other investigations and inquiries of other divisions. The final indignity was the fact that the Commissioner of Labor Statistics altered statistics collected by the women's division to the extent that the investigators refused to sign their names to the study.[93] By 1916 the Secretary of Labor, William B. Wilson, favored the reorganization of the Women's Division into a separate unit. A measure recommended by him and backed by the NWTUL, National Consumers' League, GFWC, and YWCA appeared in Congress that year but was buried in apathy. In their 1916 convention the AFL, which had supported the 1907–09 investigations, rejected a resolution calling for a women's bureau.

World War I erased the apathy and focused attention upon the industrial woman. In the surge of social-justice legislation after 1910 several states had created women's and children's divisions to check violations of the labor code; and the first minimum-wage laws were passed along with hours and work-ing-condition regulations. Emergency demands suddenly threatened these hard-won gains. The U.S. Navy Yard in Brooklyn went on a ten-hour day, breaking the eight-hour day for federal employees. In 1918 New York nearly passed a bill which threatened the entire labor code by allowing authorities to suspend existing laws while the United States was at war. The legislature passed the measure, bearing the endorsement of the president of the New York State Federation of Labor. The New York branch of the Women's Trade Union League and its middle-class allies prevailed upon Governor Charles S. Whit-man to hold hearings before signing the bill. After taking testi-mony on all sides, Whitman vetoed the measure.[94] In Vermont such a bill was signed. A team of investigators—Edith Abbott, Josephine Goldmark, and Mary Van Kleeck—from the Com-mittee on Women in Industry of the Council of National De-fense reported that conditions at the Brooklyn Navy Yard and the Frankford Arsenal in Philadelphia violated nearly every law of each state and many of the federal standards.[95]

The absence of a women's bureau to investigate permitted a bureau chief in the executive branch of the U.S. government to disregard the government's own eight-hour regulation. In April, 1917, the Women's Trade Union League and NAWSA charged Joseph Ralph, director of the Bureau of Engraving and Printing, with working women ten to sixteen hours a day; but they protested in vain. Finally they appealed to Jeannette Rankin, the first woman in Congress, who looked into the matter personally, brought the situation to the attention of Secretary William McAdoo, and threatened a congressional in-vestigation. Within two weeks the bureau was back on the eight-hour day. Mr. Ralph resigned and the bureau soon functioned with legal hours and a smaller staff with increased efficiency.[96]

Various departments affected by the influx of women workers established sections to cope with the problems—for example, the Industrial Service Section of the Ordinance De-partment, headed by Mary Van Kleeck, director of the Department of Industrial Studies of the Russell Sage Foundation. The Advisory Council to the Secretary of Labor, appointed in January, 1918, immediately recommended as an emergency war measure the creation of a special bureau to correlate all matters concerning women in industry. Congress appropriated $150,000 for a separate women's service on July 1, and the Woman in Industry Service in the Department of Labor was organized on July 9, 1918. Mary Van Kleeck and Mary Anderson of the International Boot and Shoe Workers Union were transferred from the Ordinance Department to be director and assistant director of the service.[97]

The Woman in Industry Service had no power to compel compliance with its recommendations, but had to rely upon its educational and publicity activities and enforcement of regulations by the National War Labor Board. The service's most critical problem was the prevention of the overthrow of existing protective laws in the rush for war production. The War Labor Policies Board had the service pass on all requests to override the protective laws, and it rarely consented. A significant advance was made when the service drew up a set of standards in October, 1918, for women in industry, and the War Labor Policies Board voted to insert the most important provisions into government contracts. A complete set of standards was issued on December 12, 1918, as a basis for industrial reconstruction; and the service called upon industry to cooperate. The standards were those advanced by the Women's Trade Union League and included the eight-hour day, equal pay, proper safety devices, no night work, no home work, equality of opportunity in jobs and advancement, and women supervisors for women workers. The significant fact was that the U.S. government gave its approval to an advanced set of industrial standards.[98]

The original appropriation for the Woman in Industry Service was so inadequate that the service was unable to carry out its obligations without help. Mary Van Kleeck called a conference of women trade union leaders to ask for help and cooperation. Twenty-five of them agreed to act as unofficial field agents for the service. They presented a carefully drawn budget for the service to the government which called for $300,000. One major project of the service, determining statistically the impact of war and reconstruction on the position of women workers, had to be financed through the War Work Council of the YWCA.[99]

Because the Woman in Industry Service had been created as a war measure, the end of the war threatened its existence. Antifeminist members of Congress declared their intention to kill it when the appropriations bill came up in February, 1919. Congress voted to extend the service for one year to aid in the reconstruction, but slashed the budget from $150,000 to $40,000. The women's organizations counted it a victory, but complained that the funds were inadequate. This narrow escape emphasized the need for a permanent agency, not subject to a point of order. The funds for the service were stricken in 1920 by a point of order. However, a bill to create a permanent bureau passed in June, 1920, with an appropriation of $75,000.[100]

While a permanent bureau was a cause for rejoicing, the victory was marred by congressional discrimination against the new bureau. The $75,000 was half of what the Secretary of Labor had recommended, and the scale of salaries for the employees was quite low. Congress slapped the bureau with a double discrimination on pay. It voted to exclude the women of the bureau from the general bonus of $240 given to all federal employees, and the bill limited the salaries of experts in the Women's Bureau to $1,800 a year, except for three positions at $2,000. At the same time the Bureau of Labor Statistics was provided with statisticians at $3,000 and fifteen other experts at $2,280-2,760, and similar provisions were made for other departments. When proponents of the bureau protested to individual senators, one replied, "Why, $2,000 is enough for any woman." In answer to the fear that the low salaries would drive expert women away, another senator said, "You need not fear that these employees will leave any bureau. The unemployment condition is going to be so serious that they will be glad to work there at *any* price!" [101]

A major item in the legislative agenda of the women's organizations in the 1920s was adequate and increased appropriations for the Women's Bureau, and in the first years they succeeded. The appropriation for 1920–22 was $75,000 and this was raised each year until it peaked at $107,380 for fiscal year 1924–25. Then the hand of conservatism cut it back to $100,-000, where it remained with some difficulty until it was jumped to $158,500 in 1930–31 and $179,900 for 1931–32. The reports of the director, Mary Anderson, were a continual lament over the inadequate funds. The salary improvements that came to the Women's Bureau as a result of the Civil Service Reclassification Act of 1923 reduced the money available for investigations.

The Women's Bureau became an important source of information for promoting women's rights. Mary Anderson wrote in 1921 that women had gained their citizenship rights as a result of the war but still had to win many of the economic rights. The bureau was to be an agency to gain those rights and to promote the general status of all women. While the bureau could not enforce laws, it did collect information and helped shape government policy. "It stands for equal opportunity in industry, freedom of choice of occupation, and equal pay for equal work." [102] The activities of the Women's Bureau were central to the struggle over an equal-rights amendment in the 1920s. The bureau provided the statistical information which undercut the position of the National Woman's Party, forcing them to retreat into the realm of abstract principles.

With the demand for a federal Women's Bureau came the push for state equivalents. New York created a Women's Bureau as a war measure; however, the legislature did not appropriate any funds for its operation the first year. State women's organizations paid its expenses through a private fund in 1920, and the New York Women's Trade Union League paid the salary for the state director of the bureau.[103] Continual efforts by feminists in the next decade were successful in that Virginia established a Women's Bureau in 1922, Pennsylvania raised its Women's Division to bureau status in 1925, as did

New Jersey in 1929; and Indiana also formed one in 1929. This movement for women's bureaus was an extension of prewar activities to gain recognition of industrial women's problems and stimulate the creation of women's and children's divisions or secure women members for the various industrial welfare commissions. Before 1913 Minnesota had the only separate division concerned with industrial women. Arkansas activated such a section in 1913, Pennsylvania in 1915, New Jersey and Wisconsin in 1916, Illinois in 1917, and Kansas finally in 1921. The industrial welfare commissions of California, Oregon, Washington, Kansas, and Massachusetts came to have a woman member after the war.[104]

III

The feminist movement focused its attention on winning the vote after 1910, but its interests spanned the range of social reform. World War I accelerated and accentuated the changing status of women as it expanded opportunities for service and reform and broke old stereotypes. Reforms such as prohibition and suffrage received boosts by the war, both achieving victory sooner than anticipated. The war was an exciting time for American women, and they responded with great eagerness. The sort of service they gave cannot be dismissed as meaningless and trivial. Not only did they mount campaigns to sell war bonds and conserve food, they "manned" the war plants, served as nurses, pushed to advance industrial standards, and gave volunteer duty in service organizations to soldiers. By helping to remove the suffrage barrier, the war permitted the feminist movement to return to its previous diverse interests. Indeed, the urge to serve caused business and professional women to notice their unorganized situation. They could not offer themselves collectively because they lacked the instrumentalities; consequently the war aided the development of organizations for professional women. The National Federation of Business and Professional Women's Clubs was a direct result of the effort to marshal everyone for the war. The proliferation of professional and special-interest organizations eventually weakened feminism in general and social feminism in particular. As each focused on its special concern, broader considerations were diminished. The Business and Professional Women's Clubs worked to elevate the business and professional women but became an important antagonist to the industrial women. The differences between these two elements had been muted when one or both were unorganized, but institutional development brought them into conflict and helped fragment feminism in the 1920s. The immediate post-war period saw a number of new organizations begun which sought to capitalize on the forward thrust of feminism. The vote promised to be a new instrument to win further objectives, and new opportunity and confidence urged women to move forward.

NOTES

1. Carrie Chapman Catt, "The Three I's," address to the International Suffrage Alliance, 1924, Carrie Chapman Catt MSS, box 4, Manuscript Division, New York Public Library (hereafter NYPL).

2. I have borrowed the term from Walter Lord's sprightly, impressionistic survey, *The Good Years: From 1900 to the First World War* (New York: Bantam Books, 1965).

3. The best accounts are Flexner, *Century of Struggle*; Sinclair, *The Better Half*; O'Neill, *Everyone Was Brave*; O'Neill, *The Woman Movement: Feminism in the United States and England* (New York: Barnes & Noble, 1969), 33–88.

4. The leaders who led the movement to victory made their appearance at this time and used new tactics. Harriot Stanton Blatch returned from England and organized suffrage leaders with working women. Lucy Burns and Alice Paul arrived from England imbued with the militancy of the English suffragettes. Mrs. O. H. P. Belmont became inspired by English militancy, as was Mrs. Clarence Mackay, founder of the Equal Franchise Society. Most important, Carrie Chapman Catt returned from abroad in 1912 to put her extraordinary organizational skills to work, first in New York and then as president of the burgeoning National American Woman Suffrage Association.

5. Flexner, *Century of Struggle*, 208–212, 251–259; Rheta Childe Dorr, *What Eight Million Women Want* (Boston: Small, Maynard, 1910), 166, 293–295; Harriot Stanton Blatch and Alma Lutz, *Challenging Years: The Memoirs of Harriot Stanton Blatch* (New York: G. P. Putnam's Sons, 1940), 61–63; Rose Schneiderman and Lucy Goldthwaite, *All for One* (New York: Paul S. Eriksson, 1967), 120–123.

6. Helen Woodward, *Through Many Windows* (New York: Hayne & Brothers, 1926), 147; Ishbel Ross, *Ladies of the Press: The Story of Women in Journalism by an Insider* (New York: Harper & Brothers, 1936), 114, 123–128; Rheta Childe Dorr, *A Woman of Fifty* (New York: Funk & Wagnalls, 1924), 223; Eleanor Buemel, *Florence Sabin: Colorado Woman of the Century*

(Boulder: University of Colorado Press, 1959), 61–63; Lord, *The Good Years*, 254–268.

7. O'Neill, *Everyone Was Brave*, 169–184.

8. The older view was that progressivism came to a halt when the war began; see Goldman, *Rendezvous with Destiny*; Hofstadter, *Age of Reform*; William E. Leuchtenburg, "Progressivism and Imperialism: The Progressive Movement and American Foreign Policy, 1898–1916," *Mississippi Valley Historical Review*, XXXIX (Dec., 1952), 493–504. More recent scholarship disputes that conclusion; see Allen F. Davis, "Welfare, Reform and World War I," *American Quarterly*, XIX (Fall, 1967), 515–533; Ross E. Paulson, *Radicalism and Reform: The Vrooman Family and American Social Thought, 1837–1937* (Lexington: University of Kentucky Press, 1968), 228–235.

9. William E. Leuchtenburg, "The New Deal and the Analogue of War," in *Change and Continuity in Twentieth Century America* (1964), 81–143.

10. Andrew Sinclair, *Age of Excess: A Social History of the Prohibition Movement* (New York: Harper Colophon Books, 1962), 116–128, 157–158; James H. Timberlake, *Prohibition and the Progressive Movement, 1900–1920* (Cambridge: Harvard University Press, 1963); Nuala McGann Drescher, "The Opposition to Prohibition, 1900–1919: A Social and Institutional Study" (Ph.D. thesis, University of Delaware, 1964), *passim*.

11. "Do It Now," *Woman's Medical Journal*, XXVII (Mar., 1917), 60; Emma Wheat Gilmore, "Lest We Forget," *ibid.* (Sept., 1917), 200–201.

12. Inez Haynes Irwin, *The Story of the Woman's Party* (New York: Harcourt & Co., 1921); Doris Stevens, *Jailed for Freedom* (New York: Horace Liveright, 1920); Dorr, *Woman of Fifty*, 291-296; James P. Louis, "Sue Shelton White and the Woman Suffrage Movement," *Tennessee Historical Quarterly*, XXII (June, 1963), 170–190; Caroline Katzenstein, *Lifting the Curtain: The State and National Woman Suffrage Campaigns in Pennsylvania as I Saw Them* (Philadelphia: Dorrance & Co., 1955), 196–263.

13. Carrie Chapman Catt and Nettie Rogers Shuler, *Woman Suffrage and Politics: The Inner Story of the Suffrage Movement* (New York: Charles Scribner's Sons, 1923); Maud Wood Park, *Front Door Lobby*, ed. Edna Lamprey Stantial (Boston: Beacon Press, 1960).

14. Carrie Chapman Catt, "Pickets Are behind the Times," *Woman Citizen*, I (Nov. 17, 1917), 470–471; Carrie Chapman Catt to Sue Shelton White, May 6, 1918, Sue Shelton White MSS, folder 21, Schlesinger Library, Radcliffe College (hereafter SL); Sinclair, *The Better Half*, 303–304.

15. "Patriotism—at a Price—Unmasked," *Woman's Protest*, X (Mar., 1917), 9; "The Congresswoman—Jeannette Rankin," *ibid.* (Apr., 1917), 5; "Suffrage in Relation to Patriotic Service," *ibid.* (May, 1917), 10–11; "Pulling the Pay in Patriotism," *ibid.*, XI (June, 1917), 4; "Penalizing Patriotism," *ibid.*, 5; "Suffrage vs. Patriotism," *ibid.*; "Disloyal Even to Their Sex," *ibid.*, July–Aug., 1917), 5.

16. Letter to the editor from Carrie Chapman Catt, June 19, 1917, National American Suffrage Association Papers, box 5, NYPL; see also Carrie Chapman Catt, "When Women Go a-Soldiering," *Women Lawyers' Journal*, VII (Oct., 1917), 1.

17. Mary Gray Peck, *Carrie Chapman Catt: A Biography* (New York: H. W. Wilson, 1944), 267–273.

18. "Woman Suffragists in the War Service," *Women Lawyers' Journal*, VII (Oct., 1917), 4.

19. "Cleveland Women Nobly 'Do Bit' as War Call Comes: Suffrage Party Strives to Aid U.S., Not to Get Votes," *Cleveland Plain Dealer*, Dec. 30, 1917,

Belle Sherwin MSS, newspaper scrapbook, vol. II, SL; Mrs. Andreas Ueland, President, Minnesota Woman Suffrage Association, to *Woman Citizen*, May 15, 1918, NAWSA Papers, box 5, NYLP; Ueland to Mary Sumner Boyd, Nov. 19, 1917, *ibid.*

20. Lily Lykes Rowe to Mrs. Rose Lawless Geyer, Apr. 14, 1918, NAWSA Papers, box 5, NYPL.

21. Note penned by Grace Sherwood to bottom of letter from Mary Sumner Boyd, Nov. 9, 1917, *ibid.*

22. Edith Hinkle Leaque, Secretary, Texas Equal Suffrage Association, to Mary Sumner Boyd, Nov. 24, 1917; Mrs. Bertha Cohen to Boyd, Sept. 7, 1917; Mrs. Guilford Dudley, Chairman, Tennessee Woman's Liberty Loan Committee, to Boyd, Nov. 27, 1917; Martha S. Kimball to Boyd, Nov. 16, 1917; Florence B. Cotman to Boyd, Dec. 2, 1917; Mrs. John Glover South, President, Kentucky Equal Rights Association, to Boyd, Dec. 4, 1917, *ibid.*

23. Anna B. Lawther, President, Iowa Equal Suffrage Association, to Mary Sumner Boyd, Nov. 12, 1917; Mrs. Seward S. Simons to Boyd, Dec. 5, 1917; Mrs. James Morrison, President, Chicago Equal Suffrage Association, to Boyd, Nov., 1917; Mrs. Richard Edwards, President, Woman's Franchise League of Indiana, to Boyd, Jan. 25, 1918, *ibid.*

24. Grace H. Bagby to Anna Howard Shaw, Sept. 28, 1917, *ibid.*

25. Mrs. Walter McNab Miller to local chairmen, June 26, 1917, *ibid.*

26. "Where Are the Suffragists in the War Work?," NAWSA press release, May 28, 1918, *ibid.*, box 6; see also "The Suffrage Worker and the War Worker," *Woman Citizen*, III (Oct. 19, 1918), 414-415.

27. Letter to the editor from Carrie Chapman Catt, May 5 and Oct. 1, 1917, NAWSA Papers, box 5, NYPL.

28. "Anti-Suffrage in War Relief Work," *Woman's Protest*, XI (June, 1917), 8.

29. Carrie Chapman Catt to Mary Stillwell-Kusel, June 10, 1918, Mary Stillwell MSS, Historical Society of Pennsylvania.

30. "If a War Medal Why Not a Ballot?," NAWSA press release, July 1, 1919, NAWSA Papers, box 6, NYPL; news item, *Woman's Medical Journal*, XXIX (June, 1919), 127; "American Woman Physician Decorated," *ibid.* (May, 1919), 96; *Medical Woman's Journal*, XXVII (Jan., 1920), 31; *ibid.* (Feb., 1920), 55.

31. Mrs. James Wadsworth, "For Home and National Defense against Woman Suffrage, Feminism, and Socialism," *Woman's Protest*, XI (Feb., 1918), 7; see also "Suffrage a Battle against God and Nature," *ibid.*, VIII (Dec., 1915), 10; Mrs. Joseph M. Stoddard, "The Suffrage Hypodermic," *ibid.* (Feb., 1916), 14. The NAOWS's particular conception of social revolution can be seen in the following examples: "Feminism advocates non-motherhood, free love, easy divorce, economic independence for all women and other demoralizing and destructive theories," said Ruth B. Sacks, Secretary, Missouri Anti-Suffrage League, to all candidates for office in St. Louis, June 24, 1918, Edna Fischel Gellhorn MSS, folder 14, SL; Florence Goff Schwarz's poem appeared in *Woman's Protest*, X (Jan., 1917), 5:

> Clamoring, heckling, entreating—
> Boycotting when they are peeved—
> Some of our sex are demanding
> "Rights" and are sorely aggrieved,
> Claiming that such are denied them:
> Right of free action and speech,
> Right to a public opinion,

Right in the pulpit to preach,
Right to a job or profession,
Right to ignore Fashion's sway,
Right of retaining a surname—
Pushing "Him" out of the way,
Right to political office.
Only one right is left out—
That of remaining a woman,
Which they say nothing about.

32. "Woman's Duty to Preparedness," *Woman's Protest*, VIII (Feb., 1916), 5; "Woman's Place in the War," *ibid.*, 10; "Women and Preparedness," *ibid.* (Mar., 1916), 8-9; "Anti-Suffrage—for Patriotism and Preparedness," *ibid.*, IX (June, 1916), 5-6; "Preparedness or Pacifism," *ibid.* (Oct., 1916), 19; "Suffrage versus Patriotic Service," *ibid.*, X (Jan., 1917), 1; "For Woman's Service or Woman Suffrage?," *ibid.* (Mar., 1917), 1; "How Militants Make Sport of the President," *ibid.*, 6-7; "Suffrage Fanaticism," *ibid.*, XI (July–Aug., 1917), 5-7.

33. Mabel Dodge, "An Appeal for the Defense of Democracy," *ibid.*, X (Mar., 1917), 3; Mrs. James Wadsworth, "The Wane of Feminism," *ibid.*, XI (Oct., 1917), 3.

34. Mrs. James Lees Laidlaw, "Victory in New York State, 1917, an Actual Fact," *Women Lawyers' Journal*, VII (Dec., 1917), 18; Dorinda Riessen Reed, *The Woman Suffrage Movement in South Dakota* (Government Research Bureau, Rpt. 41, State University of South Dakota, 1958), 116-117.

35. "How Pro-Germans and Pacifists Carried Suffrage in New York," *Woman's Protest*, XI (Nov., 1917), 4; see also chart, *ibid.* (Feb., 1918), 8-9; Mrs. Simeon H. Guilford, "The Suffrage Yellow and the Red," *ibid.*, V (Aug., 1914), 3-4; "The Working Alliance—Suffrage and Socialism," *ibid.*, VI (Feb., 1915), 3; George R. Conroy, "An Indissociable Alliance: Socialism, Suffragism, Feminism," *ibid.*, VII (July, 1915), 5; Margaret C. Robinson, "Suffrage and Socialism, the Kaiser's Allies," *ibid.*, XI (Feb., 1918), 10; "Woman Suffrage a Socialistic Movement," Illinois Association Opposed to Woman Suffrage, *Bull. 17* (Chicago, 1913); see also *Bull. 8* (1911), *Bull. 16* (1913), *Bull. 18* (1913); Sinclair, *The Better Half*, 322.

36. Everett P. Wheeler to members of the Man Suffrage Association, Dec. 1, 1917, Everett P. Wheeler MSS, box 8, NYPL.

37. Press release by NAOWS, Dec. 12, 1917, *ibid.*, box 10.

38. "Our New Newspaper," *Woman's Protest*, XI (Feb., 1918), 17.

39. Circular letter of American Constitutional League, signed by Everett P. Wheeler, Dec. 14, 1917, Wheeler MSS, box 10, NYPL.

40. Mrs. Benjamin Aymar Sands, Secretary, to members of the Women Voters' Anti-Suffrage Party, Apr. 15, 1920, *ibid.*

41. Warren G. Harding to Harriet Taylor Upton, June 17, 1914, Warren G. Harding MSS, box 703, folder 10, Ohio Historical Society (hereafter OHS).

42. Mary Garrett Hay to Warren G. Harding, June 22, 1920; Harding to Hay, July 7, 1920, *ibid.*, box 572, folder 435-1.

43. Woodrow Wilson to Carrie Chapman Catt, June 7, 1918, Catt MSS, box 1, NYPL.

44. "The President and Woman Suffrage Policy," *Woman's Protest*, XI (Feb., 1918), 4-5. The anti-suffragists were numerically small, but commanded the allegiance of influential members of the society including Mrs. Arthur M. Dodge, Mr. Elihu Root, Mrs. Grover Cleveland, Mrs. Charles Seymour, Mrs.

Andrew Carnegie, Mrs. Schuyler Van Rensselaer, Mrs. James Wadsworth, Ida Tarbell, Mrs. Francis M. Scott, Mrs. William F. Northrup, Mrs. William A. Putnam, Mrs. Henry Seligman.

45. Ethel M. Smith, "Senatorial Folly and the Suffrage Amendment," *Life and Labor*, IX (Mar., 1919), 62.

46. J. S. Eichelberger, field secretary of ACL, to Mary Kilbreth, Chairman, NAOWS, Apr. 6, 1920; Eichelberger to Kilbreth, Apr. 10, 1920; W. L. Marbury to Kilbreth, Apr. 17, 1920, Wheeler MSS, box 10, NYPL.

47. *Woman Citizen*, V (Jan. 8, 1921), 863.

48. George Stewart Brown, "Equal Suffrage in the Senate," *Woman Patriot*, V (July 1, 1921), 4; Carrie Chapman Catt, "A Postscript to Victory," *Woman Citizen*, VI (Mar. 11, 1922), 12.

49. Harriot Stanton Blatch, *Mobilizing Woman-Power* (New York: Woman's Press, 1918); see also O'Neill, *Everyone Was Brave*, 185–189.

50. Lorine Pruette, "Why Women Fail," in *Woman's Coming of Age: A Symposium*, ed. Samuel D. Schmalhausen and V. F. Calverton (New York: Horace Liveright, 1931), 247.

51. Blatch, *Mobilizing Woman-Power*, p. 124.

52. *Ibid.*, p. 86.

53. *Ibid.*, p. 90.

54. *Ibid.*, p. 108.

55. Compare O'Neill, *Everyone Was Brave*, 191, and O'Neill, "The Woman Movement and the First World War" (paper read for the Organization of American Historians, Cincinnati, 1966), 4.

56. O'Neill is good on Shaw's efforts; see *Everyone Was Brave*, 192–194; *The Woman Movement*, 78–79; see also Blatch, *Mobilizing Woman-Power*, 128.

57. Mrs. Walter McNab Miller to Herbert Hoover, June 5, 1917, NAWSA Papers, box 5, NYPL.

58. "To the American Woman: An Appreciation," *Good Housekeeping*, LXVI (May, 1918), 17.

59. Blatch, *Mobilizing Woman-Power*, 164–175.

60. "War Winning Girls," *Ladies Home Journal*, XXXV (Apr., 1918), 38–39. See also Howard W. Lewis MSS, Historical Society of Pennsylvania; Ethel Puffer Howes MSS, folder 139, SL; Anne Higgenson Spicer, "Hoeing Uncle Sam's Row," *Life and Labor*, VIII (July, 1918), 133–136; "Hunting a Square Hole, by a Lost Peg," *ibid.* (May, 1918), 93–94—this and subsequent issues for more than a year recount one woman's experiences in the Woman's Land Army; "Where Does the Land Army Go from Here?," *Woman Citizen*, V (Mar. 26, 1921), 1113.

61. Anne Harvey Strong, "The Need for Nurses," *Nation*, CVI (June 1, 1918), 645–646; "Doors of Business Opportunity Open to Men and Women," *Cleveland Leader*, Jan. 27, 1918, Sherwin MSS, newspaper scrapbook, vol. III, SL; "Woman Wanted at Good Pay," *Ladies Home Journal*, XXXIV (Oct., 1917), 34; Paul Van Riper, *History of the United States Civil Service* (Evanston: Row, Peterson, 1958), 260.

62. Flora Warren Seymour, "The Woman Lawyer and the War," *Women Lawyers' Journal*, VII (Dec., 1917), 17–18.

63. "Women Lawyers' Year of Opportunity," *ibid.* (Feb., 1918), 37.

64. "The Time of Fruition," *Woman's Medical Journal*, XXVII (Sept., 1917), 204; Frances C. Van Gasken, "Introductory Address. Women's Medical College, Session 1917–1918," *ibid.*, (Oct., 1917), 216–217; "Medical Association

of Greater New York Opens Its Doors to Women," *ibid.*, XXVIII (May, 1918), 114; "U.S. Public Health Service Open to Women Physicians," *ibid.* (June, 1918), 144.

65. "Medical Women's National Association: Report of the Second Annual Meeting, New York City, June 5-6, 1917," *ibid.*, XXVII (June, 1917), 141; see also "Medical Women Ready to Serve Their Country," *ibid.*, 149.

66. Editorial, *ibid.* (Aug., 1917), 184.

67. "An Executive Order Might Cut the Gordian Knot," *ibid.* (Oct., 1917), 226; Bertha Van Hoosen, "The American Press and Medical Women in War Work," *ibid.*, XXVIII (July, 1918), 154–157.

68. Editorial, "Shall We Enlist in the Volunteer Medical Service?," *ibid.* (Oct., 1918), 225.

69. Helen Hoy Greeley, "Why Army Nurses Need Military Rank," *ibid.*, XXIX (May, 1919), 83–85; Bertha Van Hoosen, "The Woman Physician and the Trained Nurse," *Medical Woman's Journal*, XXXVII (Aug., 1930), 230–231.

70. Anna Howard Shaw to Dr. Mary W. Stillwell-Kusel, May 31, 1918, Stillwell MSS, Historical Society of Pennsylvania.

71. Mrs. Raymond Robins, "President's Report," National Women's Trade Union League, *Proceedings* (1917), v–x.

72. Edith Abbott, *Women in Industry* (New York: D. Appleton & Co., 1919), 103.

73. "Women Workers in the Reconstruction Period," *Life and Labor*, VIII (Dec., 1918), 272–273; Mary Anderson, "Will Women Retire from Industry with the Return of Peace?," *Proceedings of the Academy of Political Science*, VIII (1918–20), 147; *The New Position of Women in American Industry*, Women's Bureau, U.S. Department of Labor, *Bull. 12* (Washington: Government Printing Office, 1920), 17–22.

74. "Woman's Work Is Never Done," *Good Housekeeping*, LXVI (May, 1918), 36–37; Sophonisba P. Breckinridge, *Women in the Twentieth Century* (Recent Social Trends Monograph, New York: McGraw-Hill, 1933), 104; Cleo Murtland, "Vocational Training for Women in Industry," reprint from *Bull. 32*, National Society for Vocational Education (Feb., 1920), 1; *The New Position of Women in American Industry*, 24.

75. Mary V. Dempsey, *The Occupational Progress of Women, 1910 to 1930*, Women's Bureau, *Bull. 104* (1933), Appendix A, Table I.

76. *Women at Work: A Century of Industrial Change*, Women's Bureau, *Bull. 115* (1933), 11; Janet M. Hooks, *Women's Occupations through Seven Decades*, Women's Bureau, *Bull. 218* (1947), 10, 109–135.

77. Dempsey, *Occupational Progress of Women*, 12.

78. *The New Position of Women in American Industry*, 35; Mary Elizabeth Pidgeon, *Women in the Economy of the United States of America*, Women's Bureau, *Bull. 155* (1937), 22–24.

79. Anderson, "Will Women Retire from Industry with the Return of Peace?," 147–150; "Women Workers in the Reconstruction Period," *Life and Labor*, VIII (Dec., 1918), 272–293; see also Emily Newell Blair, "Should a Woman Get a Man's Pay?," *Ladies Home Journal*, XXXVI (Apr., 1919), 39; editorial, "Reconstruction Work," *Women Lawyers' Journal*, VIII (Dec., 1918), 13.

80. Guinon Griffis Johnson, "Feminism and the Economic Independence of Woman," *Journal of Social Forces*, III (May, 1925), 612; "The Ideas of a Foreseeing Woman," *Ladies Home Journal*, XXXVI (Mar., 1919), 43; "The Ideas of a Forward Looking Woman," *ibid.* (Feb., 1919), 35; Emily Newell Blair, "Where Are Women Going?," *ibid.* (Mar., 1919), 37; Eva Wechsler, "Jobs

for Everybody," *Life and Labor,* IX (Jan., 1919), 7–9; Blatch and Lutz, *Challenging Years,* 287; "Equal Pay for Equal Work," speech at Baltimore branch of American Association of University Women, Nov. 15, 1956, Frances Tuckerman Freeman MSS, SL.

81. This issue was so glaring that the Women's Bureau investigated the problems in Detroit, Kansas City, Chicago, and Boston. See *Women Streetcar Conductors and Ticket Agents,* Women's Bureau, *Bull. 11* (1921).

82. "The Woman Street Car Conductor—Shall She Have Fair Play?," *Life and Labor,* IX (Jan., 1919), 14.

83. NWTUL press release, Dec. 12, 1918, Cornelia Bryce Pinchot MSS, box 9, LC.

84. "Women Conductors of Detroit Hold Jobs," *Life and Labor,* IX (Feb., 1919), 40.

85. NWTUL press release, Mar. 13, 1919, C. B. Pinchot MSS, box 9, LC; "Women Street Car Conductors to Be Reinstated," *Life and Labor,* IX (Apr., 1919), 98.

86. William Howard Taft, "As I See the Future of Women," *Ladies Home Journal,* XXXVI (Mar., 1919), 113.

87. Theresa Wolfson, "Trade Union Activities of Women," *Annals of the American Academy of Political and Social Science,* CXLIII (May, 1929), 120–131.

88. Mrs. Raymond Robins, *Life and Labor Bulletin,* n.s., XLIV (Feb., 1944), 1; Blatch and Lutz, *Challenging Years,* 95–98; Gladys Boone, *The Women's Trade Union League in Great Britain and the United States of America* (Columbia University Studies in History, Economics and Public Law, no. 489, New York: Columbia University Press, 1942), 224; Jessie Taft, *The Woman Movement from the Point of View of Social Consciousness* (privately published Ph.D. thesis, University of Chicago, 1915), 52–57; *Toward Better Working Conditions for Women,* Women's Bureau, *Bull. 252* (1953), 6–7.

89. Blatch, *Mobilizing Woman-Power,* 119.

90. Mary Van Kleeck, "For Women in Industry," *Survey,* XXXVII (Dec. 23, 1916), 327; Mary Anderson, "The Women's Bureau," *Woman Citizen,* V (Mar. 5, 1921), 1048–49; see also Anderson, *Woman at Work: The Autobiography of Mary Anderson as Told to Mary N. Winslow* (Minneapolis: University of Minnesota Press, 1951), 91–93.

91. Regarding the origins of the Women's Bureau, see Ethel M. Smith, "At Last—a National Women's Labor Bureau," *Life and Labor,* VIII (Aug., 1918), 159–161; Alice Henry, *Women and the Labor Movement* (New York: Doran, 1923), 167–169; Boone, *Women's Trade Union League,* 66; Agnes Nestor, *Woman's Labor Leader: An Autobiography* (Rockford, Ill.: Bellevue Books, 1954), 66–76; Mary E. Dreier, *Margaret Dreier Robins: Her Life, Letters, and Work* (New York: Island Press Cooperative, 1950), 34.

92. "Woman in Industry," *New Republic,* XVI (Oct. 26, 1918), 365-366; Henry, *Women and the Labor Movement,* xii-xv, 111–114; Kleeck, "For Women in Industry," 327; Boone, *Women's Trade Union League,* 58–62, 159–171.

93. "What Uncle Sam Does Not Do for Women in Industry," *New Republic,* VII (July 29, 1916), 324-325; Kleeck, "For Women in Industry," 328.

94. Schneiderman and Goldthwaite, *All for One,* 128–129.

95. Sophonisba P. Breckinridge to Edith Campbell, Dec. 18, 1917; "Employment of Women at Frankford Arsenal, Philadelphia, Pa., inspected November 26, 1917," Sophonisba P. Breckinridge MSS, box 3, folder W, LC.

96. News item, *Life and Labor,* VIII (July, 1918), 151; "What a Congress-

woman Did for Women Wage Earners," *Woman's Medical Journal*, XXVII
(July, 1917), 166; Henry, *Women and the Labor Movement*, 190–191;
NAWSA, "Report of Committee on Protection of Women's Labor, 1917,"
C. B. Pinchot MSS, box 3, LC.

97. Gustavus A. Weber, *The Women's Bureau: Its History, Activities, and
Organization* (Institute for Government Research, Service Monographs of the
U.S. Government, no. 22, Baltimore: Johns Hopkins Press, 1923), 1–2; Anderson, *Woman at Work*, 91–93.

98. *Standards for the Employment of Women in Industry*, Woman in Industry Service, U.S. Department of Labor, *Bull. 3* (Washington: Government
Printing Office, 1919); "The Woman in Industry Service," *Survey*, XLI (Feb.
22, 1919), 734; Anderson, *Woman at Work*, 97–98.

99. "Women in Industry," *New Republic*, XVII (Oct. 26, 1918), 366; Henry,
Women and the Labor Movement, 193; Anderson, "The Women's Bureau,"
1049.

100. NWTUL press release, Feb. 23 and Mar. 1, 1919, C. B. Pinchot MSS,
box 9, LC; circular letter, Ethel Smith to Friends of the WTUL, May 12,
1920, *ibid.*, box 11; "Continuing the Women's Bureau," *Woman Citizen*, V
(June 19, 1920), 71.

101. "The Women's Bureau," *Survey*, XLVI (Apr. 16, 1921), 74; Marjorie
Shuler, "Women and the New Administration," *Woman Citizen*, V (Mar. 12,
1921), 1063.

102. Anderson, "The Women's Bureau," 1048; Anderson, "Woman in Industry Service," *American Federationist*, XXV (Sept., 1918), 798.

103. Amey Aldrich, "New York's New Women in Industry Bureau," *Life
and Labor*, VIII (Sept., 1918), 182–183; Henry, *Women and the Labor Movement*, 185; Schneiderman and Goldthwaite, *All for One*, 222–223.

104. Henry, *Women and the Labor Movement*, 195; Florence P. Smith,
*Chronological Development of Labor Legislation for Women in the United
States*, Women's Bureau, *Bull. 66-II*, rev. (1932).

TWO

New Associations

The exhilaration of war service and the suffrage victory charged the feminist movement anew.[1] Leading feminists felt no immediate sense that the movement might lose its direction and purpose. Most women felt that *real* possibilities for change now existed; they had the key to open the door. Women would simply have to get organized and educated for the old-new tasks. They responded by creating new kinds of organizations to focus political and social action, and they cooperated more closely in their national lobbying efforts than ever before. Newly formed instrumentalities such as the League of Women Voters and the Women's Joint Congressional Committee were central to the persistent progressive thrust within feminism in the 1920s. Simultaneously, the post-war years saw a proliferation of professional groups for women. From one of the least well organized segments of society before the Great War, business and professional women rapidly acquired the attributes of professionalization. One marked effect of the developing professionalism among women was a decline in social concern and an increase in narrowly professional issues.

One of the principal attributes of a profession is a special skill, the acquisition of which is controlled by the profession itself and enforced by the sanctions of the general community.[2] For example, to practice law one had to be admitted to the bar, and standards were set through the cooperation of the lawyers and the state governments. The initial barrier to women lawyers

had been state laws barring them from practice. The first state
to admit women was Iowa in 1869. By 1902 only twenty states
had admitted them; however, the remaining states had removed
the obstacles by 1920.[3] In medicine the American Medical Association had waged a bitter battle with a host of competing
medical theories and practices in order to establish medical
standards. The AMA finally won during the progressive era
when most states adopted strict licensing laws. The education
of physicians was considerably upgraded, standardized, and extended to include a degree from an accredited school and a
period of internship in a recognized hospital. The number of
medical "schools" and "doctors" in the United States declined
substantially between 1900 and 1920 as the quack practitioners
and their schools were forced out of business.

After debating whether to admit women in osteopathic practice, the Medical Women's National Association (organized
1915) decided to require its members to join the AMA, thereby automatically excluding osteopaths. (The osteopathic wom-
en formed their own association in 1920.) By aligning itself
with the AMA, the Medical Women's National Association
adopted its advanced standards as their own; however, the
AMA requirements made admission of women to medicine
more difficult by adding to the number of possible chances for
discrimination. Medical women have complained down to the
present that they face discrimination in being accepted to
medical schools in the first place and acquiring internships
afterward. To relieve the situation women operated their own
hospitals in several major cities. In the 1920s a woman's hospital started in Chicago and Detroit, and the Medical Women's
Committee on Opportunities for Women in Medicine maintained pressure on schools and hospitals to admit women. Despite the fact that the medical profession held out great rewards to women, more entered law than medicine. Although
both faced discrimination in establishing a practice, the medical women had more difficulty in getting the required training.[4]

Another attribute of a profession is the creation of associations which spring from a sense of identity among those who possess a special skill and knowledge.[5] The existence of separate women's groups to parallel the older associations such as the AMA, American Bar Association, and the American Bankers Association revealed a group consciousness stemming from discrimination and an appreciation of the need to advance and protect the interest which women had in many professions. The first decade of the twentieth century saw the arrival of group consciousness among some professional and business women. Their first impulse was to join the established suffrage organizations about 1910, and then from 1915 on they created professional associations. World War I accelerated this development by bringing women together, providing new opportunities which required defending, and stressing the need for organization in order to serve. In addition to their central role in beginning the new profession of social work,[6] women pressed to break into established professions. They were generally excluded from the professional subculture; therefore they organized their own associations as a means to gain equal status and fulfill the need for professional and social contact.[7] Beginning before the war and running into the 1920s, a wide variety of associations developed, including public health nurses, dentists, architects, physicians, geographers, lawyers, bank women, journalists, dietitians, deans of women, teachers, preachers, X-ray technicians, medical-record librarians, and dental hygienists.[8]

The National Federation of Business and Professional Women's Clubs (NFBPWC), the largest of the lot, was a by-product of World War I. Before the war there existed a few exclusive organizations, some local clubs, and the YWCA for young business women. The "service club" phenomenon began in 1917 when a professional organizer—a man—started the Altrusa Clubs, followed by Quota and Zonta in 1919. However, these organizations fragmented women by regions and differing standards of admission.[9] The war came at a crucial time as it put increased sums of money into the hands of the YWCA; and the YWCA used the money to coordinate wartime activities of

women, promote morale, and help win the war. It believed
that the war effort would be aided by mobilizing the special
talents of the business and professional women. The federal
government had easily reached businessmen through their organizations; but no parallel to the U.S. Chamber of Commerce,
National Association of Manufacturers, or Rotary existed for
women. The YWCA sought to overcome this lack by calling
a conference of business women; and the result was the National
Federation of Business and Professional Women's Clubs.

The national conference of business and professional women
met in May, 1918, in New York with twenty-six states and
the District of Columbia represented. Three facts emerged from
the conference: there was a definite desire for a national organization, its chief purpose would be to promote the war
effort, and it was agreed that the new association would work
outside the YWCA. The YWCA agreed and continued financial and moral support of the embryonic organization, paying
nearly all the organizational expenses and trips by funding the
Business Women's Committee with $60,000. This committee,
created at the May conference, called another meeting for
July, 1919, in St. Louis to establish a national federation. In
the summer of 1918 they worked out an elaborate war-work
plan, but the end of the war forced a complete revision. In
the meantime Lena Madeson Phillips, a YWCA official, toured
the country as executive secretary of the committee to drum
up support. Thus the YWCA was the parent of the NFBPWC.

The St. Louis meeting founded the NFBPWC but a proposed merger with the Woman's Association of Commerce
failed. Gail Laughlin, a lawyer who helped formulate the constitution, became the first president. The underlying objective
of the federation was "to plan so that the young women of
the future might come into the business and professional fields
better able to cope with the conditions and with fewer handicaps to overcome than the women of today." [10] This first convention passed resolutions calling for the end of sex discrimination in civil service appointments, urged officer rank for army
nurses, called for permanent federal and state employment

agencies, and acknowledged its deep debt to the YWCA.

The YWCA funded the first year's expenses with $15,000, and the federation blossomed rapidly, growing to 25,500 members in the first year. It had to weather an internal crisis in the 1921 convention when Gail Laughlin withdrew the whole California federation over the question of incorporation, and other clubs departed when the dues were increased.[11] However, by 1925 the federation had over 45,000 members, and 56,000 by 1931.

Until the mid-1920s the NFBPWC shared many objectives with social feminism, joining the Women's Joint Congressional Committee and supporting progressive legislation. The 1920 convention endorsed suffrage, the maternity- and-infancy protection bill, and protested a bill in Congress to build canals and reservoirs in part of Yellowstone National Park. A significant decision of the 1921 convention was the resolution to remain neutral in the dispute over protective legislation for industrial women (as urged by the Women's Trade Union League, the National Consumers' League, the League of Women Voters, and the U.S. Women's Bureau) or blanket equality laws (as proposed by the National Woman's Party). In 1922 the federation's legislative committee, reflecting a weakening of social feminism in their organization, urged the NFBPWC convention to "do away with general and useless resolutionizing about justice in the abstract and confine our attention to justice in the concrete."[12] As a result the federation cut its legislation program to three items: uniform marriage and divorce laws, equal status for home economics in federal aid to states, and independent citizenship for women. The next convention added an endorsement of the child labor amendment. The 1924 convention re-endorsed it, and the 1925 session urged state federations to use every means to promote the ratification of the amendment. Because the opponents of the child labor amendment had already mounted a strong, effective campaign in the nation against it, the 1925 federation resolution provoked a heated debate. The argument resumed more fiercely the following year, forcing the NFBPWC to back away. Two entire ses-

sions of the 1926 convention were consumed in an extended
debate over the amendment; therefore the question was submitted to the state federations for "further study." The progressive impulse was not entirely gone from this organization
because the 1927 convocation gave a qualified endorsement of
the amendment, but left ratification efforts to the state federations. However, by 1928 it was a dead issue; concern for child
labor gave way to a demand for an increased tax exemption for
single persons and a protest against discrimination by Harvard's
School of Public Health.[13]

The 1920s saw the NFBPWC shift away from social feminism toward issues of more particular concern to business and
professional women. While endorsing neither protective industrial legislation nor blanket equality laws in 1921, the 1926
convention was the scene of a lengthy debate on this question.
The federation members who were also in the Woman's Party
felt strong enough to challenge the no-decision resolution of
1921. After extended discussion, the question of protective
legislation was submitted to the clubs for study. Although the
anti-protectionists were put off in 1926 and again in 1928, the
tide was running in their direction. More and more state federations lined up to oppose protective industrial laws for women,
and finally in 1937 the NFBPWC endorsed the Woman's
Party's equal rights amendment. The pivotal year was 1925–26,
when the progressive impulse faltered in the NFBPWC. While
the federation continued to recommend a federal department of
education, a federal department of health, a permanent federal
employment service, and increased aid to home economics education, the will to support social-justice reforms had been
checked. They soon found the child labor issue to be of no interest and opposed efforts to better the working conditions of
industrial women.

While the NFBPWC was a general organization, the National Association of Bank Women was an example of a very
small, specialized association. This organization was restricted
to women bank officers, automatically assuring an exclusive
group. The Bank Women was a product of the surge of femin-

ism occurring with World War I as the war unlocked the banking profession to women.[14] In the beginning the Bank Women were concerned about social feminism, but this had faded by the mid-1920s for immediate professional interests.

The founder and first president of the National Association of Bank Women, Virginia Furman, was offered a position with the Columbia Trust Company in 1915 to organize a woman's department. The vice-president was a personal friend and her father had been a bank president years before. "At the time the invitation was regarded as a pleasant gesture to the ladies, with little chance of proving of permanent constructive value." [15] Furman had no desire for a business career, but as an active suffragist she viewed this as an opportunity to advance women's rights. During World War I she chaired the Women's Liberty Loan Committee of the Second Federal Reserve District, a job which enhanced her skill and reputation. In 1919 the Columbia Trust Company considered the woman's department successful and took out a quarter-page announcement in the New York newspapers to say that Furman had been made an assistant secretary. The suffragists hailed the event; and the New York State Suffrage Party, the Women's City Club, and a number of wealthy women switched their accounts to the Columbia Trust Company. The bank was popularly known for several years as "The Suffrage Bank." Other banks quickly hired women, creating the core of the future Bank Women.

The U.S. Mortgage and Trust Company appointed Nathalie Laimbeer, who was to be the second president of NABW. She had a wide association among the wealthy families of New York. The Bankers Trust Company hired Jean Arnot Reid, later the third president of NABW. She had handled the financial affairs for Red Cross work in the war, and her work impressed officials of the bank. The fourth president of the association, Mina Bruere, entered the profession through her work as personal secretary to V. Everit Macy, a financier and philanthropist, and then as secretary to Frank A. Vanderlip, president of the National City Bank.[16]

The first meeting in early 1921 consisted of six women who

felt the need to pool their experiences.[17] None had had any
specific training for bank work before becoming involved in it.
Subsequently they adopted a name and drew up objectives
which included aid to those wanting to enter the profession.
The association grew the first year from sixteen charter members in New York City to fifty-nine scattered across the country. By 1925 it had reached 189, and then climbed to a pre-Depression peak of 247 in 1929. By 1933 it had fallen back to
the 1925 figure of 189. Many women lost their positions as
banks closed their women's departments for economy reasons;
others were carried away by the rush of bank failures.[18]

In the first year the NABW heard thirteen speakers including senatorial candidate Anne Martin, who spoke on "Feminine
Solidarity," the secretary of the New York Consumers' League,
and a speech on the "Activities of the Women's Trade Union
League." Next year they listened to women like Ida Tarbell
speaking on "Women's Jobs." These reveal broad-gauged
feminism, but as the decade passed they heard no more talks on
topics like "Feminine Solidarity." Instead they focused on
subjects like "German Reparations and Inter-Allied Debt," "An
Analysis of Insurance Trusts" (1923–24), "Saving Joyfully,"
"The First Mortgage" (1928–29), or topics in economic research useful to women in the financial field.[19]

A similar development occurred in other organizations as the
decade progressed. An increasing concentration on acquiring
special information excluded the broader concerns of social
feminism. In the 1930s a number of those specialized associations endorsed the equal rights amendment, less as a way to promote the position of all women than as a means to advance their
profession.

The organizational impulse moved in the direction of politics also. The winning of the franchise presented the suffrage
organizations with extinction. The leaders felt that the ballot
was only a tool and that it must be utilized for the good of
society. They sought ways to transform the suffrage movement into an effort for further reform. Many leaders of the
suffrage crusade had profound pacifist feelings; and some like

Jane Addams, Carrie Chapman Catt, Florence E. Allen, Anne
H. Martin, Florence Brewer Boeckel, and Mrs. James Lee
Laidlaw turned wholeheartedly to the search for peace in the
1920s. Elizabeth Glendower Evans, Harriot Stanton Blatch,
and Nora Blatch Barney urged the National Woman's Party
to throw its considerable talent into the peace crusade.[20] Since
Alice Paul was a Quaker, this seemed to be a natural direction for the NWP.

The NWP drifted while trying to decide what to do. It
invited other women's organizations to present their legislative
programs at the NWP convention in February, 1921, so that
they could avoid duplication of efforts.[21] While the invitation
said that the NWP would consider whether to disband or take
up some new program, the leaders had already settled upon
a drive against legal discriminations and hoped to sound out
support. On February 18 the Woman's Party voted to reor-
ganize and fight for legal equality. It was to be a one-plank
platform. Other women's organizations took the proposal seriously and tried to work out the implications of the proposed
sweeping equal rights laws; but when the threat to protective
legislation for women in industry could not be removed, most
moved into opposition. The NWP completed the alienation
by proposing an equal rights amendment to the Constitution in
December, 1921. From then until the 1930s the NWP was
isolated from the vast majority of organized women. However,
the situation in the thirties brought them new allies, including
the National Federation of Business and Professional Women's
Clubs.

The shrewd general of the National American Woman
Suffrage Association began planning the next step before the
suffrage amendment had cleared Congress. She feared that
her army might dissipate as state after state granted suffrage.
The organization had to remain intact to assure ratification.
At NAWSA's Jubilee Convention in March, 1919 (to cele-
brate the fiftieth anniversary of Wyoming's grant of suffrage),
Carrie Chapman Catt called for a memorial to the suffrage
struggle: "I propose . . . the most appropriate and most pa-

triotic memorial that could be suggested—a League of Women Voters to 'Finish the Fight'; and to aid in the reconstruction of the Nation." It was to be a non-partisan, non-sectarian league which would win final enfranchisement at home and abroad, end the legal discrimination against women, and make democracy safe for the world.[22] She said this could be done in five years and urged the suffragists to enlist. She reminded them that NAWSA had departed from its hoary policy of non-partisanship on controversial issues when it established committees for wartime work. These departments should be continued and more controversial issues faced. The assemblage responded by creating the National League of Women Voters as an auxiliary, which became independent at the Victory Convention in 1920.

Prototypes of the NLWV existed in New York and California. Catt had founded the Woman Suffrage Party of New York in 1909; and though it was "non-partisan" it vigorously supported a broad range of social reforms. After winning the pivotal victory in November, 1918, it converted itself into the New York League of Women Voters and continued as before. In California several suffrage leaders organized the California Civic League after their 1911 suffrage victory, and it worked under that name until 1921, when it affiliated with the NLWV.[23]

While the 1919 convention created the League of Women Voters, the next convention had to decide its path and program, as well as handle a mass of administrative details. The bearing became an issue as Jane Addams and Carrie Chapman Catt pulled in two directions. Catt sought to move the enthusiasm of the convention into participation in politics. She urged women to get into the parties and assume the responsibilities of office-holding and policy formulation. While Catt favored political activity, Addams felt women's work to be the reconstruction of their communities. She urged women to see the community as an extension of the home. A woman, she said, could no longer care for the health and welfare of her family without becoming involved in the conditions of the community. Party membership was not as important as social reconstruction. The convention compromised by embracing both positions.[24] The NLWV accepted as its mission the education of women for citizenship, training to assume a full share of governing and party membership, reforming the electorate, and promoting a more just society. To these ends they established six committees and adopted a monster platform of sixty-nine planks.[25]

The 1920 election was a tremendous disappointment. Women had worked so long for the vote and called the ballot the most precious privilege of a free society. The NLWV adopted the slogan "Every Woman a Voter." But most did not vote. Anti-suffragists gloated and suffragists were chagrined. The showing was poor in the presidential year and abysmal in the local elections of 1921 and 1922. The Minnesota LWV reported that the decline in the electorate in local elections was 60 percent; and in many townships, "women, except for one or two hardy spirits, were too timid to participate in an election where men folks made it plain they were not wanted." [26] Consequently, the task of educating for citizenship got the highest priority for the immediate future. Local and state leagues held hundreds of citizenship schools and conferences on voting, and they conducted a big "Get out the Vote" campaign before the 1924 elections. Nevertheless, the social feminism of Jane Addams remained NLWV's first love, and the 1923 convention shifted its emphasis to welfare.[27] Their program was pulled between the visions of Addams and Catt; but even when one seemed preeminent, the other was never forgotten. While citizenship training preoccupied the leagues everywhere after 1920, the greatest single effort flowed into a welfare measure, the maternity- and infancy-protection bill.

The Victory Convention of NAWSA in 1920 was both a gay and sentimental occasion. Past conventions had been serious affairs, but this final convention was quite different. It was held in February before the actual victory, but thirty-one states had already ratified and the end was in sight. "At the sound [of a large bell in the middle of the hall] old staid traditions were

flung to the winds. Cheering and singing, delegation after delegation got to its feet and began marching. . . . For a long time
it was a question whether they would ever be quiet again." [28]
Women spontaneously sang the "Battle Hymn of the Republic" and shouted hosannas to victory. When it was announced
that New Mexico had just ratified, the convention burst into
pandemonium. The bell clanged, women cheered, the "Doxol-
ogy" and "There'll Be a Hot Time in the Old Town Tonight"
contended on equal terms.[29]

Not all the enthusiasm was transferable to the new League
of Women Voters. For many NAWSA members the victory
was fulfillment. NAWSA voted to dissolve itself in favor of
its child. "The feeling that something ennobling, something
precious, had gone out of their lives" saddened many of the
old campaigners.[30] In fact, friction developed as some leaders
of NAWSA became quite active in their opposition to NLWV.
Ruth Hanna McCormick, vice-president, head of NAWSA's
congressional committee and member of the Republican National Committee, joined with Mrs. George Bass, a member of
the Democratic National Committee, in an unsuccessful attempt
to keep the Illinois Woman Suffrage Association from trans-
forming itself into the Illinois LWV.[31]

Most of the state suffrage organizations voted to dissolve in
1920–21, and at the end of 1920 the NLWV boasted it was organized in forty-six states. However, some of this growth had
no roots. When the direction of the NLWV became clearer,
many carry-overs from NAWSA faded away, and some early
growth wilted. Many desired a return to the pre-war policy of
non-partisanship and non-controversy, and wanted the NLWV
to be a study group. "I should like to belong to an organization which never takes any stand at all," wrote one dissatis-
fied member, "but which will agree to give a hearing to every
question of political and economic importance as well as to
organizations which do avowedly stand for certain definite
principles." [32] Minnesota reported that the number of county
chairmen declined in 1921, and the South Dakota LWV was
almost dead by mid-1921.[33] Although the NLWV claimed the

more than 2,000,000 members of NAWSA, it actually retained only a fraction; for example, in Cuyahoga County (Cleveland), Ohio, over 80,000 women had been members of the suffrage organizations, but only a tenth joined NLWV.[34] By the early 1930s NLWV had about 100,000 members.

The appearance of the NLWV caused deep concern in the political parties and among opponents of the Woman Movement. They charged that NAWSA was creating a woman's party. Woman suffrage was threatening enough since suffragists had been very explicit in their attacks upon political machines, but a women's bloc vote or an army of independents was cause for real anxiety.

The party regulars' fears were not groundless because women had banded together on occasion and showed bloc strength. In 1918 Senator John W. Weeks of Massachusetts was beaten after the suffragists vowed to punish him for his opposition to suffrage. The machine which dominated Columbus, Ohio, was defeated the first time women could vote.[35] In 1920 the Connecticut LWV openly opposed Senator Frank Brandegee, the New Hampshire LWV opposed Senator George H. Moses, and the New York LWV tried to unseat Senator James Wadsworth. Even the NLWV was not above suspicion since it adopted a resolution praising the women of New York for their "patriotic work of determining to send to the U.S. Senate . . . a modern-minded senator."[36] Carrie Chapman Catt assured a worried member that these actions did not mean the LWV intended to be a third party. "Of course the League of Women Voters is against Wadsworth and had so announced itself even before St. Louis [when the NLWV was begun] . . . I can leave every state auxiliary free to fight anybody he wants to."[37]

The non-partisan character of the NLWV was borne out by its critics, who accused it of "everything from Bolshevism to the most depressing kind of reaction. That's why it is accused of being secretly Republican—or secretly Democratic."[38] As concern felt by the parties about the women's bloc declined, criticism of the LWV diminished. Election losers frequently blamed their loss on the women's vote, but this soon sounded more like an excuse than an accurate appraisal. Support of the NLWV grew as they proved themselves to be responsible and sober. Albert Beveridge addressed the 1921 convention and came away greatly impressed: "No public assemblage, whether of men or women, ever appealed to me more powerfully than did that historic meeting of women. In sagacity, in dignity, in accuracy of procedure, you women approached perfection." [39] The ultimate stamp of approval came from Herbert Hoover, the women's hero since the war: "I think they are a hard-working body of earnest, studious women, and I believe that a similar organization for men would be an excellent thing for the country." [40]

Not all the league's difficulties came from politicians. It faced the hostility of women who felt the NLWV was butting into preempted territory, and the old split between the National Woman's Party and NAWSA continued to hamper organizational efforts. The California Civic League joined the NLWV in 1921, but only after some stiff opposition and continued harassment. Gail Laughlin, NWP member and master at organizational infighting, was a director of the Civic League and used her power to disrupt the transition. The Civic League voted to affiliate in May, but it was nearly wrecked by November. Laughlin and her cohorts kept important local units from joining the LWV. The president of the California LWV beat down the heckling and attacks to adopt a constitution, but she reported that they needed money badly and had only one subscribing member.[41]

The principal opposition came from local clubs of the General Federation of Women's Clubs which saw the NLWV as a threat or as superfluous. NLWV's organizers reported open opposition in many states. One NLWV official said of the opposition, "We encounter it in nearly every state in the country but the strength of the League is so great and its need so definite and assured, that no united effort of Federated Club women [can] ever really retard its growth." [42] And the fears of a raid by the NLWV had some basis since some clubs did switch to the NLWV.[43]

Significant friction in the 1920s was avoided with the election of Alice Ames Winter as president of the General Federation. She had been a social worker and suffrage leader and sympathized with some objectives of the NLWV. In the fall of 1921 she scotched further antagonism by issuing a joint letter with Maud Wood Park, president of NLWV. While the letter concerned only their common interests in conservation, it implied that each group had a place and called for cooperation. Winter's joining with Park signified GFWC approval of the NLWV, thereby relieving opposition and smoothing the way for further NLWV expansion.[44]

After forming the NLWV, its leaders moved to create a phalanx of women's organizations to achieve legislative objectives. Some device was needed to coordinate the work of the numerous groups, prevent useless duplication, and squeeze maximum benefit from the new circumstances. At the invitation of the League of Women Voters, ten organizations claiming over 10,000,000 members formed the Women's Joint Congressional Committee (WJCC) on November 22, 1920.[45] Maud Wood Park was permanent chairman. The NLWV urged its state leagues to form state equivalents, and most complied, including two which pre-dated the Joint Congressional Committee. California had had its Women's Legislative Council since 1911, and New York had organized the Women's Joint Legislative Conference with Mary E. Dreier as president in 1919.[46]

The post-war period found women's organizations trying to cooperate in order to take advantage of the new situation. Many felt that women were issue-oriented, and the WJCC was designed to focus upon particular issues. Many organizations established special committees to make contact with others, exchange information, and coordinate activities. The WJCC served as a clearing house and harmonizer of national lobbying efforts. If three (later five) groups wanted to promote some measure, they formed a subcommittee, elected a chairman to

supervise the venture, and handled all the details. The WJCC
was the formal contact point.[47] Some proposals, such as the ma-
ternity- and infancy-protection bill and the child labor amendment, received unanimous support. The membership fluctuated,
reaching a peak of twenty-one from 1924 to 1927. In 1932
there were still nineteen constituents.[48]

Friends called the WJCC "the most powerful lobby in
Washington," [49] and its enemies sometimes agreed. The AMA,
which suffered a setback on the maternity and infancy bill, reported, "Members of Congress of years' experience say that the
lobby in favor of the bill was the most powerful and persistent
that had ever invaded Washington." [50] The WJCC was particularly effective when the subcommittees were chaired by
vigorous, able women. For example, much of the strength of
the subcommittee on the maternity bill came from the determined leadership of its chairman, Florence Kelley, the general
secretary of the National Consumers' League. Later she headed
up the successful effort to have Congress approve the child labor amendment. Another example of effective leadership was
Maud Wood Park, who successfully lobbied the bill to grant
independent citizenship to women in 1922.

The Women's Joint Congressional Committee was an instrument of social feminism. It presented an organized and aroused
womanhood to Congress; and until the rejection by the states
of the child labor amendment in 1924 and 1925, measures
backed by the subcommittees passed with surprising regularity.
Some proposals, such as independent citizenship, were narrowly
concerned with women's rights, but the great majority of the
WJCC work supported social legislation. Some of their most
strenuous effort went into winning expanded appropriations
for both the Women's Bureau and the Children's Bureau in
1921, 1922, 1923, and 1924. The discriminatory salary limitations imposed on the Women's Bureau in 1920 were eliminated,
and the only Labor Department bureaus whose funds were increased by Congress in 1921 were those for which women's
organizations worked.[51] Social feminist pressure caused Congress to retain the current appropriations for administering the

minimum-wage board for the District of Columbia in 1921 in spite of the recommendations of the Budget Bureau and the attempt of the House Appropriations Committee to eliminate the funds. Women forced a reluctant Congress to approve the Sheppard-Towner Maternity- and Infancy-Protection Act in 1921 and expand its coverage to Hawaii in 1924. The WJCC had subcommittees working with other interested groups to win the Packers and Stockyards Control Act (1921), establish the U.S. Coal Commission (1921), strengthen the Coal Commission (1923), and outlaw the shipment of "filled milk" (coconut oil substituted for natural fat) in interstate or foreign commerce (1923). Civil service reclassification (1923), a federal prison for women (1924), the child labor amendment (1924), and compulsory school attendance for the District of Columbia (1925) were other successful fights of the social feminists working through the WJCC. On the negative side the WJCC lobbied against many measures which threatened previous reforms, the equal rights amendment every year after 1923, and the Wadsworth-Garrett amendment after 1925.

Many of the educational measures supported by the WJCC failed to pass in the 1920s: federal aid to promote physical education, a department of education, increased aid to home economics education. The memory of the struggle for these caused Elizabeth Tilton, a lobbyist for the Parent-Teachers Association, to recall in exaggerated fashion, " 'Don't argue with the East wind,' says J. R. Lowell, 'put on an overcoat!' The women's organizations put on raincoats and stood in the deluge, never swerving one inch from their Federal cycle of ideas; but hardly one of our special bills ever passed in all the eight years [1921–29] that I worked in Washington." [52]

The period of greatest impact of social feminism was 1920 to 1925, and some of the success in this time resulted from efforts channeled through the Women's Joint Congressional Committee. Congressmen feared a women's bloc initially; and it appeared to have taken shape in the WJCC. However, as a women's vote failed to materialize, legislators became less amenable. Politicians found that women divided like men. In addition, the 1924 elections thinned progressive ranks in Congress, and in particular the child labor amendment went down by a whopping 3 to 1 margin in Massachusetts. For reasons not entirely clear, women's organizations across the nation became either more conservative on social issues or more concerned with special-interest questions. Some of the conservatism stemmed from the merciless red-baiting of social feminists, but one still wonders why the smears were more effective in 1924–25 than they were in 1921–24. While social feminism made additional gains in the latter part of the 1920s, they were fewer and more difficult to achieve. The feminist movement worked for, and won, many social reforms; but it also reached for full citizenship as exemplified in independent nationality for women, jury service, and the rewards of office-holding.

NOTES

1. Anne F. Scott found the same phenomenon among the southern women. See *The Southern Lady*, 186 ff.

2. Ernest Greenwood, "Attributes of a Profession," *Social Work*, II (July, 1957), 45–55.

3. Willystine Goodsell, "The Educational Opportunities of American Women—Theoretical and Actual," *Annals of the American Academy of Political and Social Science*, CXLIII (May, 1929), 6.

4. *Ibid.*, 7.

5. Morris L. Cogan, "Toward a Definition of Profession," *Harvard Educational Review*, XXIII (1953), 42; see also William J. Goode, "Community within a Community: The Professions," *American Sociological Review*, XXII (1957), 194–200; Harvey L. Smith, "Contingencies of Professional Differentiation," *American Journal of Sociology*, LXIII (1958), 410–414.

6. Roy Lubove, *Professional Altruist: The Emergence of Social Work as a Career, 1880–1930* (Cambridge: Harvard University Press, 1955), 118–156.

7. Bertha Van Hoosen, "Address of the President at Second Annual Meeting of the Medical Women's National Association," *Woman's Medical Journal*, XXVII (June, 1917), 129; "Proceedings of the 11th Annual Meeting of American Woman Dentists, Buffalo, New York, Sept. 11, 1932," Stillwell MSS, Historical Society of Pennsylvania; Rosalie F. Janoer, "The Practicing Woman Lawyer's Need," *Women Lawyers' Journal*, IX (Feb., 1920), 12; Eliza M. Mosher, "United We Stand," *Medical Woman's Journal*, XXVIII (Apr., 1921), 100; "The Value of Organization to Medical Women," *ibid.*, XXIX (May, 1922), 92–93; Kate C. Mead, "Amalgamation, Not Segregation—for What Reasons?," *ibid.*, XXX (Aug., 1923), 245–247.

8. A chronological list shows the diversity:
National Organization of Public Health Nursing   1912
National Woman's Association of Commerce
    (held first national meeting in 1917)   1912

Medical Women's National Association	1915
National Council of Administrative Women in Education	1915
American Federation of Teachers	1916*
National Association of Deans of Women	1916
Altrusa International	1917
American Dietetic Association	1917
American Association of Hospital Social Workers	1918
American Association of Visiting Teachers	1918
American Association of Women [Preachers] Ministers	1919
National Federation of Business and Professional Women's Clubs	1919
Quota International	1919
Zonta International	1919
American Society of X-Ray Technicians	1920*
Association of Women in Public Health	1920
Osteopathic Women's National Association	1920
American Federation of Soroptimist Clubs	1921
American Physical Therapy Association	1921*
National Association of Bank Women	1921
American Women's Association	1922
Association of American Women Dentists	1922
Association of Women in Architecture	1922
American Dental Hygienists Association	1923
National Association of Women Lawyers (the New York–based Women Lawyers' Association, organized in 1911, expanded into a true national organization)	1923
American Dental Assistants Association	1924
Society of Women Geographers	1925
American Association of Psychiatric Social Workers	1926*
American Association of Medical Record Librarians	1928

* Men and women, but predominantly female.

9. For the history of the NFBPWC see the series by Helen Havener, "The Business Woman Awake: The History of the Federation," *Independent Woman*, n.s., VI–VII (Mar., 1927–July, 1928); see also Lena Madesin Phillips, "Getting Together," *Women Lawyers' Journal*, VIII (June, 1919), 38; Emma Dot Partridge, "What Federation Means," *Independent Woman*, X (Nov., 1926), 13.

10. Jean H. Norris, "National Federation of Business and Professional Women's Clubs," *Women Lawyers' Journal*, IX (Oct.–Dec., 1919), 1.

11. The withdrawal of the California federation crippled the NFBPWC in California for several years. A new California League of Business and Professional Women was organized and held its first convention in May, 1928. See "Our State Conventions," *Independent Woman*, n.s., VII (July, 1928), 318.

12. Havener, "The Business Woman Awake, XII," *ibid.* (Feb., 1928), 67.

13. "The Convention in Brief," *ibid.* (Aug., 1928), 361.

14. Genevieve N. Gildersleeve, *Women in Banking: A History of the National Association of Bank Women* (Washington: Public Affairs Press, 1959), 1–6; Nancy B. Staub, President, NABW, "N.A.B.W., Yesterday, Today, and Tomorrow," speech, 1954, NABW Files, folder B–3, National As-

sociation of Bank Women, Inc., New York; Anne Seward, *The Woman's Department* (Bank Department Series, New York: Bankers Publishing Co., 1924), 1–6.

15. "Presidents on Parade," *The Woman Banker*, XXII (Aug.–Sept., 1946), 4.

16. The wives of both Macy and Vanderlip were in the forefront for social welfare legislation, peace, and women's rights. What role they played in the advance of bank women is open to speculation.

17. Emma E. Claus, "Association Story," NABW Files, folder B-1, NABW, Inc., N.Y.

18. Gildersleeve, *Women in Banking*, 45–49.

19. "History of the N.A.B.W.," NABW Files, folder A-1, NABW, Inc., N.Y.; Agnes Kenny to Sophonisba P. Breckinridge, May 31, 1934, Breckinridge MSS, box 20, LC.

20. Glendower Evans to Jessie Donaldson Hodder, Feb. 2, 1921, Jessie Donaldson Hodder MSS, folder 14, SL; Blatch and Lutz, *Challenging Years*, 313; *New York Times*, Mar. 22, 1921.

21. Alice Paul to Maud Wood Park, Jan. 3, 1921, National League of Women Voters Papers, Ser. II, box 6, National Woman's Party folder, LC.

22. Carrie Chapman Catt, "The Nation Calls," address to the Jubilee Convention, Mar. 24, 1919, Catt MSS, box 4, NYPL.

23. William Theodore Doyle, "Charlotte Perkins Gilman and the Cycle of Feminist Reform" (Ph.D. thesis, University of California, Berkeley, 1960), 147.

24. "The Excursion," Dorothy Kirchwey Brown MSS, box 1, folder 25, SL.

25. Committees and original chairmen:
Women in Industry—Mrs. Raymond Robins (Mary McDowell in May, 1920)
Food Supply and Demand (later renamed Living Costs)—Mrs. Edward Costigan
Social Hygiene—Dr. Valaria Parker
Child Welfare—Mrs. Percy Pennybacker
American Citizenship (changed in 1923 to Education)—Mrs. Frederick Bagby
Legal Status of Women (later called Uniform Laws for Women)—Katherine Waugh McCullough
[Election Laws and Methods (added May, 1920, dropped in 1922)—Carrie Chapman Catt]
[International Cooperation (added 1923)—Ruth Morgan]

26. "Report of the Executive Secretary to the Annual Convention of the Minnesota League of Women Voters," Oct. 18, 1921, NLWV Papers, Ser. II, box 1, Minnesota file, LC.

27. Elizabeth O. Toombs, "The Convention at Des Moines," *Good Housekeeping*, LXXVII (July, 1923), 48.

28. Catt and Shuler, *Woman Suffrage and Politics*, 383–384.

29. Elizabeth O. Toombs, "Suffrage Jubilee," *Good Housekeeping*, LXX (May, 1920), 19.

30. *Ibid.*, 121.

31. Maud Wood Park, "National League of Women Voters—First Year (February 1920 to April 1921)—Supplementary Notes," recollection, 1943, Edna L. Stantial MSS, Dillon Collection, folder 16, SL; Katherine Philips Edson to Cornelia Bryce Pinchot, Nov. 27, 1920, C. B. Pinchot MSS, box 12, LC; Harriet Taylor Upton to Edna Fischel Gellhorn, Dec. 29, 1920, Gellhorn MSS, folder 1, SL.

32. Mrs. Glen P. Turner to Mrs. M. V. O'Shea, Aug. 30, 1922, NLWV Papers, Ser. II, box 2, Wisconsin file, LC.

33. "The Excursion," Brown MSS, box 1, folder 25, SL; Mabeth H. Paige to Mrs. Richard Edwards, Oct. 21, 1921, NLWV Papers, Ser. II, box 1, Minnesota file, LC; "Report of the Executive Secretary to the Annual Convention of the Minnesota League of Women Voters," Oct. 18, 1921, ibid.

34. Virginia Clark Abbott, *The History of Woman Suffrage and the League of Women Voters in Cuyahoga County, 1911–1945* (Cleveland: n.p., n.d.), 173.

35. Elizabeth O. Toombs, "Politicians Take Notice," *Good Housekeeping*, LXX (Mar., 1920), 14–15.

36. "The Excursion," Brown MSS, box 1, folder 25, SL.

37. Catt to Edna Fischel Gellhorn, Jan. 6, 1920, Gellhorn MSS, folder 3, SL.

38. "A Challenge to Corrupt Politics," *Woman Citizen*, V (Apr. 23, 1921), 1181.

39. Albert Beveridge to Carrie Chapman Catt, May 4, 1921, NLWV Papers, Ser. II, box 3, Catt folder, LC.

40. Quoted in Toombs, "The Convention at Des Moines," 48.

41. Mrs. William Palmer Lucas to Marie Stuart Edwards, Nov. 1, 1921, NLWV Papers, Ser. II, box 4, Miscellaneous Correspondence folder, LC; Anna C. Law, President, California LWV, to Marie Stuart Edwards, Nov. 18, 1921, ibid., box 1, California file; see also Law to Maud Wood Parks, May 14, 1921; Law to Edwards, Oct. 21, 1921; telegram, Law to Edwards, Oct. 29, 1921; report of NLWV organizer Susie W. Smith, Nov. 21–27, 1921, ibid.

42. Mrs. James Paige to Mrs. A. F. Rice, Jan. 19, 1922, ibid., box 1, Montana file; report of NLWV organizer Susie W. Smith, Jan. 16–24, 1922, ibid., Idaho file; report of Emma A. Ingalls, Feb. 21–Mar. 7, 1922, ibid.; Mabeth H. Paige to Minnie Fisher Cunningham, Oct. 21, 1921, ibid., Minnesota file; report of Liba Peshakova, Sept. 29, 1921, ibid., Mississippi file; Olive Beldon Lewis to Mrs. Charles H. Dietrich, June 2, 1920, ibid., Nebraska file; report of Olive Lewis, June 1–5, 1921, ibid.; report of Gladys Pyle, June 16, 1922, ibid.; report of Gladys Pyle, ibid., box 2, South Dakota file; report of Emma Charlotte Dumke, Oct. 31–Nov. 10, 1921, ibid., Wisconsin file.

43. Report of NLWV organizer Gladys Pyle, Nov. 5, 1921, ibid., box 2, South Dakota file; Jane Brooks to Marie Stuart Edwards, June 6, 1922, ibid., box 8, Idaho, Illinois, and Kansas file; Edwards to Brooks, June 12, 1922, ibid.

44. "The New President of the G.F.W.C.," *Woman Citizen*, V (July 10, 1920), 153; Carrie Chapman Catt to Maud Wood Park, July 13, 1921, NLWV Papers, Ser. II, box 3, Catt folder, LC; Mrs. John L. Pyle, President, SDLWV, to Mrs. Richard Edwards, Oct. 15, 1921, ibid., box 2, South Dakota file.

45. NLWV, GFWC, WCTU, PTA, NFBPWC, National Consumers' League, Association of Collegiate Alumnae (later AAUW), National Council of Jewish Women, American Home Economics Association.

46. Doyle, "Charlotte Perkins Gilman," 149–150; *Survey*, XLII (Sept. 13, 1919), 853.

47. "Joint Congressional Committee," *Woman Citizen*, V (Dec. 4, 1920), 748–749.

48. Breckinridge, *Women in the Twentieth Century*, 259–260. New members: 1921—Girls Friendly Society, YWCA, DAR, Women's International League for Peace and Freedom; 1922—National Council of Women, Service Star Legion; 1923—AFT, NEA, National Committee for Department of Education; 1924—American Nurses Association, Council of Women for Home Missions, Medical Women's National Association, National Association of Col-

ored Women; 1925—Women's Homeopathic Medical Fraternity; 1931—American Dietetic Association. In the course of the decade these withdrew: DAR, GFWC, WCTU, Women's International League for Peace and Freedom, National Council of Women, National Association of Colored Women.

49. Charles A. Selden, "The Most Powerful Lobby in Washington," *Ladies Home Journal*, XXIX (Apr., 1922), 5.

50. Editorial, *Journal of the American Medical Association*, LXXVIII (Feb. 11, 1922), 434; see also "Mrs. Catt to Name New Federal Department," *Woman Patriot*, VI (Apr. 1, 1922), 1.

51. NWTUL, *Proceedings* (1922), 57.

52. Elizabeth H. Tilton, "Autobiography," 1945, Elizabeth H. Tilton MSS, folder 235, SL.

THREE

The Struggle for Full Citizenship

Few doubted that a new day had dawned for women. The periodical literature abounded with comments on woman's "New Work," "New World," "New Society," "New Politics," "New Social Vision," and even the "New Man," who must appear as the complement to the "New Woman." [1] The impetus gained in the war brought feminism into its best years. Suffrage was won, and the movement reached for the rewards of strength. Many women assumed that the Nineteenth Amendment brought full citizenship; but in fact such was not the case, as women were barred from jury duty and office-holding, and the nationality of a married woman was determined by her husband. Women found that jury service and the right to hold office required further campaigns and the laws had to be rewritten to give women independent citizenship.

The question of independent citizenship for women was an unambiguous feminist issue. This problem was not created by World War I or the winning of suffrage; but the war had dramatized the defects of current laws, and suffrage provided the muscle to win changes. Before the Cable Act of 1922, a woman's citizenship was a function of marriage; she automatically assumed her husband's nationality regardless of her preference or place of residence. The concept of single nationality became clearly archaic once there was woman suffrage. If women were to be full and free citizens, their citizenship status could not be dependent on someone else. The desire for independent, equal citizenship was a logical next step.[2] The irony of this situation lay in the fact that the concept of single nationality was relatively new.

English common law assumed perpetual nationality regardless of marriage. In 1790 the U.S. Congress asserted that expatriation was a natural right—an obvious fact to a nation of immigrants; but it retained the common-law concept of separate citizenship.[3] As waves of people migrated and international marriages multiplied, the concept of permanent citizenship became inconvenient, resulting in dual nationality. Perpetual nationality gave way to the principle of single nationality, determined by the husband. The first law code to embody this was the Code of Napoleon in 1804. England took a half-step in 1844 when it gave British nationality automatically to women who married British subjects. The United States adopted the same rule in 1855.[4]

No act fully covered American women who married aliens. In order to conform to the general international standard the United States adopted in 1907 the principle of single citizenship: "Any woman who marries a foreigner shall take the nationality of her husband." It was automatic, and the woman could not determine her own citizenship as long as the marriage lasted.[5] While tardy in adopting this rule, the United States did so when the status of women was changing dramatically; and the law was an affront to feminism. It took World War I to demonstrate the absurdity of the law.

Having one's citizenship removed did not cover the range of difficulties. By 1907 numerous states had laws which penalized aliens, prohibiting them from inheriting property or buying real estate. Others closed certain professions and occupations; New York, for example, disbarred aliens from the law. Many states forbade them to teach school or practice medicine. A woman who lost her citizenship by marriage was barred from state or federal civil service exams or from holding any elective or appointive office in government.[6] When the war came, many women who had never been outside of the country, but who had married resident aliens from the Central Powers, found themselves classified as enemy aliens. Their property was seized and they were subject to government surveillance for the duration. An example was the case of an American woman who married an Austrian years before World War I. He was killed in a mine accident in Washington and the unnaturalized widow was paid compensation under the state's workmen's compensation act. When the United States entered the war, the woman, though born in and a permanent resident of the country, was declared an enemy alien, and the compensation money was seized and held by the alien-property custodian.[7]

Prominent, but not pitiful, was Gladys Vanderbilt, who saw her property seized under the Alien-Property Act because she was married to Count Szecheny, who was later the Austrian ambassador to the United States.[8] Others caught by the 1907 law included the militant suffragist Inez Milholland Boissevain, Harriot Stanton Blatch, and daughters of William Jennings Bryan and Mrs. O. H. P. Belmont, the militant head of the Woman's Party.

Anomalies could be worked out with special acts of Congress, but the granting of private naturalization acts violated the constitutional scruples of congressmen. The Constitution declared that Congress was empowered "to establish an uniform Rule of Naturalization," and special acts seemed to contravene a uniform rule. Consequently, Congress balked at further acts despite numerous petitions for relief. The appeals demonstrated the clear need for change, and suffrage provided the lever for women to move Congress to enact the Married Women's Independent Citizenship Act on September 22, 1922.[9]

As early as 1910, Congressman Edward Taylor of Colorado submitted a bill to Congress to eliminate the 1907 act, but the bill died in committee. The Association of Women Lawyers was the only women's organization working for a bill before 1920.[10] Ellen Spencer Mussey worked ceaselessly to get a bill introduced and passed, and such a measure appeared every year from 1913 through 1920 without success. In 1920 the National League of Women Voters adopted a resolution urging that the laws be changed so that a resident American woman would not suffer loss of citizenship by marriage and that alien women be naturalized by the same procedure as men.[11] Representatives from this and other women's organizations appeared before the platform committees of the national political parties to ask their endorsement, and the major parties agreed.

Senator Charles Curtis moved in December, 1921, to redeem the convention pledge. However, in April, 1922, an omnibus immigration bill also was submitted which incorporated Curtis's proposals along with a host of controversial provisions which endangered the bill. Maud Wood Park and the Women's Joint Congressional Committee wanted the question of independent citizenship to get a hearing on its own merits; therefore they opposed the omnibus bill. Also the Curtis bill encountered certain objections, so Congressman John L. Cable introduced a bill drawn up in consultation with Maud Wood Park. Park was the chief spokesman for the women in the hearings on the bill. "A woman is as much an individual as a man is, and her citizenship should no more be gained or lost by marriage than should a man's. To forfeit or acquire citizenship," she argued, "by the mere fact of marriage without regard for the desires or the qualifications of the individual affected, belittles both the individual and the sacred right of citizenship." [12]

During the 1922 hearings the WJCC kept up the pressure until the House Committee on Immigration and Naturalization approved the bill and submitted it to the House for action. Then the women interviewed each congressman to win his support and the House approved overwhelmingly on June 20, 1922. Supporters of the Cable Act in Congress agreed that World War I had demonstrated the inadequacies of the principle of single nationality, and that woman suffrage called for separate citizenship if it were to be meaningful.[13] John Jacob Rogers confessed that suffrage had changed the whole situation: "In my judgment there was no particular force in the demand for this bill until the nineteenth amendment became a part of the organic law of the land." [14] After having been ignored for years before suffrage, the bill passed on the first attempt in 1922. The bill's sponsor, Congressman Cable, gave complete credit to the women, describing the WJCC as "the most energetic lobby ever concentrated on Capitol Hill." [15]

Senator Curtis withdrew his bill in deference to the Cable Bill, which moved through the House in a month. However, it ran into opposition and heavy traffic in the Senate Committee on Immigration and lay untouched until September, when Congress began its mad rush for adjournment. The women feared their bill might be lost, but Maud Wood Park and others rounded up a quorum of the Senate committee and got them to vote the bill out on September 8. The Senate passed the measure on a voice vote the next day. President Harding signed the act on September 22, 1922, and sent Park the pen used for the signing.[16]

The Cable Act, hailed as a great victory for women's rights, actually had granted citizenship grudgingly. In view of the limited opposition to the bill, the WJCC and Maud Wood Park were too conservative in their demands. They should have asked for citizenship identical to men.[17] Park pointed out some of the defects in the committee hearings, but the primary thing was to establish the principle that a woman had the equal right to choose nationality. The faults could be eliminated later. One provision of the act contradicted the very idea of the bill and reflected the racist thinking which produced the immigration restriction laws of the 1920s. This clause stripped citizenship from a native American woman who married a foreigner ineligible by race for naturalization, and she could not be repatriated as long as the marriage lasted. American-born women of those ineligible groups who were citizens by birth but who married aliens of their own group not only lost their citizenship but also forfeited the right ever to recover it! No similar laws applied to men.[18] The law changed the status of a native American woman married to an alien to that of a *naturalized* citizen. Hence, she faced the same restrictions as a foreign-born naturalized citizen. The most onerous of these was the presumption that she renounced her American citizenship if she lived abroad with her alien husband for more than two years at a time. At no time was a native American man ever subjected to this presumption.

A beneficial aspect was the provision for shortening the process of naturalization for a repatriated person from five to one year's residence. However, in 1924 Congress passed the Immigrant Quota Law, which required a returnee to come as a quota immigrant. If the quota of her husband's country were filled, she could not gain entry even for the purpose of repatriation. Furthermore, when a woman was admitted and tried to take advantage of the shortened process, she had to prove that she was back permanently in order to meet the residence requirements—something which was difficult to show, especially if she had a husband and children still overseas. The imperfections imbedded in the law were eliminated in 1930 and 1931, and the WJCC did the main lobbying on the measures. However, the problems of nationality were international inasmuch as American laws created a limbo for foreign-born women who automatically lost their native citizenship but who did not automatically acquire American citizenship. These were stateless until they qualified.[19] The United States tried unsuccessfully to get other countries to agree to independent, equal citizenship at the Hague Conference for Codification of International Law in March, 1930.

Most women assumed that winning suffrage would give them the right to hold public office and to serve on juries. Voting and office-holding were deemed inseparable, but some states ruled women off the ballot. New Hampshire's attorney general issued an official statement saying that under common law a woman could not hold office, but in 1920 New Hampshire elected two women to the state legislature anyway. On the other hand in Arkansas a woman had to withdraw her candidacy because the state law disqualified her. Twenty-three states elected women to the legislature or some other office in 1920 and several others had already had women officials. In order to clarify their status, feminists lobbied for specific legislation granting the right to hold office. The question was settled in Michigan by a Detroit circuit judge. An opponent of women's rights sued for the removal of a woman justice of the peace on the grounds that since she was married, she was a chattel and not a person, "woman by law not being permitted to exercise a judicial office and to discharge the duties thereof, she being sexually unable to do so as a matter of nature and as a matter of law." The judge cut off the attorney's plea and dismissed the case with the remark that the Nineteenth Amendment settled all that. Elsewhere the issue dragged on for years; Iowa amended its constitution in 1926, Oklahoma in 1942! [20]

Of the sixteen states with full enfranchisement before the Nineteenth Amendment, only five (Idaho, Kansas, Michigan, Nevada, and Utah) ruled that the ballot entitled women to jury duty. Even here, anti-suffragists sometimes challenged the Attorney General's ruling and the courts had to decide. In Michigan, for example, jury service was considered automatic in 1918, but its validity was not certain until December, 1920, when the Michigan Supreme Court agreed. In two more old suffrage states, Washington and California, women were disqualified by legal opinion until special legislation removed the barrier. Of the remaining thirty-two states fully enfranchised by the amendment, seven (Indiana, Iowa, Ohio, Delaware, Kentucky, Pennsylvania, New Jersey) permitted service automatically. The bar lay in the fact that most state constitutions and statutes said that juries and office holders must be men. The decision to admit women turned on rulings as to whether "men" was a generic term or excluded women. Since states with nearly identical statutes came to opposite conclusions, the ruling depended in the final analysis upon the bias of the legal authorities. Most ruled against women, agreeing with New Hampshire that "the 19th Amendment applies solely to voting." North Carolina's attorney general ruled: "The term jury at the time of the enactment—had a known and definite signification —as follows: a jury is a body of *men*. The only way that women could be liable to jury service is by act of legislature." [21] Such decisions outraged women and set off a drive in each case to have the constitution or statute changed. Arkansas passed such an act in 1920; and Louisiana, Maine, Minnesota, North Dakota, Oregon, and Wisconsin followed in 1921.

On appeals of attorney general decisions the bias of the judges was supreme. Two court decisions illustrate the wide discrepancy. In 1920 the Michigan Supreme Court held that common law did not apply and that the word "men" in the state constitution was a generic term which means "male" and "female." The Massachusetts Supreme Court in 1931 barred women from jury service despite the fact that state law made no mention of sex: "A person qualified to vote for representatives of the General Court shall be liable to serve as a juror." The court ruled that a literal translation was invalid, that one had to take into account common law, the history, times, and customs when the statute was passed. In short, the court ruled that women were not voters when the law was passed; therefore they could not serve on juries without a special act of the legislature.[22]

If the rulings were negative and the women failed to reverse them almost immediately, they were condemned to an extended battle for the basic right to serve on a jury. The Illinois attorney general ruled that the words "electors" and "legal voters" in the jury statutes did not include women since they had not been electors when the statute was enacted. The Illinois Supreme Court agreed, and the women struggled for years to overcome these rulings. A bill to grant jury service was defeated in 1923, 1925, 1927; and the 1929 General Assembly referred the issue to the electorate in a referendum for November, 1930. The women won but the Illinois Supreme Court ruled the referendum unconstitutional. The denial was a bitter defeat to Illinois women, who then had to wait until 1939.

The effort in Connecticut lasted until 1937. In this case the proponents had to outlive the anti-suffrage generation and wait for Republican domination of the state to be broken in the Great Depression. The Republican party in Connecticut was essentially anti-suffrage: the governor refused to summon the special session which would have made Connecticut instead

of Tennessee the thirty-sixth state, and Senator Frank Brandegee was on NAWSA's "Most Wanted List" because of his stub-
born opposition to suffrage. The suffragists attacked in 1920
when the Connecticut Woman Suffrage Association declared
its opposition to the Republican party and actively campaigned
to defeat Brandegee. The Republicans swept the state and at
this early date learned of the political weakness of social feminism. As a result women had a difficult struggle for all progressive legislation and for jury service in particular until the
1930s.

When women were ruled out of the jury box, the Connecticut League of Women Voters spearheaded the effort to
overcome this decision, but they were defeated every session
from 1921 to 1937. The Republican party dominated the state
so thoroughly that no opponent even appeared to testify in
hearings on the bill until 1927, and then opposing testimony
was probably prompted by the fact that the Senate voted its
approval in 1925. Starting in 1927, important Republican
women testified against the bill. Katherine Bryne, vice-chairman of the State Republican Central Committee, reported that
she had canvassed thousands of women all over the state and
none favored jury duty: "Laissez faire—let it alone, gentlemen." Alice Coe, Republican member of the legislature, added:
"Women should be more concerned over the breaking down
of homes than over the breaking down of the jury system."
She argued that women were less fitted mentally and physically
for jury service.[23] One Republican representative said the jury
box was no place for a lady, except some hard-boiled women.
Jury service would "unsex" a woman, not to speak of the im-
propriety of women having to stay overnight when a jury
was locked up.[24] In 1929, in spite of the fact that women had
served on juries in twenty-one states for most of the decade, a
Republican state senator remarked: "Connecticut is conservative and does not run after every fad and notion." [25] However,
the stock argument from 1921 was simply that Connecticut
women did not want jury service.

The proponents argued that jury duty was not a question

of desire, but rather the obligation of full citizenship. Furthermore, they maintained that a woman could not receive equal justice from a jury that was not a cross section of the entire community. Replying to the argument that women should not be subjected to unseemly testimony or were too emotional and illogical, the proponents demanded they be treated as mature adults and pointed to the experience of women in other states. Judges and attorneys in jury states testified that women served as well or better than men. In fact, in Bayonne, New Jersey, in 1927 an all-female jury had functioned so successfully that the judge said he doubted he even wanted male jurors again.[26] The women pointed out that women helped make the laws and were present in the courts as lawyers, witnesses, and litigants. They demanded jury service as a matter of justice: "Jury service for women is another step toward the attainment of that universal standard of justice for which the American nation stands." [27]

The Senate majority leader scoffed at the advocates, saying that obviously Connecticut women did not care since they did not punish the Republican party for its record on the issue.[28] And, while the Republicans controlled both houses, the bill usually went down by 5 to 1 margins. In the late 1920s even the Democratic party dropped the plank from its platform. However, the Depression destroyed Republican control of the state, and the Democrats captured the governorship and the Senate. Finally, in 1937 the governor threw his influence behind the jury bill and it passed. Present at the signing were representatives of the Connecticut LWV.

By the end of 1921 twenty states had put women on their juries, but the forward momentum collapsed. Most legislatures held biennial sessions, and when they convened in 1923, the drive for jury service had ground to a halt. Ohio made statutory her attorney general's ruling, and only the Territory of Alaska represented a new victory. The LWV tried to get jury service in twelve states in the 1927 sessions. Congress voted service for the District of Columbia and Rhode Island joined the ranks that year, but from then until 1935 no other states extended the right.

The effort to get jury service was a partial measure of feminist power in the 1920s. Most victories were made in an atmosphere of uncertainty about the extent of the women's vote. Before 1922 when this power was unknown, twenty states gave jury service; but as the uncertainty began to evaporate, only three jurisdictions (only one state) granted it from 1922 to 1935. In states like New York and Connecticut, where the women attempted a bloc power play in 1920 and failed, the opponents realized the limits of the threat and jury service was denied until the late 1930s. As no discernible women's vote materialized elsewhere, legislators became less pliant. In fact, opponents initiated efforts to cut back women's participation; for example, in Pennsylvania in 1923 such a bill was on its way to swift passage until the LWV blocked it.[29]

II

One reward of power was position, and the coming of suffrage brought an increase in the number of women holding significant places in government.[30] Before suffrage seemed inevitable only Julia Lathrop held a major executive office in the federal government. President Taft had appointed her chief of the Children's Bureau in 1912. In the last years of his administration, President Wilson moved to attract the female vote by elevating several women to responsibility.[31] Upon recommendation of his Attorney General, he placed Kathryn Sellers on the Juvenile Court of the District of Columbia in October, 1918. "The President frankly said that he was making an experiment of the woman judge. . . ."[32] He was satisfied and assigned a woman to the U.S. District for San Francisco, one of the heaviest working districts in the country; and he appointed Annette Adams as Assistant U.S. Attorney General. In a direct gesture to the suffragists Wilson appointed Helen H. Gardener, NAWSA vice-president, to the U.S. Civil Service Commission in 1920. Mary Van Kleeck headed the Woman in Industry Service during the war; Mary Anderson succeeded her in 1919 and became chief of the Women's Bureau in 1920. Wilson appointed women to the District of Columbia Commission, the D.C. Rent Commission, and the U.S. Employees' Compensation Commission.

President Harding repaid the women's election support with some significant appointments, assistance for key items in their program, and by refusing to dismiss married women from government service when some proposed it as a way to economize. In 1921 Harding chose for important offices two women who had the overwhelming support of progressive women. Since Mary Anderson was a Wilson appointee, party regulars felt that a deserving party figure should get her place as head of the Women's Bureau. She was reappointed after a number of prominent Republican women supported her, notably Harriet Taylor Upton and Mrs. Douglas Robinson, the sister of Theodore Roosevelt. The question of her reappointment never came up again until her retirement in 1944.[33] Julia Lathrop carried to fruition her idea of a maternity- and infancy-protection bill and wanted to retire. Mrs. Harry Kluegel of San Francisco mounted a campaign to get herself appointed,[34] and this effort disturbed social feminists. Katherine Philips Edson, progressive member of the Executive Committee of the Republican National Committee, telegraphed her strong disapproval of Kluegel: "She has no backing from women's organizations in the West where she is known per past experience. . . . California women would deeply resent her appointment to Children's Bureau as their representative. . . . Please prevent this appointment." Harriet Taylor Upton, vice-chairman of the Executive Committee of the Republican National Committee, relayed it to Harding with her agreement.[35] She also advanced the name of Grace Abbott, saying that Lathrop had wanted to resign for months but wanted to be certain that Abbott would be her successor.[36] Secretary of Labor James J. Davis was delighted to escape the pressure from Kluegel when he became aware of Grace Abbott: "I had forgotten she had served in the Bureau." [37] She was appointed and Hull House alumnae continued to dominate the Children's Bureau.

Helen Gardener's appointment to the Civil Service Commission came under attack from politicians of both parties who sought to have her replaced. Each charged her with belonging to the other party, but she denied any partisanship: "I had been put on the Commission not as a political factor but to secure on that body the woman's point of view in the civil service." [38] Harding resisted the pressure and retained her. When she died in 1925, President Coolidge appointed another woman, Jessie Dell.

When Harding promised a social welfare department most people assumed a woman would head it.[39] He was spared the decision since the department never emerged. The next chance for cabinet rank came in 1930 when many women hoped President Hoover would select Grace Abbott as his Secretary of Labor when James Davis resigned, but she lacked enough political influence. Finally, Frances Perkins became the first woman cabinet officer as President Roosevelt's Secretary of Labor.

The NLWV convention of 1921 passed a resolution urging Harding to recognize women as an integral part of government by appointing them "on all boards and commissions dealing with or investigating international relations." [40] He promised to give it every consideration, and the opportunity to make good came sooner than expected. Senator William E. Borah had introduced a resolution in Congress in December, 1920, requesting the President to convene an international conference on the reduction of naval expenditures. He reintroduced it in April, 1921, in the special session called by Harding. While Harding did not favor the idea, he retreated in the face of pressure; and the resolution passed in July. The NLWV sought to collect on the promise, and they were joined by other women's organizations who urged that a "just representation" would include a woman in the delegation.[41] However, Helen Gardener admonished Harding not to appoint a woman simply as a gesture, but to choose one who was qualified or none at all. "Women are on trial as men are not and we feel that many years of our future success or failure are in your hands," she declared. "Far better have no woman appointed . . . one 'wrong' woman will hurt us more than the appointment of a hundred inefficient men." [42] Congresswoman Alice Robertson, the lone female in Congress and an anti-suffragist, declared that no woman should be appointed because none were qualified, but she nominated one anyway. [43]

Harding asked the advice of Harriet Taylor Upton. She replied that it would not be advisable to appoint a woman as a delegate but "it would be great politics" to appoint some to the Advisory Commission; "you could relieve the tension in three circles by appointing Mrs. [Raymond] Robins." She would represent women, labor, and the progressives. [44] Gardener and Upton concluded that best choices were Carrie Chapman Catt and Maud Wood Park, but Harding said that "there is no likelihood of both of them being appointed." [45] Neither was chosen; instead he picked four Republican women for the twenty-one-member Advisory Commission. [46] The women joined such notable men as John L. Lewis, Samuel Gompers, Herbert Hoover, General John J. Pershing, and Colonel Theodore Roosevelt. While women were honored by this choice in 1921, they had to wait until 1930 before a woman was appointed as an actual delegate to an international meeting.

To please women the Division of Home Economics was raised to bureau status in early 1923, and Harding appointed Dr. Louise Stanley as chief, thereby making three bureaus headed by women. In place of Annette Adams he chose Mabel Walker Willebrandt as Assistant Attorney General. Mabel Reinecke became Internal Revenue Collector in the Chicago office, second largest in terms of volume in the United States. When she took over in 1922 the office had a "poor" efficiency rating, but soon ranked as "excellent." [47] With some prodding from prominent women, Harding opened the Foreign Service. [48] Lucille Atcheson pioneered the way, passing the exams in July, 1922, and receiving appointment in December. Her preliminary period in the Department of State was extended from the usual three to six months to two years before receiving her overseas assignment. Some speculated as to whether she would ever be permitted to serve overseas, but in April, 1925, she was assigned to the Berne legation as Third Secretary. After 1925 four more women received appointment in the 1920s—a small number but each found it easier than her predecessor.[49] Women reached ambassadorial rank in the Roosevelt administration.

In the decade women entered nearly every aspect of the government. Bessie Parker Brueggman was made chairman of the U.S. Employees' Compensation Commission, Anna C. Tillinghast became the first woman U.S. Commissioner of Immigration, Annabel Matthews was appointed to the U.S. Board of Tax Appeals, several women became assistant trade commissioners in American consulates around the world, and Ruth Shipley was chief of the Passport Division of the Department of State. A growing number of women received judgeships, sometimes over the active opposition of male lawyers. Genevieve R. Cline was appointed justice on the U.S. Customs Court in New York in spite of being opposed by a committee of customs lawyers, the first instance of opposition to any appointment. The National Association of Women Lawyers tried to get a woman appointed in every state department of justice and as assistants to all U.S. district attorneys.[50]

Yet in relation to the number of places available and the large number of women employed under civil service, the position of women was inferior. The Woman in Industry Service discovered in 1919 that women were excluded from 60 percent of the civil service exams. Within a week of this exposure the Civil Service Commission opened all exams.[51] However, they left the discretion to the department head to specify the sex when requesting certification of eligible persons. Women clamored for removal of this hedge and to require the selection to be made from the top three scores on exams. The Harding administration passed the Veterans Preference Act, which qualified veterans with much lower scores; and since the veterans were men, the women retreated to the old practice in order to get any woman appointed.[52]

Investigation also revealed that of the 3,270 women appointed in 1919 only 5 percent got salaries over $1,299 per year, while 46 percent of the 4,689 men appointed got over $1,299. Of all women 91 percent held clerical positions. Most women assumed that the preponderance of women in the lower brackets proved discrimination. Helen Gardener, however, suggested that women must bear part of the blame. Admittedly women had faced sex barriers, but the old restrictions and prejudices were being eliminated; and the chief problem now lay in the qualifications of the women. If 91 percent were in clerical positions, these figures reflected the general qualifications of the vast majority of those applying. The fact remained that many women took the clerical exams, while few took technical tests; for example, in 1920 seventy-seven men and seven women took exams as patent examiners, and appointments went to sixty and five. More training was needed, not "resentment that their general abilities are not duly recognized."[53]

Women lawyers complained that discrimination was being practiced against them in several departments. The Women's Bar Association of the District of Columbia investigated the complaints and sent a delegation to present the evidence to the President. They noted that despite the fact that fourteen women passed the exams none was appointed as law clerk, but received clerical positions with half the salary. Of the 155 persons employed as solicitors, attorneys, assistant solicitors, and law clerks, only seven were women, although one was Assistant Attorney General Mabel Walker Willebrandt. A Treasury Department official declared that no woman could earn more than $1,200 per year and dismissed or cut the salary of the few women who earned more. The Patent Office refused a promotion to a woman with the comment that no woman should have so high a position, and women did not receive deserved promotions in the Income Tax Claims Office. The lawyers charged that the situation was worse than under the Wilson administration.[54]

Despite the fact that he presided over a general spoils raid on the government service, it is to Harding's credit that he refused to surrender to a movement to dismiss married women

with husbands in government service. Senator Porter J. Mc-
Cumber introduced a bill in April, 1921, which he said was
meant to redeem election pledges for government economy.
The bill established priorities for trimming the government
payroll and permitted the head of any government establishment to discharge anyone with a spouse in the government's
employ. However, the bill died in the Committee on Civil
Service, so McCumber urged Harding to carry out the plan by
executive order. His intent was clear as he said that married
women should be dismissed first. Harding responded only to
say that cutting the rolls was a difficult job and unfairness and
hardship had to be avoided.[55] Secretary of Labor Davis also
favored the removal of married women, commenting, "You
know, there are a large number of them working in the Department here." [56]

While Harding made no pronouncement, Postmaster General Will Hays showed the best side of the administration. He
ruled that a woman postal employee lost no rights by marriage.
Previously when a woman married while holding a postmaster
position, she was obliged to secure a new appointment, execute
a new bond, and pass the civil service exams in competition with
others, with the result that some lost their places. "The ruling
of the Postmaster General Hays will set a precedent in the
Federal Service and will no doubt have an important effect in
establishing for women the full rights of citizenship intended
to be conferred by the Nineteenth Amendment to the Constitution." [57]

The case of Harriet Reid illustrated the new muscle of women
at the state level. She was certified as an industrial arbitration
agent in November, 1918, after passing the state civil service
exams, but received no appointment for two years. In July,
1920, she learned of an opening in the Arbitration Commission;
but even though she topped the list, the Industrial Commission
refused to consider a woman. The Civil Service Commission
then called for new examinations. Reid caused a great uproar by
appealing to prominent Illinois women, such as Catherine
Waugh McCullough, a leading woman lawyer in Chicago,

Mary McDowell, head of the University of Chicago Settlement House and former president of the Chicago Women's Trade Union League, Agnes Nestor, current president of the Chicago WTUL, and Jane Addams of Hull House. Women's organizations from Cairo to Chicago protested so loudly that Governor Frank Lowden intervened and Reid got her appointment. Even then, they sent her into an area of Illinois dominated by a political boss who consistently opposed equal rights for women. Her hard work and integrity won him over, and later he told her that he had been told to refuse to submit any compensation cases to her. She held the position until 1937.[58]

The offices gained by women showed improvement in the 1920s; however, some were those which might fall within a traditional notion of woman's sphere, such as public welfare, charities, and corrections. Governor Pinchot of Pennsylvania appointed Dr. Ellen C. Potter to head the Department of Public Welfare in 1923, making her the first woman to hold a cabinet position in any state.[59] In Massachusetts Esther Myers Andrews achieved cabinet rank when appointed the first woman on the Governor's Council in 1927. She declared it was a victory for women.[60] A number of women headed the women's and children's bureaus which were established in this period, especially after the passage of the Sheppard-Towner Act in 1921. Others served as industrial commissioners. Most famous was Frances Perkins, who was industrial commissioner in New York from 1919 to 1921 and 1923 to 1933, serving as chairman of the State Industrial Board from 1926 until she became Secretary of Labor for F.D.R.

In the federal government until 1918 only one woman, Julia Lathrop, held a major position; by 1929 nearly 200 were ranked as "administrative" and "supervisory." From 1913 to 1916 only seventy-one women received appointments to professional and scientific categories. From 1922 to 1925, 185 got such appointments. The numbers were small but increasing.[61] New departments and the Foreign Service opened, and the Bureau of Home Economics and Women's Bureau were created and women dominated them. Women sought increasing responsibilities in government at home and abroad, and continued to fight for the rights and obligations of full citizenship. Many of those women who received appointments were social feminists who wanted to carry out their reform objectives. Still others sought to reform the political parties and win elective office.

NOTES

1. Anna Howard Shaw, "The New Man," speech, n.d., Lucy Anthony MSS, Dillon Collection, folder 81, SL; Mary Van Kleeck, "The Working Woman and the New Social Vision," *Life and Labor*, IX (Dec., 1919), 320–323; Mary Stewart, "The New Politics," *Good Housekeeping*, LXXI (July–Aug., 1920), 49; "New Women for Old," *Woman Citizen*, V (June 5, 1920), 19–20; Dudley Harmon, "The American Woman's New Work," *Ladies Home Journal*, XXXVI (Jan., 1919), 22; W. L. George, "Woman and the New Society," *Good Housekeeping*, LXVIII (Apr., 1919), 42–43.

2. Grace Abbott, "After Suffrage—Citizenship," *Survey*, XLIV (Sept. 1, 1920), 655–657; see also resolution of Stockton (Calif.) section of Woman's National Democratic League, Dec. 10, 1919, C. B. Pinchot MSS, box 12, LC.

3. Raymond Fowler Crist, "What Constituted an American Citizen," *Congressional Digest*, IX (Nov., 1930), 258.

4. U.S. Congress, Senate, Committee on Immigration, *American Citizenship Rights of Women*, hearings before the subcommittee, 72nd Cong., 2nd Sess., on S. 992, S. 2760, S. 4169, Mar. 2, 1933 (Washington: Government Printing Office, 1933), 14–15 (hereafter cited as Hearings, *Citizenship Rights*); see also Burnita Shelton Matthews, "Woman, Wedlock, and Nationality," *Equal Rights*, XVI (Feb. 22, 1930), 21; Emma Wold, "The Ins and Outs of a Woman's Citizenship," radio talk on NBC, Jan. 20, 1930, *ibid.* (Feb. 8, 1930), 3.

5. Hearings, *Citizenship Rights*, 11. The section relative to women was only a section in a longer bill dealing with the question of citizenship, and in the debate in the House nothing was said about the status of women; *Congressional Record*, 59th Cong., 2nd Sess., 1463–67. One reason for the inclusion of a section stripping American women of their citizenship if they married aliens was the numerous and notable marriages between impecunious titled aliens and the daughters of wealthy American businessmen. The fierce nationalism of the country in the period was affronted by this spectacle, and so the law was passed to punish those women. This same question was brought up by Fiorello LaGuardia in 1930 when amendments to the 1922 Cable Act were being debated; see Ruby A. Black, "Cable Bill Passed by House," *Equal Rights*, XVI (May 3, 1930), 100–102.

6. Idella Gwatkin Swisher, "Program of the National League of Women Voters," *Congressional Digest*, IX (Nov., 1930), 265; see also John L. Cable, "The Citizenship of American Women since 1830," *Atlantic Monthly*, XLII (May, 1930), 649–653.

7. Hearings, *Citizenship Rights*, 26–28.

8. *Women Lawyers' Journal*, XII (Oct.–Nov., 1922), 5.

9. Hearings, *Citizenship Rights*, 25.

10. *Women Lawyers' Journal*, VII (Jan., 1918), 29; "Bills in Congress," *ibid.*, IX (Oct.–Dec., 1919), 8.

11. Swisher, "Program of the National League of Women Voters," 265.

12. *Ibid.*

13. *Congressional Record*, 87th Cong., 2nd Sess., LXII, 9040–41.

14. *Ibid.*, 9047.

15. Hearings, *Citizenship Rights*, 28.

16. Maud Wood Park to Harding, Sept. 28, 1922, Harding MSS, box 203, folder 260–1, OHS; "Woman's Work is Never Done," Stantial MSS, Dillon Collection, folder 5, SL.

17. Johnson, "Organized Women and National Legislation," 194.

18. Wold, "The Ins and Outs of a Woman's Citizenship," 3.

19. Sophonisba P. Breckinridge, *Marriage and the Civil Rights of Women* (Social Service Monograph 13, Chicago: University of Chicago Press, 1931), 24.

20. "In Michigan Women Are People," *Woman Citizen*, V (Jan. 8, 1921), 865; Martin Gruberg, *Women in American Politics: An Assessment and Source Book* (Oshkosh, Wis.: Academic Press, 1968), 159.

21. Alice Stone Blackwell, "Common Law Handicaps on Women's Citizenship," *Woman Citizen*, V (Jan. 22, 1921), 909; see also Mary Sumner Boyd, "Must Women Voters Serve on Juries?," NAWSA pamphlet, n.d., Grace H. Harte MSS, Dillon Collection, folder 8, SL.

22. "In Michigan Women Are People," *Woman Citizen*, V (Jan. 8, 1921), 865; news item, *Woman Voter's Bulletin* (Connecticut League of Women Voters), XII (Jan., 1932), 6; "Massachusetts Rules against Women Jurors," *Women Lawyers' Journal*, XIX (Fall, 1931), 6–7.

23. *Woman Voter's Bulletin* XI (Apr. 15, 1931), 1.

24. "The Hall of Fame," *ibid.*, IX (Apr. 12, 1929), 1; *ibid.*, III (Feb. 17, 1923), 4.

25. *Ibid.*, IX (Apr. 5, 1929), 1.

26. "An All-Woman Jury," *Independent Woman*, n.s., VII (Jan., 1928), 15.

27. Jennie Loitman Brown, "Ladies and Gentlemen of the Jury," *Woman Voter's Bulletin: Legislative Edition*, V (Mar. 13, 1925), 1; see also "All Support for Jury Duty for Women," *Legislative Bulletin No. 3 of the Connecticut League of Women Voters*, I (Feb. 25, 1921), 1–2; *Woman Voter's Bulletin*, III (May 19, 1923), 1; "Arguments for H.B. 429: Women on Juries," *ibid.*, V (Apr. 10, 1925), 1–4; "Objections Overruled," *ibid.*, VII (Jan., 1927), 3.

28. "The Hall of Fame," *Woman Voter's Bulletin*, IX (Apr. 12, 1929), 1.

29. "Halting the Schantz Jury Bill Shows League's Efficiency," *Bulletin of the Pennsylvania League of Women Voters*, III (Feb., 1923), 2; see also an effort defeated in Minnesota: "Jury Service Deferred," *Woman's Journal*, XIV (Feb., 1929), 28.

30. The most complete listing can be found in Gruberg, *Women in American Politics*, 117–218.

31. Winifred Mallon, "Uncle Sam and the Ladies," *Independent Woman*, n.s., IX (Sept., 1930), 398.

32. Lily Lykes Rowe, "Judge Kathryn Sellers: The First Woman Appointed to the Federal Judiciary," *Ladies Home Journal*, XXXVII (Jan., 1920), 138.

33. Anderson, *Woman at Work*, 173–174.

34. James J. Davis, Secretary of Labor, to George B. Christian, Secretary to the President, May 4, 1921, Harding MSS, box 33, folder 15-14, OHS.

35. Telegram, Edson to Harriet Taylor Upton, May 18, 1921; memorandum, Upton to White House, May 19, 1921, *ibid.*

36. Upton to Harding, Aug. 1, 1921, *ibid.*

37. Memorandum "Re: Miss Abbott and the Children's Bureau," James J.

Davis to George Christian, n.d.; Davis to Harding, Aug. 19, 1921, *ibid.*

38. Helen H. Gardener to Senator Kenneth McKeller, Aug. 21, 1921, *ibid.*, box 2, folder 2-2.

39. See the many petitions and letters of recommendation in *ibid.*, box 223, folders 312-1 through 312-4.

40. "Resolution passed by the NLWV, Cleveland, April 15, 1921," *ibid.*, box 203, folder 260-1.

41. Emma Wold, Chairman, Women's Committee for World Disarmament, to George B. Christian, July 23, 1921, *ibid.*, box 170, folder 172-1.

42. Gardener to Harding, Aug. 16, 1921, *ibid.*, folder 172-2.

43. Carrie Chapman Catt, "Nominating a Woman," *Woman Citizen*, VI (Aug. 27, 1921), 12; cross-reference sheet of letter from Alice M. Robertson to Harding, Aug. 14, 1921, Harding MSS, box 170, folder 172-2, OHS.

44. Upton to Harding, received at White House Aug. 16, 1921; Memorandum, Upton to Harding, n.d., Harding MSS, box 170, folder 172-3, OHS.

45. Gardener to George B. Christian, Sept. 28, 1921; Harding to Gardener, Sept. 30, 1921, *ibid.*, folder 172-2.

46. Mrs. Charles Sumner Bird, leader in both the Massachusetts Republican party and LWV; Katherine Philips Edson, a Hiram Johnson supporter, California LWV, member of the Executive Committee of the Republican National Committee, and well-known progressive on the California Industrial Welfare Commission; Eleanor Franklin Egan, regular party member from New York; Mrs. Thomas W. Winter of Minnesota, president of GFWC and lukewarm party member.

47. Mae Teressa Holder, "A Custodian for Uncle Sam," *Independent Woman*, n.s., VII (Dec., 1928), 539.

48. Mary Anderson to Cornelia Bryce Pinchot, Apr. 20, 1920; Pinchot to Anderson, Apr. 26, 1921, C. B. Pinchot MSS, box 14, LC.

49. Winifred Mallon, "Women in Our Foreign Service," *Independent Woman*, n.s., VIII (Sept., 1929), 387–388.

50. Lucy Somerville-Howorth to Mrs. B. F. Saunders, Sept. 7, 1923, Lucy Somerville-Howorth MSS, folder 236, SL; "Justice Cline to the United States Customs Court," *Women Lawyers' Journal*, XVI (July, 1928), 2; see also "Judge Jean Norris," *ibid.*, IX (Feb., 1920), 12; news item, *ibid.*, XI (Mar., 1922), 21; Anne Shannon Moore, "When Women Sit in Judgment," *Good Housekeeping*, LXX (Apr., 1920), 46–47; "Women in Business," *Ladies Home Journal*, XLV (Sept., 1928), 31; *ibid.* (Nov., 1928), 69; Breckinridge, *Women in the Twentieth Century*, 307–310.

51. "The Discrimination against Women in the Government Service," *Life and Labor*, X (Jan., 1920), 13.

52. Even though the Veterans Preference Act undermined the principle of civil service, the women were able to make the best of it until Jessie Dell became Civil Service Commissioner. She was a member of the NWP, and the NWP wanted Congress to take away the right of a departmental head to stipulate the sex of appointees and force them to select strictly on the basis of civil service exam scores. With veterans qualifying at lower scores a woman would rarely have a chance. Dell finally convinced President Hoover to remove the stipulation by executive order. It lasted one year, until Franklin Roosevelt became President. Mary Anderson and others got the order countermanded because in practice it discriminated against women; see Anderson, *Woman at Work*, 153.

53. Helen H. Gardener to Ethel Smith, Mar. 28, 1921, Harding MSS, box 2, folder 2-1, OHS.

54. Ellen Spencer Mussey to Harding, Feb. 15, 1923; Marie K. Saunders to Judge Mary O'Toole, Jan. 17, 1923; cross-reference sheet of letter from O'Toole to Harding, Dec. 29, 1922, *ibid.*, box 203, folder 260-1.

55. Porter J. McCumber to Harding, June 18, 1921; Harding to McCumber, June 25, 1921, *ibid.*, box 3, folder 2-6.

56. James J. Davis to George B. Christian, Nov. 7, 1921, *ibid.*, box 31, folder 15-2.

57. News release, "Women Postmasters Lose No Rights by Marriage," Nov. 25, 1921, *ibid.*, box 203, folder 260-1.

58. Harriet Reid, typescript reminiscence, 1942, Harriet Reid MSS, folder 1, SL; see also folder 2 for letters and newspapers of the 1920 incident; "Triumph of Equal Rights," *Life and Labor*, X (Dec., 1920), 328.

59. "Commissioner of Public Welfare of the State of Pennsylvania," *Medical Woman's Journal*, XXX (Sept., 1923), 274. Potter was an executive in the Pennsylvania LWV and later president of the Medical Women's National Association.

60. *Boston Globe*, Nov. 3, 1927; see also *News Letter on Women and Children in Industry*, no. 7 (Mar., 1925); *ibid.*, no. 10 (Sept., 1926), Ethel M. Johnson MSS, folder 6, SL.

61. Grace Abbott, "The Changing Position of Women," in *A Century of Progress*, ed. Charles A. Beard (New York: Harper & Brothers, 1933), 286.

FOUR

The Lady and the Tiger

There was a young lady of Niger
Who smiled as she rode on a tiger—
They returned from the ride
With the lady inside
And the smile on the face of the tiger.[1]

Political organizations feared the advent of suffrage, partly because it introduced an unknown factor into an arena which desired predictability, but mostly because suffragists openly threatened them. A high-priority article of business of many social feminists was the purification of politics and the elimination of such things as blind party loyalty, the boss politics, and political machines. Until it ascertained the actual strength of the women, the "tiger" tread softly and absorbed some beatings. When it found that women were "fools because God made them to match the men," [2] it swallowed them.

Political reform was a major dimension of the progressive era, and suffragists continually maintained that woman suffrage would help the reformation process and purify politics. In 1888 Frances Willard, dynamic head of the WCTU, wrote that the mission of women was "to make the whole world homelike." She predicted that woman "would come into government and purify it, into politics and cleanse its Stygian pool, for woman will make homelike every place on this round earth." [3] Anti-suffragists declared that, indeed, women should stay home and clean house. *Ladies Home Journal* retorted, "They can. And they will. . . . Let them shake the dust off from a few of our political fixtures and see what is underneath. Let them drive the rats out of the public pantry. . . . Will American women clean our political houses for us? Heaven speed the day when they begin!" The legislative hall would be "made clean when woman is allowed to exercise that God-given right of equal suffrage." [4]

Some claimed that women would not vote like men, that they would vote independently and unpredictably. Supposedly, they did not have a man's concept of party loyalty and never would. The parties would have to scramble to attract this uncommitted vote. Party labels meant nothing; but issues like health, education, and maternity and infancy protection drew women together. Elizabeth Frazer, a *Good Housekeeping* political writer who was usually wrong or outdated, predicted, "There is little doubt that within twenty years the corrupt city machine as we now know it, with its party bosses, its inner cliques and grafting gangs, will be a thing of the past, as extinct as the dodo." She explained, "The present trend shows clearly that women are going to clean up the cities and oust the machines if they do nothing else." [5]

Enfranchisement made a noticeable difference in the reception given women at first. They entered the political parties with fanfare and much motion. In early 1920 the Democratic National Committee doubled its size to include a man and woman from each state, but the man appointed the woman. Emily Newell Blair, vice-chairman of the Democratic National Committee (1921–28), recalled that the women originally selected were generally of the highest type, reflecting the respect the men felt for the new voters. The national Democratic convention that year voted that both men and women should be elected in the same fashion. "What had been given the appointees by courtesy now became theirs by authority." [6] At first the Republicans tried to work through a Woman's Division, but by 1924 they had adopted the complete Democratic system. While the 50-50 plan gave women a special status, it opened the male stronghold. Women attempted to have it duplicated on the state level; and by 1928 eighteen states had this arrangement. Where the plan existed, women exercised some power; Iowa even had a woman chairman for a while. Men on the committees endured women at first, but later came to value their advice. In the South, where no state adopted the plan, no women were on the state committees; and in the West the women usually had only auxiliary status.

Another example of new activity was the number of women attending the national conventions as delegates or alternates. In 1916 there were twenty-two women delegates and alternates to the Democratic convention and fourteen at the Republican convention. In 1920 the Democrats seated 299 and the Republicans 156. The number peaked in 1924 with 509 at the Democratic convention and 397 at the Republican convention. The totals dipped in 1928 and returned to 1924 levels at the 1932 conventions.[7]

Both parties made a special effort to capture the women's vote in 1920. The Democrats stressed the fact that the suffrage amendment passed under the Wilson administration. President Wilson gave significant appointments to women, and the Democratic platform incorporated twelve of the NLWV's fifteen planks. The Republicans replied that the amendment passed only because of overwhelming Republican support in Congress and that twenty-nine of the thirty-six ratifying states were Republican-controlled.[8] The Republicans won the contest.

Perhaps Warren G. Harding attracted the female vote by his handsome appearance, but he left nothing to chance as he followed a carefully planned approach. His front-porch campaign consisted mostly of special "days" to appeal to blocs of voters. He staged Social Justice Day for women. "October 1 was not to be Suffragettes' Day, but rather, Respectable Women's Day." He wanted to exclude the newly formed League of Women Voters. A selected list of women were invited to give lots of respectability, some non-partisanship, and a touch of progressivism. Among those present were Mrs. Douglas Robinson (Theodore Roosevelt's sister), Mrs. Leonard Wood, Mrs. William C. Sproul (wife of Pennsylvania's governor), Mrs. James P. Goodrich (wife of Indiana's governor), Mary Roberts Rinehart (writer for *Ladies Home Journal*), Florence Kelley, Alice Roosevelt Longworth, Cornelia Bryce Pinchot, Esther Everett Lape (New York LWV and WTUL), Lena Lake Forrest (NFBPWC president), and Mrs. Minnie E. Keyes (Grand Secretary of the Grand Chapter of the Order of the Eastern Star).[9]

The Harding managers asked prominent Republican women to arrange delegations to visit Harding in Marion; but Mrs. Richard Edwards, also the treasurer of the NLWV, accepted only on condition that "the candidate would prepare to go further than the platform and so supplement some of the disappointments the women have met. . . ."[10] The Republican platform had accepted only five of the least controversial of the NLWV planks. Mrs. Gifford Pinchot was asked to select a delegation, and she rounded up some of her liberal friends from the WTUL and elsewhere, hoping to secure an endorsement of an eight-hour day for women, minimum-wage legislation, maternity and infancy protection, and equal pay for equal work.[11] Harriet Taylor Upton urged Harding to make no slip with the women and suggested that he submit advance drafts of his remarks for censoring to Mrs. Raymond Robins, who in addition to being the president of the National Women's Trade Union League was a member of the Woman's Division of the Republican National Executive Committee, or Mrs. Richard Edwards, or Mrs. Adah E. Bush, secretary to Governor Goodrich of Indiana. Upton declared that the women's vote was going to be an enormous factor in the election.[12] Harding declined to be censored.

Upton's worries were misplaced because Harding scored a tremendous success by going well beyond the disappointing Republican platform. He called for equal pay for equal work, an eight-hour day, extension of the Children's Bureau, the end of child labor, enforcement of prohibition, prevention of lynching, maternity and infancy protection, appointment of women to state and federal employment boards, payment of a living wage (the basic argument for minimum-wage laws at that time), help for farm workers, a national standard for social justice to employees and employers, the promotion of health, and the creation of a department of social welfare. His social-justice proposals astonished social feminists and defused many progressive critics. What many overlooked in the speech was Harding's stress on governmental efficiency, his emphasis on instruments rather than programs.[13]

Harding skillfully courted the Republican progressives and succeeded in winning the support of many. Gifford Pinchot interviewed him and "decided to support the Republican Party completely and unreservedly. . . ."[14] The Social Justice Day speech convinced the skeptical Mrs. Pinchot, who had considered Harding very weak. She wrote to a LWV county chairman: "Did you read Harding's speech which he made on Social Justice Day at Marion last Friday? It takes practically the whole program of the League of Women Voters."[15] To Mrs. Harding she wrote: "Hitherto some . . . women have been unaccountably reluctant to committing themselves to either party, but this makes a clear cut issue that it is hard to see how the more progressive ones can hesitate any longer."[16]

Women cast only about one-third of the total vote in 1920, most voting for Harding; however, their party loyalty was uncertain. Where the woman voter would go had been a question which concerned both politicians and suffrage leaders. Social feminists saw the ballot as a key to further reform; politicians feared some kind of antagonistic bloc, woman's party, or large non-aligned faction. "Nothing but trouble, confusion, wreck; and the stoutest-hearted captain of wards looked with gloom upon the future."[17] When the National American Woman Suffrage Association created the NLWV in 1919, the St. Louis *Globe Democrat* said that war between the sexes had all but been declared: NAWSA was establishing a woman's party.

Carrie Chapman Catt tried to allay these fears immediately in a final, extemporaneous speech to the 1919 convention.

"There has been much talking about as to whether the League of Women Voters is a woman's party, antagonistic to men." She replied, "It is not a party. . . . It is, above all, not sex segregation. . . . They are to work with men." However, she warned that the NLWV was not "a parlor uplift movement. . . . They will not hesitate to use their ballots fearlessly whether it is for or against the party of their inheritance." [18] Catt returned to the question in her presidential address to NAWSA's 1920 convention. She emphasized that women must join the regular parties and that the National League of Women Voters was not a party. She declared that party membership was a means to advance the Woman Movement. The mass of women were timid and lacking in self-respect. "You must stimulate those women to self-respect. You have got to urge them on, to show them that they are not emancipated until they are as independent within the party as men are." The winning of suffrage was only one round in the fight for women's progress; party membership was next: "We are not going to be such quitters as to stay on the outside and let all the reactionaries have it their way on the inside. . . . You must go into the parties." However, Catt warned against the twin evils of conservatism and blind partisanship. Women must convert the parties, and the NLWV should show the way. "If the League of Women Voters hasn't the power and the vision to see what is coming, and what ought to come, and to be five years ahead of the political parties, then our work is of no value." [19]

The *Woman Citizen*, official journal of the NLWV, warned women that joining a party did not admit them to the inner circles which made policy, and it urged them to keep their conscience when they entered. In order for the women's program to be advanced, the parties had to be transformed, and independent voting could only be a protest gesture.[20] Emily Newell Blair and Harriet Taylor Upton, each a party official, encouraged women to belong to both a party and the NLWV; and Carrie Chapman Catt, professing no party allegiance, agreed with them. However, a minority of the NAWSA leadership, like Ruth Hanna McCormick, wanted women to join a party and nothing more.

Catt felt that a woman voter's organization was needed temporarily as a means of catching up with the present inequities of legislation enacted from the male point of view. Women needed an extra lever to compensate for their disadvantage in working with men in the parties or obtaining legislative objectives because they lacked representation.[21] After a couple of years, she concluded that even this temporary device was a mistake. She felt that the charge that the NLWV was a woman's party could be dispelled while creating a great non-partisan political force for progress. All this could be accomplished by dropping "Women" from the name and extending "a strong and urgent invitation . . . to independent-minded men to become members and unite in an independent political policy for the Nation." [22] The leaders declined but the suggestion recurs periodically.

NAWSA traditionally had been non-partisan and the new NLWV proclaimed its non-partisanship, but deeds spoke more loudly at first. While parent and child pushed issues, their components openly campaigned for people.

In 1918 Senator John W. Weeks of Massachusetts was upset in his re-election bid by David I. Walsh. This was Weeks's first outing since the adoption of the Seventeenth Amendment, and he collided with a coalition of labor, suffragists, and the Jewish community. His record was negative: he opposed the sixteenth, seventeenth, eighteenth, and nineteenth amendments, the appointment of Louis Brandeis to the Supreme Court, the creation of the Federal Trade Commission, the Shipping Board, the excess war profits tax, the Clayton Anti-Trust Act, the Rural Credits Act, extension of the parcel post, and a government-owned steel plant to turn out armor plate. He supported a bill to turn over public water-power rights to private interests.[23]

The Massachusetts Woman Suffrage Association helped mobilize the Jewish community and labor against Weeks. They did this through their Non-Partisan Committee of Women. The committee mailed a flier of Weeks's record to every registered Republican and Progressive man in the state in addition to approaching a picked list of 35,000 suffragists. Catholic women appealed to suffragists to oppose Weeks on the suffrage issue alone. Trade Union women contacted the labor unions and distributed handbills at factories. While touring the state in three cars, the trade union women made speeches in all major cities. Jewish women did the same, operating from two automobiles. Finally the committee published Weeks's negative record in sixteen of the largest Republican newspapers.[24]

In New York that same year women helped defeat at least four old antagonists in the legislature. One was State Senator Elon R. Brown, the author of the bill to remove protection from women and children in industry in wartime. (The bill passed, but Governor Whitman vetoed it.) Before the primaries, the New York State Suffrage Party and other women's groups blanketed his district with anti-Brown literature and speeches; he decided to retire. The Women's Trade Union League and the Women's Non-Partisan League banded together to upset the chief opponent to minimum-wage legislation. Sweetest of all was the replacement of two opposing assemblymen by women. One woman ran for the sole purpose of defeating a man with a record of opposition to child labor laws and other social legislation. Another opponent of woman suffrage and hours laws for women fell to a woman who campaigned for equal pay and child labor laws.[25]

The Franklin County Woman Suffrage Association initiated and led an effort in 1919 in Columbus, Ohio, which upset George F. Karb, mayor for sixteen years and potential gubernatorial candidate. The city had a wide-open reputation; therefore, the women threw out the boss in their first chance after receiving municipal suffrage. Karb had expected to breeze over his three opponents until the feminists intervened. The association called a meeting with the YWCA, WCTU, and representatives of nearly all women's clubs. While condemning Karb, they did not endorse anyone. The Karb organization retaliated by calling them a "shrieking sisterhood" and accused them of defaming the city. The women reassembled, endorsed James Thomas, and appointed a steering committee of three to direct the women's effort: a Socialist, a Democrat, a Republican. With $68 and 500 volunteers, they concentrated on thirteen of the sixteen wards, registering women and instilling a desire to vote. By casting the campaign as one against vice and corruption, the women picked up allies in the Ministerial Alliance, YMCA, and Federation of Churches. Thomas won the election by 19,000, and the women had signed up 21,000 new voters.[26]

The Connecticut Woman Suffrage Association ignored NAWSA's plea for non-partisanship and specifically opposed the Republican party in the 1920 elections. The Republican state convention in March, 1920, endorsed suffrage but nominated the very people who had been opposing it, in particular Senator Frank Brandegee. Brandegee's record was much like that of his erstwhile colleague Weeks: opposed the Seventeenth, Eighteenth, and Nineteenth amendments, the extension of parcel post, the Rural Credits Act, the eight-hour railroad bill, the Federal Reserve Act, and child labor laws. The Woman Suffrage Association called for his defeat under the slogan of "Place Principle above Party."[27] He won despite their efforts and served until 1924, when he committed suicide. Even that brought no respite to social feminists, as his seat went to Hiram Bingham, who shared Brandegee's view of the world.

The most widely publicized effort of the feminists came in New York, where they hoped to derail Senator James Wadsworth, whose record paralleled that of Weeks and Brandegee. Moreover, his wife was the president of the National Association Opposed to Woman Suffrage. When Wadsworth opposed suffrage after New York voted for it, the suffragists vowed to repay him if he ran in 1920. He announced his candidacy; and Mary Garrett Hay charged that the Republican machine was forcing better men to withdraw. At a meeting called by her and Mrs. Frank A. Vanderlip, chairman of the New York LWV, the LWV formed the Non-Partisan Senatorial Committee. They appealed to the Democratic Party to nominate a candidate acceptable to the women. Women present included Mrs. Ogden

Mills Reid, Mrs. V. Everit Macy, Alice Duer Miller, Mrs. Louis F. Slade, Ruth Morgan, Mrs. Raymond Brown, Mary E. Dreier, Mrs. George Pratt, Mrs. Casper Whitney; most were Republicans. The *New York Times* chided the LWV for attacking a man who remained unmoved by pressure: "Shouldn't woman suffragists show broad-mindedness, a spirit above political grudges, revenges, and punishments?" [28]

In violation of the primary laws of New York, the Republicans held an "unofficial" nominating convention. Mary Garrett Hay denounced the whole procedure and said that women were getting their first real lesson in politics; they were being excluded from all the real business, which was conducted in closed conferences at the convention. She demanded equal participation for women. Many women delegates attacked Wadsworth, but Mrs. Douglas Robinson defended him. The convention endorsed Wadsworth for senator and Nathan Miller for governor. Social feminists resented Miller because of his attitude on social legislation, but Mrs. Robinson said Miller was a man "who stands for the principles for which Theodore Roosevelt stood." [29] Mary Garrett Hay, NAWSA vice-president and former chairman of the Women's Executive Committee of the Republican National Committee, broke with the party to support the Democratic candidate for senator, Harry C. Walker, and Harriet May Mills for Secretary of State, the only woman nominated by either party for a major office. Hay was particularly irritated at men in her party who said that no woman should be Secretary of State because no woman had the ability.[30]

Mary Livermore, of NAWSA's board of directors and the Republican Executive Committee of New York, appealed to women voters of the state to put aside suffrage considerations and vote for party candidates. Her statement dramatized the great split in Republican and suffrage ranks as both she and Hay were officers in the New York Suffrage Association, NAWSA, and the Republican party. Livermore urged the election of Wadsworth so that Harding would have a Republican Senate that would support his policies. This appeal brought a direct response from the suffrage generalissimo, Carrie Chapman Catt.

Catt said that Harding did not need Wadsworth. If Harding won the election, he would carry the Senate without New York. Besides, the record indicated that Wadsworth would not support Harding anyway. On suffrage Wadsworth had bucked the wishes of local, state, and national Republican committees and chairmen. The Republican-dominated state legislature even requested him to vote in favor, but he refused. Furthermore, in the event he agreed with Harding, Wadsworth was unlikely to be present to cast his vote since he had a high absentee record. Finally, a vote for the man was a vote for his awful record, which showed unfailing support of special interests and opposition to the public good. Theodore Roosevelt had said of him, "It is rarely that a public man champions the right of big business to do wrong as openly as Mr. Wadsworth." [31]

Wadsworth and Miller both won in the November landslide. Jean Burnett Tompkins, chairman of the Women's Non-Partisan Committee, assessed the damage. She said that women got the vote but did not make a ripple in the election. Furthermore, "the result was disastrous to women." The spirit of cooperation that had characterized the struggle for suffrage had been dissipated. "Women . . . have been seduced by the dominant parties." No sooner had they won the vote than they divided their strength to join the old parties on the advice of the suffrage leaders. The result in New York was that the Republicans threw a few committee positions to the women but refused to nominate a woman. The Democrats nominated Harriet Mills and then abandoned her to her fate. She ran behind the rest of the ticket, failing to get even the support of the women. Worst of all, Mills, a superior candidate, had run against a mediocre party hack. The answer, according to Tompkins, was a woman's pressure party which would vote only for women but not run candidates: "By forming, for a time, at least, a woman's party," the non-partisan women's bloc could squeeze nominations from the parties.[32] Carrie Chapman Catt disagreed, arguing that the nomination of Harriet Mills was an achievement in itself. She reminded women that achievements could not be measured only by offices won or enemies defeated. Instead she pointed to certain negative election results: prominent anti-suffragists ran well behind the rest of the ticket while winning. Moses in New Hampshire, Brandegee in Connecticut, and Penrose in Pennsylvania trailed and had reduced margins.[33] As for Wadsworth, he lagged behind Harding's winning total by over 700,000 votes.

Besides suffragists, Wadsworth's principal opposition came from prohibitionists. While they failed in 1920, this combination sank him in 1926. He was the organization candidate again and victory seemed certain. The New York League of Women Voters announced that it would not oppose him, but said that most of its members would vote for Robert Wagner. The *Woman Citizen*, by then an independent magazine, advertised Wadsworth's negative record, saying, "His strongest 'pro,' next to his party allegiance is militarism." His party regularity had prompted talk in Republican circles of Wadsworth for President in 1928 or 1932.[34] What seemed sure in the spring turned into defeat by November. Mary Garrett Hay said that the women voted against Wadsworth because of his stand against any progressive legislation, but in fact he was beaten in a dry revolt. Both Wadsworth and Wagner were wets, so dry Republicans ran Franklin W. Cristman as an independent Republican, and he drew enough votes away so that Wagner won.[35]

Anti-suffragists chortled over the failure of the feminists to defeat any well-known opponent and declared that suffragists could not even protect their friends.[36] Governor Roberts of Tennessee, who had defied the anti-suffragists in calling the special session which led to the final ratification of the Nineteenth Amendment, lost in 1920. Roberts's defeat was noteworthy since the Republicans won the governorship for the first time since 1868. Actually he had alienated the farm and labor blocs. In addition, Republican men encouraged women to vote, whereas in Democratic areas the women were discouraged; for example, in one Democratic town of 10,000 only fifty women registered to vote. As a result, the east Tennessee counties rolled up tremendous Republican majorities while the Democratic areas failed to cast enough votes to overcome them. In Democratic areas the vote varied little from 1916 while in Republican sections it nearly doubled.

In a contest where the suffrage vote was the issue, women saved Harry T. Burns from defeat. At twenty-four Burns cast a dramatic vote for suffrage in the ratification session. He had been counted a sure negative vote until the roll call, when he stood, removed the red rose (the anti-suffrage symbol) from his lapel, dropped it to the floor, and voted for suffrage to please his aged mother. Both party organizations in his district vowed to punish him and his party refused to endorse him. Consequently he had to work up his own organization, and women from both parties went to his rescue, including the chairman of the county Democratic women's association, who resigned to help the Republican Burns.[37]

On lower levels the LWV pointed to bright spots amid the general failure. They defeated three of their most vigorous opponents in Delaware. In Erie, Pennsylvania, they spearheaded a drive to unseat the regular Republican candidate for Congress. Erie had been dominated by a bipartisan political organization for fifteen years and its candidate for Congress ran on both tickets. The women backed and elected an independent. Florence E. Allen ran for judge of the Common Pleas Court of Cuyahoga County at the urging of members of the Cuyahoga County Woman Suffrage Party, who circulated her petitions. The Cleveland Business and Professional Women's Club, labor unions, and the Cleveland LWV directly endorsed her. She led the entire slate of candidates and credited the women with her election.[38]

One result of the 1920 election was renewed attacks upon the LWV. Non-partisanship was a threat to those to whom party regularity and allegiance were virtues. Mrs. Ralph Easley of the National Civic Federation rejected the LWV on the grounds that it was fostering independent voting, which she said weakened party allegiance, bringing the disintegration of the party system, "in our opinion the direst calamity that could befall our country." [39] The National Civic Federation warned its members against the trends of non-partisanship. It was bad enough, but the independents had "a more or less radical, sentimental program for the so-called betterment of women in industry and it is supporting 'Proportional Representation' as well as other radical political proposals." [40]

The New England leagues reported political opposition, and they expected the traffic to increase as the LWV offended additional special interests. "Now we are antagonizing many, and we shall find ourselves fought by many powers that we did not know existed." An organizer in Connecticut reported "strong Republican opposition" to her efforts, and mild Republican obstruction appeared in Nebraska and Kansas. Democrats in New York mounted a letter-writing campaign to magazines warning that the LWV had gone over to the Republicans "boots, saddles, and dragoons." [41] These charges were especially interesting in view of New York Republican attitudes.

Since the New York LWV tried and failed to defeat Wadsworth in the 1920 elections, the Republicans counterattacked in early 1921, hoping to scatter them. The Women's Republican Club of New York declared that the LWV was a political party acting under the cloak of non-partisanship regardless of party principles, hence it was "a menace to our national life and un-American in principle." Concerning citizenship training, a Republican leader remarked, "My advice to the League of Women Voters is to disband immediately and let real politicans give them an education in politics." [42] Finally, Governor Miller attacked the enemy in its own quarters.

The New York LWV held its annual convention in January, 1921, at Albany and invited the governor to address them in accordance with their usual practice. He accepted on condition that he be permitted to tell where he disagreed with them, and they consented. Despite the fact that he had to rearrange his schedule to make the appearance and was suffering from a bad cold, Miller arrived at the appointed hour with three male stenographers who took down his words. Every few minutes one would leave with notes and type them in the next room. When the address was ended, it was already on the press wires so that the whole state learned of Miller's attack on the LWV. He departed immediately, leaving the women in stunned silence.

"There is no proper place for a *league of women voters*," he declared, "precisely as I should say there was no proper place for a *league of men voters* . . . any *organization* which seeks to exert political power is a *menace to our institutions,* unless it is organized as a political party." He maintained that the American government had been framed so that the two-party system was essential, and he repeated that any association which sought to exert political pressure and was not a political party "is a *menace to our free institutions and to representative government.*" He advised women to withdraw. Not stopping here, he condemned the legislative program of the New York LWV, saying that night-work laws were false in theory and injurious in operation and that federal aid to education was an unconstitutional invasion of states' rights. Furthermore, he asserted that there was no need for health insurance or old-age pensions since it was not a function of the state to put a premium on getting sick, making life comfortable, or taking care of poor working people regardless of their thrift. "I say that if you are to have the stimulus which is necessary for human progress you must leave to the individual himself the *provision for his old age, or for his unemployment, or for his sickness.*" [43]

Miller did not remain for a reply, but Carrie Chapman Catt delivered an extemporaneous rebuttal. A remonstrance was drawn up and signed by the Republican women, who comprised 127 of the 157 present; and the convention formally condemned Miller the next day. Much of the press comment on his speech called it nonsense. When he found himself the target of a host of irate Republican women, he retreated, saying that he had been misunderstood. "I do not deny your right to work as a group outside the political party for political measures. . . . I do not condemn non-partisan groups." [44] The immediate effect of Miller's speech was the resignation of a number of women from the LWV, but far more joined as a result. Miller never made peace with the LWV, and he failed to get re-elected in 1922.

Whether as a result of their failure to score heavily in 1920, because of criticism, or because women were now in the political parties, the LWV did not repeat its 1920 election approach. It never again tried direct opposition or endorsement of particular candidates; instead, it remained issue-oriented and promoted its objectives by making voters conscious of certain issues and the candidates' positions on them. While the New York LWV detested Wadsworth, it did not oppose him directly in 1926 but tried to generate opposition over issues and principles, especially prohibition and welfare legislation. Elections occasionally turned on a female revolt, and the decision usually came in the primaries instead of the general elections, which meant that women were struggling inside of the parties.

Led by the president of the Women's Democratic League of St. Louis, women tried and failed to block the renomination of Senator James Reed in 1922. They opposed his record on suffrage, the Sheppard-Towner Act, and party irregularity during the Wilson administration. Democratic women in Mississippi helped upset Theodore Bilbo in the 1923 primaries, one of the only two elections he lost in his entire career. In Indiana in 1922 the regular party apparatus rejected Albert Beveridge for senator, but he got heavy support from the women and won the nomination anyway. While once progressive, Beveridge was by now quite conservative; and he lost in the November contest to the Democratic opponent. Perhaps the most noteworthy upset came in Pennsylvania, where Gifford Pinchot defeated the organization candidate for the gubernatorial nomination. Pinchot gave full credit to the women.[45] Although backed by the progressive women of the state, Pinchot's election was hardly a clear-cut progressive victory. His principal plank was prohibition enforcement, which earned him the ardent support of the WCTU, the most highly organized body of women in the state.[46] The contest was not liberal versus conservative but insider against outsider. The most liberal and the most conservative people ended in the same camp in opposition to the regular party apparatus.

When Boies Penrose died in December, 1921, the various factions of the Republican party vied for control: the Vare machine in Philadelphia, the Leslie organization in Pittsburgh, the Eyre group in Chester, Andrew Mellon of Pittsburgh, W. W. Atterbury, president of the Pennsylvania Railroad, and Joseph R. Grundy, president of the Pennsylvania Manufacturers Association. Each had his own candidate for the governor's chair in 1922. The prize was not only political dominance, but some "honest graft"—$50,000,000 worth of road contracts which the state expected to give in the next few years. The contest was wide open until Pinchot announced his candidacy; most of the factions composed their differences. On the last day for filing petitions they met and nominated Pennsylvania Attorney General George Alter, an honest machine politician.

Mrs. Barclay Warburton, vice-chairman of the Republican State Committee, refused to agree to the power play, declaring that the machine nomination of Alter was a challenge to Pennsylvania's direct primary system. A third candidate, Grundy's choice representing the most conservative elements in the party, withdrew in favor of Pinchot so that "the forces of good government should not be divided." In doing so, the issue became one of good government versus boss rule. Pinchot clubs sprang up all across the state; and although men and women were members, women did most of the intensive campaigning, including door-to-door and telephone canvasses. Surveys of organizational women showed that 75 to 90 percent were Pinchot backers: Women's Republican Clubs, LWV, WCTU, Pennsylvania Federation of Women's Clubs. The machine was contemptuous of the "petticoat vote," but it elected Pinchot. Governor Sproul explained the defeat of the organization: "He got a good start upon us and was able to capitalize the enthusiasm of the newly enfranchised women and to corral all of the disaffected elements in the state. . . ." [47]

The Harding administration was disturbed by the upsets in Indiana and Pennsylvania, but Harriet Taylor Upton assured the White House that neither could be interpreted as anti-administration actions, only rebuffs to the particular state organizations for being insensitive to women's demands. "The machine politician to this date has not admitted to himself that women have arrived. He expected women to act politically as negroes do— come out once a year and vote and disappear." She argued that women do not want bosses or machines, and that the Indiana and Pennsylvania victories were proof that they could stop a machine. However, there would never be a women's bloc, only a tendency to vote on certain issues. She said that political machines need not fear women, just admit them and give them some significant work.[48]

The anti-machine women proceeded to create their own. Out of the election experience grew the Pennsylvania State Council of Republican Women. The Pinchot women observed that in Pennsylvania in 1922 the Republicans elected 80 percent of all offices and the primaries determined most of them; therefore, the Pinchot-for-governor clubs expanded in order to maintain a voice in Republican party affairs. The leaders were Cornelia Bryce Pinchot and Mrs. Barclay Warburton.[49]

Warburton was one of those women pulled into politics in 1920 by men to attract support. She was appointed mainly be- cause she was the daughter of old John Wanamaker, former Republican treasurer and Postmaster General under Benjamin Harrison. While seeming to have impeccable credentials, she was tinged with heresy. Regarding the Progressive party platform of 1912, she "thought it the most magnificent document ever penned by man." [50] Because the Pennsylvania LWV saw its role as one of promoting good government, fiscal reform, and effi- ciency, but not social legislation, Mrs. Pinchot turned to the party to promote progressive legislation.[51] The Council of Re- publican Women outdistanced the LWV by endorsing child labor laws, an eight-hour day, a minimum wage, and other pro- tective legislation for women.

The council began in February, 1923, in a meeting of 500 enthusiastic women and grew rapidly. The foremost critics were Mrs. George H. Lorimer, an ardent Pinchot supporter and presi- dent of the Republican Women of Pennsylvania, and Mrs. John O. Miller, an Alter backer and president of the Pennsylvania LWV. Both the LWV and the pre-existent Republican Women of Pennsylvania felt threatened. The council tried to win Lorimer by making her a vice-president.[52] While the council wanted to include all shades of opinion to avoid being labeled a "Pinchot machine," Mrs. Pinchot intended it to be an organization to support her husband.[53] The best plans were eroded by time, and by the late 1920s the council had been domesticated by the regular machine. Mrs. Pinchot and her liberal friends ceased to have a major influence, and she left the council in disgust. However, she was politically ambitious and ran for Congress three times. Gifford Pinchot failed to win the senatorial nomination for the second time in 1926 but won the governorship again in 1930, serving until 1935.

Women, of course, did not confine their efforts to electing men; some ran for office themselves. The number of women trying for federal office in any year never reached fifty during the 1920s, and most of them were minor party candidates who never had a chance; for example, Rose Schneiderman, president of the New York WTUL, polled about 60,000 votes in 1920 when Wadsworth was winning with 1,025,000.[54] Women usually lost, but the number of winners increased in nearly every election. While the total was small, the election of a woman ceased to be a rarity.

Jeannette Rankin, elected in 1916, became the first woman in Congress; but she lost in 1918 trying for a Senate seat. She returned to Congress in 1940 and cast the only vote against war after the Pearl Harbor attack. No women served in the Sixty-sixth Congress, which passed the Nineteenth Amendment. In 1920 seven women ran for Congress; one won. Two were of the majority party of the district, but Republican men preferred a male Democrat to a female Republican. One astonishing upset put Alice M. Robertson of Oklahoma in Congress, but feminists took no pleasure in this. She had been president of the Oklahoma Anti-Suffrage Association until early 1920, and her election was a fluke. She did not campaign except to mail out little printed notices from her small cafeteria. In Congress she opposed everything the Women's Joint Congressional Committee wanted. To the relief of the feminists, she was defeated next time. Harding appointed her a social worker in a veterans' hospital in 1923.

Two more women eventually served in the Sixty-seventh Congress, filling out the terms of their husbands. This became the principal road to office in the 1920s. Of the thirteen women who served in the House of Representatives up to March, 1933, seven took seats previously held by their husbands. Two more, Ruth Hanna McCormick and Ruth Bryan Owen, were daughters of famous politicians. Ruth McCormick was also the widow of Senator Medill McCormick. A third "Ruth," Ruth Pratt, was the widow of a millionaire partner of the Standard Oil Company and prominent Republican party leader. Yet five of the thirteen won re-election. Two held office for decades: Edith Nourse Rogers held her seat from 1925 to 1961, and Mary T. Norton served from 1924 to 1951. The pre-Depression peak came in the Seventy-first Congress (1929–31) when nine women were members; the Depression reduced their number to six.[55]

The number of women in state legislatures followed a similar pattern, hitting a peak in 1929 and tapering off with the Depression. The NLWV estimated that about sixty women had served from time to time between 1896 and 1920, but the number increased notably after suffrage. Still, the numbers were small compared to the thousands of seats available. Women held only 1.8 percent of the 7,542 seats in the forty-eight states in 1925.[56]

No advantage was derived from being a prominent suffragist. Anne Martin, legislative chairman of the National Woman's Party, ran for senator from Nevada as an Independent in 1918 and 1920. She ran well enough in 1918 for some Republican leaders to consider her for their candidate in 1920. Belle Kearney lost in the primary in Mississippi in 1922; Harriet Taylor Upton failed in Ohio in 1924; and Cornelia Bryce Pinchot lost in Pennsylvania in 1928. The experience of Minnie Fisher Cunningham of Texas was typical. She ran a poor fifth in a field of six. She constantly confronted the tune, "She can't win because she's a woman." It caused votes to shift to other candidates who were supposed to have a chance.[57]

Florence E. Allen failed to win her primary fight for senator, and her defeat was deeply felt by feminists who supported her.

She proved her ability to win in non-partisan races by becoming the first woman to sit on a state supreme court, having beaten a strong contender by nearly 50,000 in 1922. She was re-elected by a margin of 350,000 in 1928. She won because of the support of the women of the state. For example, in 1922 the Republican party tried to prevent its women from working for Allen for judge. They imported Mabel Walker Willebrandt from Washington to halt Republican women; but two prominent women on the Woman's State Republican Committee resigned rather than stop, and one county Republican leader said she simply stacked anti-Allen literature in her basement rather than distribute it. She won non-partisan elections, but not the Democratic primary in 1926. She tried to replace Senator Atlee Pomerene, who had announced his retirement. Then at the last moment he entered and defeated her by 20,000. This defeat was especially galling because Pomerene had opposed woman suffrage and nearly everything the WJCC wanted. "Judge Allen's defeat was more than the failure of an individual candidate. It was a reverse in a cause which, to many women, [she] embodied."[58]

Ruth Hanna McCormick won the Republican primary in Illinois in 1930 by 200,000 votes, and many women thought they might at last see a woman elected senator. She had won a congressman-at-large race in 1928 which showed she had statewide potential. However, economic collapse had withered Republican chances by 1930 and she lost to J. Hamilton Lewis.

In the period under consideration two women were appointed to the Senate; all who ran for office lost. Rebecca Felton served one day in 1923, and Hattie Caraway was appointed in 1931 to serve out her husband's unexpired term. She was twice re-elected in the 1930s. The seating of Rebecca Felton was a chivalric gesture. Senator Thomas E. Watson died in September, 1922, and the governor appointed Felton, an eighty-eight-year-old veteran of reform battles, to the unexpired term. She was the first woman to stump Georgia on behalf of prohibition and maternity and infancy protection, and the first to appear on a public platform for suffrage. She led the fight in Georgia for

child labor laws, compulsory school attendance, and state re-
formatories for children. The appointment was wholly honorary
because Congress was not in session and the November election
permanently filled the seat with Walter George. Except for extraordinary circumstances she would never appear in Congress.
Women of the country tried to turn the honor into reality by
petitioning the President to call a special session, and then they
prevailed upon the real senator to stand aside until after the
woman appointee had been seated. When Congress convened in
January, 1923, the opening session was immediately adjourned
out of respect for the memory of Watson, as was the custom as
soon as the formal announcement of death was made. The following day, Felton presented her credentials, was sworn in, made
a little five-minute speech, and received tributes and congratulations. This was all done without precedent only because Senator
George withheld his credentials to give her the honor. Once this
was done, he was sworn in, and Felton ceased to be senator.[59]

While Rebecca Felton was certainly honored by the proceedings and some women saw it as an honor to all women, others
viewed it as a farce. "In the history of woman's politics, scarcely
has there been a more significant revelation of the failure of suffrage in its essentials," said one commentator. "To accomplish
this event, established precedent was set aside and the woman
senator held court for an hour on the Senate floor in the midst
of flowers and congratulations, while national affairs awaited her
exit." The writer bitterly noted that the whole episode revealed
that women would accept high political places on any terms,
"even to the extent of being seated illegally and impotently." [60]

Every level of office in state and local government had a
woman occupant in the 1920s. They served rather well with a
few jarring exceptions. Florence Knapp, elected New York's
secretary of state in 1924, was the first woman to win high
elective office in the state; and her plurality topped the entire
ticket. On inauguration day, January 1, 1925, she was honored
second only to Governor Smith (the only Democrat to survive
the Republican sweep). Feminists rejoiced in her victory. "This
is the day we were looking forward to when we were working

so hard for the vote in this State years ago," said Mrs. Alexander McEwan, a prominent suffragist. Gertrude Conner, a leading Democrat in New York City, wrote to Knapp, "I know you are going to show the men of this State that women are just as capable in office as they are." [61] Knapp, however, proudly declared that she did not get into politics by agitating for the vote or joining any "so-called feminist movements." She gave the seconding speech nominating Senator Wadsworth in 1920 and ran in 1924 at his urging. She credited him with securing her nomination by forcing recalcitrant delegates to accept her.[62] In short, she was no social feminist.

Suffragists had said that women would purify politics and reform political practices. True to form, Knapp pushed the use of voting machines, an election reform greatly favored by the NLWV. Because of her work in education and politics she received an honorary degree from Illinois Women's College. She did not run in 1926. Then in 1927 the Democratic administration probed her handling of the funds for the 1925 New York census. The evidence looked bad, but the *Woman Citizen* urged everyone to suspend judgment until both sides were heard since Knapp had not replied to the charges. When she was formally charged with grand larceny, the *Woman's Journal* made the best of the awkward situation by urging that Knapp be judged exactly as a man. Her conviction would hurt the advance of women, but the number of successful women was too great for Knapp's failure to matter ultimately. When she was convicted, *Woman's Journal* said it was a just conviction and that she must not escape punishment because of her sex. "Women would suffer, not gain. Appointment or election of women would be less likely" if women were judged and punished by a different standard.[63] The court sentenced her to thirty days in jail.

Before Mrs. George Wallace was elected in 1966, only two other women had ever been governor of a state, and one was, like Mrs. Wallace, a substitute for an ineligible husband. In 1924 Miriam A. Ferguson was elected governor of Texas. She ran for her husband, who had been impeached. Both had been antisuffragists, and he manipulated her term in office so badly that officials threatened her impeachment too. The usual tradition of giving a governor a second term was broken in her case as the party refused to nominate her in 1926. But "Ma" Ferguson was not finished in Texas; she won a second term in 1932 and fired her husband as "advisor."

All the feminists could say was, "Thank God for Nellie Ross!" In 1924 Wyoming elected Nellie Taylor Ross. She took her husband's place after he died and established a record of economy and efficiency, even reducing taxes. She served as spokesman in Washington for the states of the Colorado River basin in a question of distribution of water rights. She carved out a successful record despite the fact that the Republicans controlled the legislature and held all the other elective offices. She was the Democratic candidate in 1926, but lost. She had the consolation of running far ahead of the rest of her party and losing by 1,500 votes.[64]

In addition to public office, women sought a meaningful place in the party apparatus. Many suffragists expected to make some telling and immediate contribution by joining the parties. Women were certain a new era was upon them, but many were soon disillusioned because the impact was much less than expected. They received a pseudo welcome by the parties. "As voters they witnessed . . . a great many political flourishes in their honor, empty flourishes for the most part, that got them exactly nowhere in party councils."[65] The New York LWV cautioned women to expect to be relegated to the subordinate places in the parties and that men would try to keep them there, but "as women progress, they will not remain satisfied with an inferior status." Women with pride of sex and a sense of justice would fight for equal rights within the parties. "Let us all remember the duty we owe to our sex as well as the duty we owe to our party, and labor to make political equality apply not to voting but to [all party activities]."[66]

Women office holders felt that men did not want women in politics, except to vote on election day. Consequently, some put aside political aspirations. Others were denied nominations because of their sex. Sue White charged that in the South women had been discouraged from party participation. Artificial leaders of women were created by the men "not to lead women but to fool them." [67] As for offices, the more important the office, the less likely a woman would be nominated. "Political offices are the assets of the political machine. In general, they are too valuable to give to women." [68]

The limited space given women in the parties led some extreme feminists to endorse the idea advanced by Jean Burnett Tompkins after the Wadsworth fiasco in 1920. Anne Martin had appealed to both men and women in her 1918 and 1920 campaigns, but by 1925 she had concluded that the advice given by the suffrage leaders to join the big parties was wholly wrong. "There is no doubt that Mrs. Carrie Chapman Catt sounded the doom of feminism for many years to come when she urged the newly enfranchised women to humbly 'train for citizenship,' to join the men's parties, 'to work with the party of your choice'. . . ." She called upon women to support only women candidates and not to cooperate with the big parties. Until half of the legislators were women, true equality would not exist.[69]

More extreme was Mrs. O. H. P. Belmont, National Woman's Party president, who predicted the coming of the women's dictatorship. This was to be a benign dictatorship which would bring permanent peace, protection, and prosperity under the Woman's Party. The NWP would impose its will and program upon the world, but its work would be for the good of humanity. The party would be for women only; no men allowed at any level. She felt that women must be freed from the indignity of belonging to the old political parties. "I do not want to see any woman in the Senate as a Republican or a Democrat." She argued that it was useless to try to change the man-made world with the man-made parties. Only by segregation and sex consciousness would women elevate themselves and redeem the world. The men were so bad that she could not understand why any woman, now that she could be self-supporting, should want to marry one! [70]

Carrie Chapman Catt agreed that women had been manhandled; but "a bride going into her mother-in-law's house has small choice of keeping it in her way." The same was true of women entering the male-dominated parties. Many women who tried to clean them up received only knocks. "All over the country, women loyal to their party and intelligent toward their party duties as well as voters' rights have been peremptorily discharged, without reference, from posts they eagerly accepted expecting an opportunity for party services." [71] But Catt refused to be daunted and said that women had to stay in the parties and fight. Grace Abbott agreed and said that while women were not feared as voters, their presence had made a difference. As a woman official she found that her work commanded more interest and respect than formerly. "The Nineteenth Amendment provided a ticket of admission to the political fairgrounds. It does not admit us to the races nor to the side shows, nor does it insure us a place on the committees which award the prizes." [72]

The editor of *Ladies Home Journal* concluded that a decade of woman suffrage had made little difference in the parties or the quality of office holders because 1928 was really the first year women began to be alive to political questions and play a substantial part in the election.[73] Many thought that Hoover owed his election to the women's vote, yet he generally ignored them in dispensing rewards. A major example was his passing over Grace Abbott in naming a new Secretary of Labor to replace James J. Davis. She was supported by the American Association of University Women, National Urban League, NWTUL, National Federation of Settlements, National Conference of Social Work; and Hoover was presented with several petitions bearing thousands of names. Despite this support, Abbott lacked real political backing. Social workers and women had little political punch in Hoover's estimation.[74]

Women hoped to dismantle the political machines, but the political analyst Frank Kent claimed, in *The Great Game of Politics*, "The undeniable fact is that in every city in the country and in every state woman suffrage has increased the power of the political machine and political bosses. . . ." [75] He said that the machines captured the women's vote by lining up all the female relatives of the organization men and seeing that they supported the machine. Others were granted favors and jobs to win them. Many states required the election of men and appointment of women to the party committees. The men tried to pick compatible women, including anti-suffragists sometimes. For example in Connecticut, Mrs. Samuel R. Prentice was appointed vice-chairman of the Republican State Committee. Mrs. Prentice, a friend of Senator Brandegee, had maintained during the suffrage fight that women should have nothing to do with politics.[76] Political organizations knew by the mid-1920s that a women's bloc did not exist; women divided just like men. One writer declared that the ward captains who feared wreck and ruin in 1920 were happy men by 1924—"it is the same old thing, but more of it." [77]

Various party women believed that the tiger had eaten the lady. Irma Johnson, a Democratic leader in New Jersey, said that women were adopting the whole rationale of the machine. Emily Newell Blair and Harriet Taylor Upton agreed, saying that the fright of the bosses over the coming of women into politics was rapidly disappearing. Winifred Starr Dobyns, first chairman of the Republican Women's Committee of Illinois, gave up trying to reform the party from the inside, arguing that it was hopeless. Women accomplished nothing by going into the parties—not because they were women, but because they were outsiders. They had no influence. "Once in the organization, we could be controlled. Our nuisance value was gone." She felt that machines bowed to external, not internal, pressures. Party members as a rule had less influence on candidate selection than the independent voters.[78]

The tiger may have swallowed the lady, but he was never quite the same again. Women had the ballot and were in politics to stay. The 1920s was the period of most substantial expansion of office-holding for American women; the levels reached in that first decade of suffrage have remained fairly constant.[79] Women joined the regular parties, and ordinary women exerted as little influence as ordinary men. On the other hand, extraordinary women, such as Nellie Nugent Somerville in Mississippi, Sue Shelton White in Tennessee,[80] Cornelia Bryce Pinchot and

Emma Guffy Miller in Pennsylvania, Belle Moskowitz in New York, Ruth Hanna McCormick in Illinois, and Eleanor Roosevelt, had access to power. Neither the golden age promised by expansive suffragists nor the doom predicted by the Anti's materialized. The question "Is woman suffrage a failure?" was possible only because more had been promised during the heat of the suffrage struggle than could be delivered. Yet some leading feminists were not surprised at the outcome. Carrie Chapman Catt had been coldly realistic about the prospects; in fact, the idea of a League of Women Voters reflected this awareness. She knew that women were complete novices in politics. Moreover, Rose Schneiderman recalled that she never expected a great change with the vote "as men had it all these years and nothing of great importance had happened." [81]

NOTES

1. *Woman Citizen,* XI (Jan., 1927), 20.

2. Alice Stone Blackwell to Carrie Chapman Catt, Sept. 4, 1929, quoted in Sinclair, *The Better Half,* 344.

3. Quoted in Aileen Kraditor, ed., *Up From the Pedestal: Selected Writings in the History of American Feminists* (Chicago: Quadrangle Books, 1968), 318–319.

4. "The Editor's Page," *Ladies Home Journal,* XXXVII (Mar., 1920), 1; see also "Suffragists Would Clean Nation with Ballot Broom," *Philadelphia Press,* Dec. 2, 1913, Caroline Katzenstein MSS, newspaper scrapbook, Historical Society of Pennsylvania; Stephen A. Doyle to Jane Addams, Feb. 23, 1920, Jane Addams MSS, microfilm reel 5, Swarthmore College Peace Collection; Elizabeth Frazer, "The Political Organization," *Good Housekeeping,* LXXV (Aug., 1922), 66.

5. Elizabeth Frazer, "A Political Forecast," *Good Housekeeping,* LXXV (Sept., 1922), 159; Marie Cecile Chomel, "Does the Wife Vote Like Her Husband?," *Ladies Home Journal,* XXXVI (May, 1919), 92; Elizabeth Frazer, "This Thing Called Party Loyalty," *Good Housekeeping,* LXXIV (May, 1922), 37.

6. Emily Newell Blair, "Women in the Political Parties," *Annals of the American Academy of Political and Social Science,* CXLIII (May, 1929), 218; Breckinridge, *Women in the Twentieth Century,* 336–337; Scott, *The Southern Lady,* 203.

7. Breckinridge, *Women in the Twentieth Century,* Table 52, 289.

8. Carrie Chapman Catt, "Which Party Did It?," *Woman Citizen,* V (Sept. 18, 1920), 422–427.

Senate	Yes	No	House	Yes	No	States	Yes	No
Republican	36	8	Republican	201	21	Republican	29	1
Democrat	20	17	Democrat	105	70	Democrat	7	7

9. Randolph C. Downes, "The Rise of Warren Gamaliel Harding, 1865–1920" (book manuscript, 1966), 585, 629–630. The NLWV wanted to avoid Harding too; see Marie Stuart Edwards to Katharine Ludington, Sept. 21, 1920, C. B. Pinchot MSS, box 13, LC.

10. Marie Stuart Edwards to Mrs. Arthur Livermore, Executive Committee, Republican National Committee, Sept. 25, 1920, C. B. Pinchot MSS, box 13, LC.

11. Alice N. O'Halloran to Cornelia Bryce Pinchot, Sept. 28, 1920; Pinchot to Ruth Trombly, Sept. 22, 1920; Esther Everett Lape to Pinchot, Oct. 4, 1920, ibid.

12. Harriet Taylor Upton to Warren G. Harding, Sept. 20, 1920; Upton to Harding, Sept. 25, 1920, Harding MSS, box 525, folder 4148-1, OHS.

13. Downes, "The Rise of W. G. Harding," 631. This approach dominated the actual administration, and his most spectacular promise, a department of social welfare, was lost in a thicket of argument over governmental reorganization and efficiency.

14. Cornelia Bryce Pinchot to Catherine Philips Edson, Sept. 13, 1920, C. B. Pinchot MSS, box 12, LC.

15. Pinchot to Mrs. Theodore Fillmore, Oct. 6, 1920, ibid. In August she had written of Harding and his opponent, James Cox, "I quite agree with you as to the neolithic qualities of our peerless leaders. . . . The only advantage of weakness such as Harding's is that some good may be able to be crammed through him." See Pinchot to Cornelia S. Parker, Aug. 6, 1920, ibid., box 13.

16. Pinchot to Mrs. Warren G. Harding, Oct. 10, 1920, ibid., box 12.

17. Charles Edward Russell, "Is Woman-Suffrage a Failure?," Century Magazine, n.s., XXXV (Mar., 1924), 724.

18. "Address at St. Louis Convention," Mar., 1919, Catt MSS, box 4, NYPL.

19. Quoted in Margaret Curry, "The Victory Convention," Life and Labor, X (Mar., 1920), 70–72. Catt never joined a political party or accepted any invitations from partisan women's organizations to speak or dine. See Carrie Chapman Catt to Sara McPike, May 4, 1929, Catt MSS, box 1, NYPL.

20. "When You Get into the Parties," Woman Citizen, V (Aug. 7, 1920), 249; Rose Young, "Party Affiliation for Women," ibid. (Nov. 20, 1920), 678.

21. "League of Women Voters Launches Big Program," ibid., 694–695; Katherine McCormick to Cornelia Bryce Pinchot, Mar. 29, 1920, C. B. Pinchot MSS, box 13, LC.

22. Carrie Chapman Catt to Mrs. George Gellhorn, Mrs. Richard Edwards, and Elizabeth H. Hauser, Feb. 17, 1921, NLWV Papers, Ser. II, box 3, Catt folder, LC; see also Robert A. Shanley, "The League of Women Voters—a Study of Pressure Politics in the Public Interest" (Ph.D. thesis, Georgetown University, 1955), for a discussion of this proposal and that of the Atlanta (Ga.) League of Women Voters.

23. Leaflet, Stantial MSS, Dillon Collection, folder 17, SL.

24. Teresa A. Crowley to Maud Wood Park, Nov. 6, 1918; Blanche Ames to Park, Nov. 5, 1918, ibid.

25. "Indemnities to the Suffragists," Life and Labor, VIII (Dec., 1918), 258–260.

26. Elizabeth O. Toombs, "Politicians Take Notice," Good Housekeeping, LXX (Mar., 1920), 14–15.

27. Katharine Ludington, "Association Will Oppose State Republicans," Suffrage News Bulletin, VI (June–July, 1920), 1; "Against Those Who Are against Suffrage," Woman Citizen, V (June 19, 1920), 70–71; political advertisement by Connecticut Woman Suffrage Association, 1920, Florence C. Kitchel MSS, box 6, folder 166, SL.

28. *New York Times*, July 26, 1920; see also *ibid.*, July 24, 1920; "The Crusade Beings," *Woman Citizen*, V (July 31, 1920), 221–222.

29. *New York Times*, Sept. 6, 1920.

30. *Ibid.*, Sept. 10, 1920.

31. Carrie Chapman Catt, "An Open Letter to Mrs. Arthur Livermore," *Woman Citizen*, V (Oct. 2, 1920), 475; *New York Times*, Sept. 24, 1920.

32. Jean Burnett Tompkins, "Women's Void in Politics," *New York Times*, Nov. 21, 1920.

33. *New York Times*, Nov. 21, 1920.

34. Cora Rigby, "The Seeking Senators," *Woman Citizen*, X (May, 1926), 5–7.

35. Huthmacher, *Wagner and the Rise of Urban Liberalism*, 52–53.

36. Mary Kilbreth, "The New Anti-Feminist Campaign," *Woman Patriot*, V (June 15, 1921), 2.

37. "Where the Suffrage Issue Counts," *Woman Citizen*, V (Nov. 20, 1920), 682.

38. "The Housewife's Broom in Erie," *ibid.*, VI (July 2, 1921), 12; Florence Ellinwood Allen, *To Do Justly* (Cleveland: Western Reserve University Press, 1965), 41–51; Abbott, *History of Woman Suffrage in Cuyahoga County*, 75.

39. Mrs. Ralph Easley to Mrs. Frank A. Vanderlip, Dec. 1, 1922, National Civic Federation Papers, box 60, NYPL.

40. "Confidential Memorandum," n.d., *ibid.*, box 91.

41. Carrie Chapman Catt, "A Teapot in a Tempest," *Woman Citizen*, V (Feb. 5, 1921), 949; report of NLWV organizer Helen Seymour, Sept. 22, 1921, NLWV Papers, Ser. II, box 1, Connecticut file, LC; report of NLWV organizer Olive B. Lewis, May 29–June 1, 1921, *ibid.*, Nebraska file; Alice Stone Blackwell, "Massachusetts League of Women Voters," *Woman Citizen*, V (Dec. 11, 1920), 770.

42. Interview with Mrs. Olive Stott Gabriel, *New York Evening Post*, Feb. 24, 1921, Mary Lee MSS, folder 7, SL; "The Excursion," Brown MSS, box 1, folder 25, SL.

43. Miller's remarks quoted in "A Tempest in a Teapot," *Woman Citizen*, V (Feb. 5, 1921), 950–951; see also *New York Times*, Jan. 28, 1921; "Are Women a Menace?," *Nation*, CXII (Feb. 9, 1921), 198.

44. *Woman Citizen*, V (Feb. 19, 1921), 1009; William A. Willis, "Practical Politics," *Ladies Home Journal*, XXXVIII (May, 1921), 53.

45. Gifford Pinchot, "The Influence of Women in Politics," *Ladies Home Journal*, XXXIV (Sept., 1922), 13.

46. The WCTU decided according to the liquor issue regardless of whatever else might be in their platform; consequently in 1922 they opposed for re-election liberals and conservatives ranging from Robert La Follette and Hiram Johnson to Henry Cabot Lodge, Atlee Pomerene (Ohio), and William Henry King (Utah).

47. "Sproul's Statement, May 18, 1922." Gifford Pinchot MSS, box 447, LC; "The Women Did It," *Woman Citizen*, VII (June 3, 1922), 7–8; M. Nelson McGeary, *Gifford Pinchot: Forester-Politician* (Princeton: Princeton University Press, 1960), 277–285.

48. Upton to George B. Christian, May 17, 1922, Harding MSS, box 703, folder 10, OHS; Harriet Taylor Upton, "The Machine and the Woman," *Ladies Home Journal*, XXXIX (Oct., 1922), 13.

49. "Women Voters Organize," *North American* (Philadelphia), Mar. 8, 1923, C. B. Pinchot MSS, box 30, LC.

50. Cornelia Bryce Pinchot to Lady Johnstone, Jan. 20, 1920, *ibid.*, box 12.

51. "Women Voters and State Legislation," *Woman Citizen*, VI (June 4, 1921), 24; Cornelia Bryce Pinchot to Maud Wood Park, Apr. 22, 1920, C. B. Pinchot MSS, box 13, LC; Pinchot to Miss [Martha] Thomas, Feb. 28, 1921, *ibid.*, box 17; Pinchot to Marie Stuart Edwards, May 24, 1922, *ibid.*, box 21.

52. Telegram, Minnie Warburton to Cornelia Bryce Pinchot, Feb. 21, 1923, C. B. Pinchot MSS, box 37, LC; Pinchot to Warburton, Mar. 3, 1923, *ibid.*; Pinchot to Mrs. George H. Lorimer, Jan. 30, 1923, *ibid.*, box 33.

53. Cornelia Bryce Pinchot to Herbert Croly, Oct. 21, 1922, *ibid.*, box 21.

54. Geneva M. Marsh, "Campaigning for Senator with Rose Schneiderman," *Life and Labor*, X (Dec., 1920), 303–305.

55. Breckinridge, *Women in the Twentieth Century*, 296–301; women in Congress: 65th=1, 66th=0, 67th=3, 68th=1, 69th=3, 70th=3, 71st=9, 72nd=6; Gruberg, *Women in American Politics*, 118–123, 151–156.

56. Breckinridge, *Women in the Twentieth Century*, 322–326; women in legislatures: 1921=37, 1923=98, 1925=141 in 38 states, 1927=127 in 36 states, 1929=149 in 38 states, 1931=146 in 39 states, 1933=131 in 33 states; see also Gruberg, *Women in American Politics*, 169–170; Sue Shelton White, "Woman's Research Foundation: Women in State Legislatures," May, 1925, White MSS, folder 13, SL.

57. Minnie Fisher Cunningham, "Too Gallant a Walk," *Woman's Journal*, XIV (Jan., 1929), 12–13; Anne Martin to Caroline Katzenstein, Dec. 20, 1918, Katzenstein MSS, Historical Society of Pennsylvania.

58. Breckinridge, *Women in the Twentieth Century*, 303–304; Agnes Bryant Dickinson, "Judge Allen's Glorious Defeat," *Woman Citizen*, XI (Oct., 1926), 10; Allen, *To Do Justly*, 65–68.

59. Willie Snow Ethridge, "The Lady from Georgia," *Good Housekeeping*, LXXVI (Jan., 1923), 27; Minnie Anderson Hale, "Rebecca Felton," *Women Lawyers' Journal*, XII (Oct.–Nov., 1922), 6; Frances Parkinson Keyes, "Letter from a Senator's Wife," *Good Housekeeping*, LXXVI (Feb.,1923), 28.

60. "Ascent of Women's Suffrage," [1923], C. B. Pinchot MSS, box 19, LC.

61. *New York Times*, Jan. 2, 1925.

62. Florence E. S. Knapp, "A Woman Politician and Proud of It," *Ladies Home Journal*, XLIV (May, 1927), 37.

63. Editorials, "Mrs. Knapp," *Woman Citizen*, XII (Nov., 1927), 24; *Woman's Journal*, XIII (Feb., 1928), 23; *ibid.* (July, 1928), 21–22.

64. Between 1930 and 1932 three other women ran for governor but lost: Elizabeth Upham Yates (Democrat) in Rhode Island in 1920, Alice Lorraine Day (Non-Partisan League) in South Dakota in 1921, Gladys Pyle (Republican) in South Dakota in 1930.

65. Editorial, "The Present Moment," *Woman Citizen*, V (Dec. 25, 1920), 813; Emily Kneubuhl and Emma Woytinsky, "How Do You Like America?," [ca. 1939], Emily Kneubuhl MSS, folder 13, SL.

66. "The Woman in Politics," *Women Lawyers' Journal*, IX (Feb., 1920), 15.

67. Sue Shelton White to Mary Dewson, Nov. 23, 1928, White MSS, vol. I, SL.

68. Quoted in Breckinridge, *Women in the Twentieth Century*, 302; see also Katherine Braddock to Alton B. Parker, Feb. 8, 1926, National Civic Federation Papers, box 91, NYPL; Ruth Bryan Owen to Carrie Chapman Catt, Dec. 1, 1932, Catt MSS, box 1, NYPL; Margaret S. Roberts to Gertrude Foster Brown, Oct. 11, 1922, Margaret S. Roberts MSS, folder 7, SL.

69. Anne Martin, "Feminists and Future Political Action," *Nation*, CXX

(Feb. 18, 1925), 185–186; see also Ruth McIntire Dadourian, "Why Get Out the Vote?," *Woman Citizen*, XII (Sept., 1927), 16–17. Demands that half of Congress, legislatures, and so forth be made up of women have recurred down to the present. A number of leading feminists, such as Betty Freidan, founder of the National Organization of Women (NOW), Congresswomen Shirley Chisholm and Bella Abzug, and Fannie Lou Hamer, leader in the Mississippi Freedom Democratic Party, came together in July, 1971, to form the Women's Political Caucus with the goal of making the political parties select women for 50 percent of their delegates to the nominating conventions in 1972, getting women on the U.S. Supreme Court, and winning at least 50 percent of all elective offices within a decade; see *Newsweek*, LXXVIII (July 26, 1971), 29–30.

70. Mrs. O. H. P. Belmont, "Women as Dictators," *Ladies Home Journal*, XXIX (Sept., 1922), 7; *Evening Public Ledger* (Philadelphia), May 21, 1921, Katzenstein MSS, Historical Society of Pennsylvania.

71. Carrie Chapman Catt, "What Women Have Done with the Vote," *Independent*, CXV (Oct. 17, 1925), 447–448.

72. Grace Abbott, "What Have They Done?," *ibid.* (Oct. 24, 1925), 476.

73. Loring A. Schuler, "Ten Years of Suffrage," *Ladies Home Journal*, XLVII (Aug., 1930), 22; see also Eunice Fuller Barnard, "Madame Arrives in Politics," *North American Review*, CCXXVI (Nov., 1928), 551–556; Sarah Schuyler Butler, "After Ten Years," *Woman's Journal*, XIV (Apr., 1931), 10–11; Breckinridge, *Women in the Twentieth Century*, 247–256, 268.

74. J. Prentice Murphy to Dorothy K. Brown, June 24, 1930, Brown MSS, box 1, folder 28, SL; Julia Lathrop to J. Prentice Murphy, June 20, 1930, *ibid.*; editorial, "A Woman in the Cabinet," *Boston Herald*, June 13, 1930; editorial, "Grace Abbott," *Daily News* (Washington), Nov. 8, 1930.

75. Frank R. Kent, *The Great Game of Politics* (New York: Doubleday, 1935), 168; Kent, "Women's Faults in Politics," *Woman Citizen*, XI (Mar., 1927), 23; see also Ida Tarbell, "Ten Years of Woman Suffrage," *Literary Digest*, CV (Apr. 26, 1930), 11.

76. "Fooling the Women in Politics," *Ladies Home Journal*, XL (Sept., 1923), 159.

77. Charles Edward Russell, "Is Woman-Suffrage a Failure?," *Century Magazine*, n.s., XXXV (Mar., 1924), 730.

78. Winifred Starr Dobyns, "The Lady and the Tiger," *Woman Citizen*, XI (Jan., 1927), 20–21.

79. See the catalog of names and positions in Gruberg, *Women in American Politics*, 117–218.

80. Scott, *The Southern Lady*, 203–205.

81. Schneiderman and Goldthwaite, *All for One*, 121–122.

FIVE

The Progressive Imprint

The Woman Movement became one of that host of reform efforts called the Progressive Movement during the first decades of the twentieth century, but the two movements were never identical. The feminist movement had objectives which benefited women first of all and were sought as a matter of justice: the vote, jury service, office-holding, independent citizenship, property rights, access to professions, and the end of sex discrimination. However, most women involved in the Woman Movement were social feminists who put social reform ahead of simple rights of women. The inequities facing women made many sympathetic to demands for social reform; indeed, some of the most prominent leaders of the social-justice wing of progressivism, the "spearheads for reform," were feminists, such as Jane Addams, Florence Kelley, and Lillian Wald. For the most part women's reform efforts reflected the traditional idea of woman's sphere: Home and Motherhood, which included the morals, health, education, and welfare of children. Hence, Frances Willard would declare that woman's objective was to make the whole world "homelike"; and the major innovation of advanced social feminists in the late nineteenth century in trying to cope with urban ills and poverty was the settlement house movement. The reforms which won the greatest support among women before and after the suffrage interlude were those which concerned children, mothers, and the home. Women strongly supported prohibition and were its principal defenders even after it was destined for repeal. Congress experienced its first great blizzard of telegrams and letters in support of pure food and drug legislation. Women were among the most staunch and persistent proponents of child labor legislation, and only because of feminist pressure did Congress ever pass a maternity- and infancy-protection bill in the 1920s. Social feminists worked up an agenda for reform in the Progressive Era and in the 1920s which required the emergency climate of the New Deal for passage.

The coming of the 1920s did not see the end of the reform drive among the women's organizations, but the growing resistance to further reform in the New Era had its reflection in a weakening of the impulse in many organizations. New organizations such as the League of Women Voters and the Women's Joint Congressional Committee appeared in order to undertake new efforts, and many social feminists viewed enfranchisement to be the starter's gun for a new race. Nevertheless, the commitment to progressive change varied. Professional women's groups increasingly focused on professional advancement, and the hard-core feminists in the Woman's Party openly combatted social feminists on the issue of protective industrial legislation for women. On the other hand, to varying degrees the National Consumers' League, Women's Trade Union League, League of Women Voters, American Association of University Women, General Federation of Women's Clubs, Parent-Teachers Associations, YWCA, and others carried the progressive impulse through the 1920s.

During the final years of the crusade for suffrage the National American Woman Suffrage Association had swelled to more than 2,000,000 members. With the winning of the vote, the feminist movement returned to its former diversity and size. NAWSA's offspring, the National League of Women Voters, advanced a broad platform of reforms throughout the 1920s, but retained less than one-tenth of NAWSA's millions. Of course, not all defections were due to the progressive stance since it cost only a dime to belong to NAWSA while the NLWV charged real dues; and some former leaders, such as Ruth Hanna Mc-

Cormick, Mary Livermore, and Mrs. George Bass, rejected the concept of a non-partisan political organization. From its inception the NLWV felt an urgency to solve the pressing problems of discrimination facing women everywhere, underpaid women laboring in sweatshops, a million children working in mills, mines, factories, and commercial agriculture (400,000 under age fourteen). One fourth of the men called by the military draft were rejected as physically unfit and another fourth were illiterate. America had one of the highest maternal and infant death rates of civilized nations. In the 1920s the NLWV fought for maternity and infancy protection, government ownership and operation of Muscle Shoals, federal regulation of marketing and distribution of food, the cooperative movement, aid to education, and pure food and drugs. It adopted a liberal labor platform including collective bargaining, hours and wages laws, equal pay for equal work, federal employment service, and prohibition of child labor.[1]

Of the membership groups, the NLWV was the strongest of the more progressive organizations which included it, the National Consumers' League, and the National Women's Trade Union League. Naturally the NCL and NWTUL fought for protective legislation wherever possible, but these organizations had neither large membership nor presence in all states. On the other hand, the League of Women Voters existed in all but two states by 1930, and it formed the nucleus of the many women's legislative councils. For example, in 1922 the NLWV reported that thirty state leagues had a chairman for women in industry and many had legislative programs.[2] The state efforts ranged over the whole terrain of election laws, eugenics, labor legislation, mothers' pensions, children's codes, city manager government, equal rights, marriage laws, birth control, anti-lynching, fiscal reform, governmental reorganization and efficiency, school attendance, jury service, vice repression, and appointment of women to state boards and commissions.[3] However, the progressive impulse of the NLWV failed to penetrate to certain state leagues. This difficulty stemmed in part from the broad platform which allowed varied interpretations and divisions of interest.

Although Governor Pinchot of Pennsylvania was sympathetic
to labor, he never controlled the legislature. He supported the
Consumers' League's minimum-wage proposal and the Women's
Trade Union League's eight-hour bill, but neither passed in the
1920s. The only success of the decade for feminists was the elevation of the Women's Division of the Industrial Board to
bureau status in 1925. Political attitudes were not conducive to
labor legislation. Pennsylvania was the scene of major strikes in
the 1920s, home of powerful open-shop organizations, and residence of leading opponents of child labor legislation, such as
Henry Moore of the Pennsylvania Manufacturers Association
and Raymond Pitcairn of the Pittsburgh Plate Glass Company.
Most people still breathed the atmosphere of the Red Scare.
"Here people still talk in terms of bombs and anarchy, as if
Bolshevists and Trade Unionists were one and the same." [4] "You
can't imagine how medieval Pennsylvania is on the subject of
labor," Mrs. Pinchot wrote her cousin Lady Nancy Astor; "it
will stagger them to the very roots of their being to see some-
body like you actually admit that trade unions are not bolshevist
groups organized to deposit bombs at the doors of the wealthy." [5]

In this conservative climate, the Pennsylvania League of
Women Voters was a mirror, not a beacon. The league was
headed by Mrs. John O. Miller, the hold-over president of the
suffrage association. She was an able woman, eminently respectable; but a conservative person interested in government frugal-
ity, efficiency, and honesty. Mrs. Pinchot urged Miller to adopt
a liberal program. "I can not see that there is any reason at all for
the League of Women Citizens to exist unless it is going to stand
for a program far ahead of what either political party will be apt
to accept within the next five years. . . . It is only if they
refuse to have this purpose that I feel the organization will be
absurd." [6] The Pennsylvania League refused, however, to take
a stand on the eight-hour bill, minimum wage, meat-packer control, or a proposed child labor law. Miller even tried to persuade
Joseph Grundy, one of the most conservative men in the state,
to finance the LWV. In desperation Mrs. Pinchot appealed to

Maud Wood Park, NLWV president, to intervene in the situation because the state league "is not doing the work for which it is organized." Park replied she could not unless requested by the Pennsylvania LWV itself.[7] Most distressing was Miller's refusal to appoint a woman in industry committee, thereby slicing off a major portion of the NLWV platform.[8] Pinchot turned to the Consumers' League, YWCA, and WTUL in the fight for labor legislation. "It is all the more important that those women who believe that the State has a responsibility to the workers . . . stand together and put their whole strength behind the movement."[9] Finally, after the 1922 elections, she organized the Pinchot-for-Governor clubs into the Pennsylvania State Council of Republican Women to promote the sort of legislation that the LWV refused. Even this did not last, as the regular organization absorbed the council.

The NLWV found the Pennsylvania problem elsewhere. A league organizer reported that the president in Wichita was "splendid on arranging for a formal patriotic meeting with emphasis upon the Gettysburg address and the flag but not big enough for a real constructive job of nation building."[10] The problem in Montana was worse: the president was described as very conservative, "a disgrace to the League of Women Voters," and the vice-president was characterized as an "old W.C.T.U. worker, is very reactionary, resting on the laurels of the old Suffrage party."[11] The concern of these leaders of the Montana LWV was to keep the "radicals" from seizing control of the state and the LWV. The Butte DAR wanted to revive a free school for the education of immigrants but was opposed by the mining companies and the local business college. On the Women's Council in Butte only the president of the Montana LWV opposed the school (she was the wife of the president of the business college). She declared that they were not "under obligation to educate all the ignorant Europeans who wanted to come here, let them go out and pay for what they get. . . ." In the 1922 campaign the Montana LWV did nothing until its president and others organized the Home Guards and declared that if the Non-Partisan candidates won, "the women of the state would be nationalized, the babies snatched from their mother's arms and placed under state care." [12]

Such division of perception had parallels within the officers of the National League also. Robert La Follette usually backed the legislation that women wanted, but important members of the NLWV feared him. Marie Stuart Edwards, NLWV first vice-president in 1922, said, "I cannot think of LaFollette in any light but a horrible menace." Her friend, Mrs. William G. Hibbard, regional director of the NLWV, wrote, "I . . . feel the state is better off with LaFollette in Washington than in the state. . . . LaF. can't live forever so the Lord may help us out." [13] However, the Woman's Division of the Progressive campaign in 1924 included significant NLWV women: Mabel Costigan, chairman, Jane Addams, Elizabeth Glendower Evans, and Florence L. Kitchelt.

The most advanced social feminist organizations, the National Consumers' League and the Women's Trade Union League, suffered the worst in the 1920s; and survival itself became a question. [14] In the New Era the NCL saw its income drop and membership drift away. Florence Kelley practically wore herself out fighting reactionary court decisions and the equal rights amendment of the NWP. In addition, the NCL was viciously red-baited because Kelley was a Socialist. The prosperous days of the NWTUL were before 1920, when it had an expanding membership, adequate finances, active union organizers and legislative representatives, and a monthly magazine. In the 1920s the WTUL was red-baited by rightists, and generally ignored by other labor organizations. Meeting biennially became too costly so they switched to triennial conventions after 1920. *Life and Labor* became the *Life and Labor Bulletin*, a cut-down version which appeared irregularly. By 1925 most of the local leagues were in deep financial trouble, union organizing had virtually ceased, and the national league had only about 1,000 members. The NWTUL saw its income reduced, and an increased proportion came from wealthy allies instead of dues-paying members. Ethel Smith resigned as national legislative chairman in 1926 but stayed on parttime until 1928, after which the NWTUL was without an effective legislative representative in Washington.[15] Rose Schneiderman, who became NWTUL president in 1926, declared that the twenties were "fruitful years," but her account suggested that this was personal, rather than an organizational experience.[16]

The General Federation of Women's Clubs, the largest women's organization until surpassed by Carrie Chapman Catt's NAWSA, supported conservation, women's labor laws, civil service reform, and pure food a decade before it endorsed suffrage in 1914. Its enthusiasm for progressive reform hit a peak in the period 1920–24. It helped organize the Women's Joint Congressional Committee and established a social welfare committee in 1920 to advance the federation's efforts for children and health. The 1922 program included a child labor amendment, enforcement of prohibition, department of education, honest labeling of cloth and clothing, independent citizenship for women, and regulation of billboards.[17] The legislative ardor cooled, and a chairman at the 1924 biennial noted that "the clubs were returning to the literary program." [18] The child labor amendment caused internal dissension after 1924, but the federation continued its endorsement. The issue of legislative lobbying was debated at the 1926 and 1928 biennials. The Kentucky delegation requested the GFWC to abandon its social and legislative activities and return to cultural uplift. The GFWC agreed to withdraw from WJCC, but refused to cease legislative lobbying.[19]

Even the DAR had a reform phase which climaxed when it joined the WJCC and backed the Sheppard-Towner Act in 1921. Before World War I, in addition to its usual patriotic and historical concerns, the DAR had supported conservation, playgrounds and clubs for children, and vocational education, called for the establishment of the Children's Bureau, denounced militarism in the schools, and opposed child labor. It endorsed prohibition in 1917 and the League of Nations in 1919. But in the 1920s the DAR moved to extreme militarism, nationalism, and isolationism. In 1921 it helped pass the Sheppard-Towner Act, which its leaders denounced as Bolshevism by 1927. It endorsed federal aid to education in 1920, but soon it resisted such efforts on constitutional grounds and came to support censorship of books, ideas, and teachers. The transformation was complete by 1928, when the society expelled internal critics of its course.[20]

Even though the DAR slipped into reaction, the Consumers' League and the Women's Trade Union League struggled for life in the late twenties, and the General Federation's zeal for reform declined, the progressive impulse continued within feminism. The League of Women Voters and the American Association of University Women were growing, vital organizations with a commitment to reform. These and nearly two dozen others were members of the Women's Joint Congressional Committee in the nation's capital and formed the multitude of state legislative councils and committees. The peak of their effort and impact was reached in the first half of the decade; the period from then until the coming of the New Deal was mainly one of holding back the tide of reaction and laying the basis for further reforms in a more favorable situation. A survey of some of the areas of concern suggests no lessening of effort by social feminists in the 1920s. By contrast to the winning of suffrage, the grinding fights for city managers, school and labor laws, educational reforms, and consumer interests seem colorless and routine. However, it is only the brilliance and spectacle of the suffrage victory which makes the subsequent work of social feminists seem less than it really was.

Support for the City Manager Movement

Progressivism was born in the cities, and the city received extensive attention from the reformers. Attempts to reform urban political and administrative machinery and practices were as characteristic of the Progressive Movement as any activity. Even so, municipal reform got support from varied sources including old-fashioned Good Government conservatives, businessmen wanting "business-like" government, wealthy and middle-class citizens tired of corruption and waste, and chambers of commerce and minority party politicians wanting to rearrange the power relationships.[21] Among the programs to rid the city of corruption and bossism and to create efficiency and order, the movement for city manager government seemed to be very promising. The spread of this form continued from 1910, with the 1920s as a period of substantial expansion. In 1918 only 98 cities had the city manager form; 403 had it by 1933.[22] In the New Era the social feminists especially promoted the plan.

Ohio, with its large number of urban areas, was a particular arena of struggle. In 1913 Dayton had become the first important city to adopt the city manager plan, and then in 1921 Cleveland became the first great city to accept the plan. The League of Women Voters was in the center of nearly every effort and continued when others surrendered. They helped win in Oberlin, Painesville, Lima, Middletown, Cleveland, Cleveland Heights, Cincinnati, Hamilton, Ironton, and Piqua. They saved Dayton's city manager charter in 1921, and worked in Toledo from 1923 to 1935, when they finally won.

Cleveland had had good government under Tom Johnson and Newton D. Baker, but after 1912 the city suffered from old-fashioned boss rule. A group of substantial citizens, calling themselves the Committee of Fifteen, began an investigation in 1917. The committee (no women on it) reported in 1920, favoring a city manager. The Cleveland voters elected a commission in 1920 headed by Baker to write a new city charter. The women's organizations rallied behind the plan and supplied most of the workers to canvass for votes. Voters approved a charter in November, 1921, which abolished the old ward system and provided for a twenty-five-man council elected from four districts by proportional representation. Executive responsibility was given to a city manager hired by the council.

The first election under the charter came in November, 1923. The results revealed that fourteen of the thirty-three old wards had no councilmen; the old-line organizations saw their power clipped. They set out to repeal the new plan, especially proportional representation. Thus began a running fight that finally brought repeal of the new charter in 1931. In every election city

charter government was the major issue, and the machines eventually wore out the proponents.

In 1925 the LWV conducted a door-to-door canvass, sponsored rallies in the park, and provided a motor pool to drive
voters to the polls. Proportional representation was saved by 804
votes out of 41,300 cast. In 1927 the machines were led by
Harry L. Davis, former mayor and governor of Ohio. From a
supporting role to the lead part, the LWV moved to save the
city manager plan. They fought almost single-handedly and won
by 3,232 votes. The battle resumed in 1929 and again the LWV
took the lead. Having spent $8,000 in 1927 beating the machine,
the LWV could not afford to do it alone; therefore they helped
organize the Progressive Government Committee and provided
the vice-chairman and most of the workers. The committee was
essentially a LWV vehicle but generated wide support. They
won by 3,004 votes at a cost of $70,000. They lost in 1931 as
even Newton D. Baker joined the opposition and took most
progressive Democrats with him. People were weary of the issue,
and it had become clouded by the revelation of corruption and
mismanagement by the first city manager, who was removed in
1930. He had come to terms with the political organizations in
a deal to split job appointments on a 60-40 percent basis. The
LWV led the defense again, but lost by 9,000 votes.[23]

The charter reform movement in Cincinnati found the women
supplying much of the muscle. For years the city was in the
grip of the Republican machine of Rudolph K. Hynicka; and
although the city adopted a charter in 1917, Hynicka dominated
its old-style mayor-council of thirty-two councilmen elected
from the wards. City manager advocates sprang from the Cincin-
natus Association, a group of substantial citizens who agonized
over the waste of tax money. They began a study in 1920, and
in 1924, led by men like Charles Taft, they organized to pass
a new charter for city manager government. They hired Emily
Kneubuhl as director of the City Charter Committee. Kneubuhl
was state director of political education for the Minnesota LWV
and secretary of the National Municipal League.

In the campaign men took the lead but the Women's City

Club and the LWV did most of the work through hundreds of volunteers. The charter won 92,500—41,000 despite the attempt of the city council to confuse the voters by cluttering the ballot with competing and similar amendments. The Charter Committee ran a slate of nine for the new reduced council and won six seats. However, the Hynicka machine dominated Hamilton County and limited the effectiveness of the manager in the city. Manager advocates saw they would have to control the Republican political organization in the county if the city government was to function properly. They organized the Citizens Republican Committee to compete with the regular apparatus and were so successful that the machine had to come to terms. Because the Committee's women worked so hard and were so successful, the Republican party tried to create a permanent organization to attract them, but they viewed one another with suspicion.[24]

Many of the same forces combined to bring city manager government to Rochester, New York.[25] The plan climaxed civic reform efforts dating back to the Good Government movement of the 1890s, but emerged in the 1920s from a combination of women's concern for civic betterment and a crisis caused by the death of the long-time Republican boss George Aldrich in 1922. After winning suffrage, women concentrated on the city government, persuading the city council to hold public hearings on the city budget and undertaking an intensive two-year study of the government. They found that the city charter had fundamental faults; for example, no fixing of responsibility for spending and a grossly undemocratic ward-representation system. The women turned to the city manager idea as a solution. The Woman's City Club used the period 1922–23 to educate the public by bringing speakers for public meetings and study groups. They imported Emily Kneubuhl from Cincinnati to conduct classes in political education for club members and to train city manager speakers. In the meanwhile, Aldrich had died and his henchmen scrambled for control of the party machinery. Their revival of the broad use of patronage endangered all the gains made by civic reformers since the 1890s and caused deep concern among civic leaders. The first director of the Bureau of

Municipal Research, Leroy Snyder, joined with his successor, Stephen B. Storey, and Helen Probst Abbott, president of the Woman's City Club, to work for a city manager charter for Rochester. They organized the City Government Plan Committee in 1923 with the backing of George Eastman, enlisted the bureau's services, and drafted a series of charter amendments.

In 1924 the combined leadership began the City Manager League (with Abbott as vice-chairman) and hired Kneubuhl. Under her direction the league quickly enrolled 24,000 members. McKelvey reported, "Indeed, the campaign acquired such momentum in 1925 that despite the hostility of leaders of both political parties, the City Council reluctantly passed the amendments, hoping, sullenly, to see them defeated or set aside in the courts." [26] The courts, however, upheld the home-rule laws of the state. The City Manager League conducted an intensive house-to-house canvass, largely done by women, that resulted in an unprecedented registration of 104,000. Women held a mass meeting for the charter on the Saturday night before election, and they won by more than 13,000 votes. The first council under the new charter was not elected until November, 1927, but a pro-manager Republican slate dominated it. The new government began operations on January 1, 1928, and named Stephen Storey as city manager.

Emily Kneubuhl moved next to Minneapolis, where she helped organize a losing effort of the LWV for a city manager in 1928. After this she spent full time as executive secretary of the National Federation of Business and Professional Women's Clubs until 1935, when she became the special assistant to the administrator of the Rural Electrification Administration.

Educational Concerns

The draft in World War I revealed a shockingly high rate of illiteracy; therefore, social feminists turned to federal solutions to national educational problems. Most of the plans failed in the 1920s. Highest on the list was the creation of a department of education. The National Education Association began its agitation for a department of education in 1866, and its hopes soared as the idea picked up supporters after the war. Altogether, twenty-six organizations including members of the WJCC and the AFL came to endorse the idea, but a federal role in education had powerful enemies. Aside from various reactionary or states' rights groups like the Sentinels of the Republic, Massachusetts Public Interests League, Maryland League for State Defense, Woman Patriots, and American Constitutional League, the proposal offended the U.S. Chamber of Commerce and the National Catholic Welfare Council.[27]

Unfortunately for the program, it became snarled during the Harding administration in the problem of executive reorganization and Harding's proposed department of social welfare. During that period when the women's vote was a threat, the main chance became lost in secondary issues. The NEA supported a bill which would create a department of education with an appropriation of $100,000,000 for elimination of illiteracy and "Americanization" of immigrants, development of physical education programs in every school, teacher-training, and the equalization of educational opportunities. The money was to be given to states as matching grants.[28] On the other hand, the Harding administration proposed its department of social welfare (or public welfare), which would have assistant secretaries of education, public health, social services, and veterans administration and include the Women's and Children's bureaus.[29]

During the 1920 campaign, social feminists had been thrilled by Harding's promise of a department of social welfare; but when it turned out to be only a reorganizational gimmick, many opposed it. In fact, nearly every aspect of the proposed department offended someone, even those it was supposed to impress. Such organizations as the American Constitutional League and the Woman Patriots denounced the plan as unconstitutional or Bolshevistic. The American Legion opposed placing the Veterans Administration in the department; medical associations feared it meant "socialized medicine"; defenders of the Women's and Children's bureaus wanted the bureaus to remain in the Labor Department; NEA and GFWC wanted a separate department for education; and finally, many objected to the suggestion that a woman would be appointed to head the new department.[30] Carrie Chapman Catt urged proponents to accept the combined department rather than squabble and lose both.[31] Harding had only slight interest in the thing; and when opposition developed, he dropped it. Only Charles Sawyer, White House physician, wanted to pursue the matter.[32] Even the NLWV lost interest and dropped the question from its 1926 platform. At last in 1953 the combined department appeared as the Department of Health, Education and Welfare.

In addition to a department of education the women asked for parity for home economics training. The Smith-Hughes Act of 1917 provided federal aid to states for training in agriculture, trade, and industrial pursuits—fields mainly for men. Women felt it discriminated and demanded equal appropriations for home economics. Oddly enough, the women could not obtain it while they massed their support, but in 1929, after most had lost interest and ceased to agitate, parity was granted.[33] The Joint Congressional Committee had a subcommittee which worked to secure compulsory school attendance in the District of Columbia and won it in the lame-duck session in January, 1925. The Women's Trade Union League supported increased teachers' salaries for the District also. The AAUW broadened its concern from higher to elementary education after 1923.[34] In fact, support of public education increased noticeably in the 1920s, partly due to the attention given by the women's organizations.

Consumer Interests

Women evinced a higher concern for consumer legislation and protection than anyone else, and progressive women promoted federal solutions to key problems. The NLWV Cost-of-Living Committee asked the national political conventions in 1920 to endorse increased aid to home economics and federal regulation of marketing and distribution of food. The former was achieved in 1929, but the latter was a broad proposal which had to be embodied in specific acts. The NLWV joined the NCL and

NWTUL in demanding federal regulation of the packing industry. They organized a WJCC subcommittee and cooperated with the American Livestock Association, the Farmers' National Council, and the farm bloc in Congress to win passage of the Packers and Stockyards Control Act of 1921. Of the various proposals to regulate the meat packers, the WJCC supported George Norris's bill, which placed the jurisdiction of control under the Federal Trade Commission. The women strongly supported the FTC and were sorely disappointed when the Packers Control Act did not give the FTC jurisdiction.[35] In 1923 the women joined the farm bloc to win the "filled milk" bill, which prohibited the interstate shipment of doctored milk. The agricultural interests promoted these bills out of economic self-interest; they were producers trying to strengthen their position against merchandizers. The women's interest had nothing to do with agricultural politics and economics; instead they wanted lower consumer costs, safe food, and an end to *caveat emptor*. The farm bloc wanted higher prices for farmers; the women wanted lower prices for consumers. To this end the WTUL and NLWV called for laws favoring the spread of the cooperative movement in addition to the creation of public markets, milk depots, and other terminal facilities.[36]

Led by their goal of lower production costs through the intervention of government, the NLWV became the only citizens' organization in the 1920s to endorse and campaign for George Norris's dream for the Tennessee Valley. During the war the federal government had constructed two nitrate plants for munitions, but the dams authorized by Congress were incomplete when the Harding administration began. Controversy swirled over whether the dams should be completed and whether the government should retain ownership of the nitrate plants. Norris called for government ownership and operation of the nitrate plants to produce inexpensive fertilizer. In 1920 the Chicago LWV endorsed his program, and the 1921 NLWV called upon Congress to complete the dams, produce fertilizer, and furnish electricity for the regions in the South around the dams.[37]

In 1922 Henry Ford offered to buy the facilities and produce cheap fertilizer. The NLWV momentarily favored this, and the 1922 convention nearly passed a resolution urging the government to accept the offer. Mabel Costigan, a progressive of impeccable credentials, stopped the move by presenting the case for government ownership; and the NLWV accepted the plans advanced by Norris. As Norris shifted from fertilizer to public power, the NLWV shifted with him, so that by 1926 "the program of the League read like a blue print for the TVA." [38] In the years from 1924 to 1928 the NLWV conducted an intensive study of power development and regulation in the United States. As a result practically every chapter in the country undertook a local investigation and education program. In Indiana, one small town's utility franchise was about to expire and Samuel Insull wanted it. The LWV held an open meeting in which Insull's agent presented his case and David Lilienthal spoke for public ownership. As a result of the meeting, Insull failed to get the franchise.[39]

The 1925 NLWV convention adopted the platform that Muscle Shoals be treated as a national asset. The Pennsylvania delegation, one of the most conservative in the entire LWV, tried to put Muscle Shoals back on the "study program," but Mabel Costigan argued for positive action and carried the convention.[40] The NLWV believed that the government should own and operate Muscle Shoals as a yardstick in the generation and distribution of power as well as the production of nitrates. Ann Dennis Bursch, NLWV Cost-of-Living Committee member, addressed the American Academy of Political and Social Science on the issue of electric power and asked, "Oughtn't the United States government to run Muscle Shoals and produce electricity there, do the same thing at Boulder Canyon and give us a yardstick so we can measure whether our home use of electricity is costing us a reasonable amount?" [41]

NLWV activities on behalf of public ownership greatly alarmed the private power interests. Their staff members infiltrated the LWV to spy on its activities. Stenographers attended league meetings to take down speeches made by the leaders on Muscle Shoals, and letters circulated warning that the LWV was a menace to the electric industry. One letter said that Mrs. Harris Baldwin, who directed LWV efforts for Muscle Shoals after 1928, should not be allowed to come into Michigan because she was dangerous to the private power interests.[42] In general the industry wanted to halt efforts on behalf of public power and "educate" the LWV to its view. The NLWV did not campaign for any of the various Muscle Shoals bills until 1928, when they shifted into a massive educational campaign to popularize Norris's plan.[43] It gained enough momentum to be passed twice and vetoed, first by Coolidge in 1928 and then by Hoover in 1931. The attempt to override Hoover's veto failed by a few votes. Finally TVA won in the first hundred days of the Roosevelt administration, and the only non-governmental person present at the signing was Belle Sherwin, NLWV president, who received one of the pens.

In the attempt to override Hoover's veto, seven lame-duck senators provided the margin of defeat. Norris had proposed an amendment to eliminate the lame duck back in December, 1922, and it actually passed the Senate in 1923, only to die in the House. The NLWV endorsed it in 1925 but did nothing to promote it until 1928. The loss of the TVA plan in 1931 served to spur efforts for the amendment, and it finally passed Congress in March, 1932. The NLWV and the American Bar Association were Norris's chief backers and were the only non-governmental groups represented at the proclamation ceremony in February, 1933.

The Primary and Civil Service

Progressives sought to democratize government and make politics more responsive to the popular will. In this effort the NLWV and others advocated election-law reforms, short ballot, proportional representation, use of voting machines, permanent registration, and the direct primary. Progressives advanced the direct primary as a means to break boss control of nominations; however, beginning in 1919 the primary system came under a growing attack which actually gained momentum as women got

the vote. Party regulars feared that women would be independent in their voting, hence they wanted to get rid of the primary
before the women used it. In 1920 the New York Republican
party put repeal in its platform and Governor Nathan Miller
pressed the measure. In 1921 at least eight states tried to dismantle the primary, but succeeded only in New York. In
Indiana, Tennessee, Vermont, Delaware, North Carolina, Wisconsin, and West Virginia primary advocates fended off the
repealers. In West Virginia the governor attempted to repeal the
primary in a special session. The principal opposition came from
the LWV and the Federation of Women's Clubs. The bill was
withdrawn; and the Wheeling *Register* said: "It was the ladies—
the dear, dear ladies—who by showering the legislature with
telegrams of protest saved the primary law from repeal." [44] In
Ohio a special referendum to repeal the primary was defeated in
1926, and Maine sustained hers in a special election by a substantial majority in 1927 despite the opposition of all the major
newspapers in the state. A political science professor complained
in attacking the NLWV, "Every effort to get rid of the direct
primary in this country in the past few years has been blocked
by the League of Women Voters." [45]

Civil service reform was standard fare for progressives, and
social feminists remained among the most faithful proponents
throughout the 1920s. Reform had a dimension beyond good
government and efficiency because it held the prospect of advancing women's rights. The Woman in Industry Service spot-
lighted various abuses in the public service in 1919, including the
exclusion of women from 60 percent of the exams, discriminatory appointment practices, and unequal pay. While the tests
were immediately opened, the other problems persisted. [46]

Until 1920 the only law of importance for civil service was
the Pendleton Act of 1883. Almost from the beginning federal
employees had agitated for a retirement program. More than
seventy bills had appeared in Congress from 1886 to 1914, and
a retirement plan had become a key plank in the program of the
federal employee unions after 1917. In March, 1919, Congress
appointed the Joint Commission on Reclassification of Salaries,

which investigated pay and classification of the service. Its report in March, 1920, condemned the inequities in the matter of equal pay for equal work and recommended a federal pension plan and a thorough reclassification. Under the current system about a dozen different pay rates existed for the same job. The NLWV and the NWTUL endorsed the proposals of the commission, considering the retirement plan to be a necessary step toward equal pay and equal opportunity. Congress passed the Sterling-Lehlbach Retirement Act in May, 1920.

The opposition to these reforms came from the economy bloc in Congress, who wanted to pare government expenses and who felt pensions and reclassification created a class of public pensioners, caused employee dissatisfaction with wages, and increased government expenses. The Retirement Act felt the niggardly hand of fiscal conservatives as all contributions until 1929 came from the employees themselves. The plan cost the government almost nothing for several years. Likewise reclassification was delayed until 1923 and won by compromise after a bitter fight against the economizers led by Reed Smoot of Utah. Even then, Smoot managed to thwart the intent of the law for several years.

The NLWV recommended in 1920 and 1921 a comprehensive civil service program which served as their platform well into the 1930s. It included the retirement plan, reclassification based on job qualifications and skills, merit system for promotion, minimum wage in federal and state civil service, expansion of the classified service, enlargement of all civil service commissions to include representatives of employers, general public, and administrative officials, and the delegation of full power to the commissions to maintain an efficient, non-political service.[47] In the 1920 national conventions the NLWV got the Democrats to endorse the reclassification plan, while the Republicans accepted the idea of equal pay for equal work, regardless of sex.

Congressman Frederick Lehlbach introduced the reclassification bill in the House in October, 1921, and it passed in December. A WJCC subcommittee of nine (including NLWV, NWTUL, AAUW, GFWC, NFBPWC, and NCL) joined the

AFL, the National Federation of Federal Employees, and the National Civil Service Reform League in support of the bill.[48] Ethel Smith, Harriet Taylor Upton, Maud Wood Park, and others testified in committee hearings. Park vigorously attacked the idea that sex or marital status had any bearing on the question; and Upton contended, "Women don't work as married or unmarried, nor is their ability to work determined by that particular condition." "Pay employees what they are worth, regardless of whether they are men or women." [49] Although the bill easily passed the House, Senator Smoot blocked it in the Senate until March, 1923. When Smoot's proposals were soundly defeated, a compromise Lehlbach bill became law. It called for grades of employment determined by skill and duties, and uniform wages and salaries set by grades, regardless of sex.

The compromise forced by Smoot provided the means to thwart the intentions of the reformers. Instead of giving the task of establishing classification to the Civil Service Commission, a Personnel Classification Board was created, composed of the heads of the Civil Service Commission, Budget Bureau, and Bureau of Efficiency. The latter two were dominated by men who shared Smoot's concern for dollars-and-cents economy. Government employees had expected reclassification to result in a pay raise, but the action of the board denied it. The bill intended the board to develop detailed job specifications with wages being set by the nature of the work. However, the Personnel Classification Board took the current pay scale and attached ranks to it. This meant that everyone with the same pay got the same rank and title, regardless of what he did or the skill involved. As a result, economists and statisticians in the Department of Commerce and Agriculture received professional grades while statisticians in the Women's and Children's bureaus got the rank of minor clerk since their pay was so low. Pay determined rank instead of the reverse as the law intended. This held down the cost to the government, but failed to resolve the inequities. Salaries rose only slowly, and the implementation of equal pay for equal work was delayed. In 1928 the act was amended to grant a general salary increase. Smoot himself dominated two of the members of the Classification Board and only the Civil Service Commissioner held out for the spirit of the law.[50] Consequently, Congressman Lehlbach introduced an amendment to put classification authority in the Civil Service Commission, and the women supported this move. Finally, the Economy Act of 1932 abolished the Classification Board and gave the power to the Civil Service Commission; and the following year the commission's chief antagonist, the Bureau of Efficiency, was legislated out of existence.

Although Smoot flawed the women's victory, the principle of equal pay for equal work was established in the public service. The law was a significant step forward for working women everywhere. The National Women's Trade Union League maintained that the pay scales of the government and private industry were interdependent. Women received low pay in private industry, and the government had taken the easy way and paid less also. Women were paid less because they were women. The NWTUL argued that the government, as the largest single employer, should set the example instead of following. It would promote improvement everywhere. The Reclassification Act took the first step.[51]

Protection of Women and Children

While some progressives endorsed the labor movement, most feared it more than monopolies.[52] Consequently, the struggle to aid industrial women, even the effort to unionize them, usually was justified in traditional terms—the protection of motherhood and family. Some attempts to aid working girls were basically anti-union. For example, the YWCA courageously adopted an industrial action program in the face of threats from conservative businessmen to refuse donations. "The fight against the adoption of this program was probably the most bitter that has ever been waged within any organization similar to the Y.W.C.A. . . ."[53] Some members of the national board resigned in protest. The YWCA endorsed the eight-hour day, forty-hour week, the right of collective bargaining, and prohibition of night work and child

labor. However, it hoped to be a substitute for trade unions.
"There seems to be no reason why the Industrial Centers of the
Association should not take the place of trades unionism and
more than fill it." The writer argued, "The girls are brought
together in a closer spiritual contact than any union could give
them. . . . They believe in collective bargaining, but in the
Association they are not likely to be led astray by class emotion-
alism from their own best interests. . . ."[54]

Support for labor legislation tested the mettle of social feminists as they had to fight opponents who called them Bolsheviks,
retrogressive court decisions, a hostile and unsympathetic general
public, and hard-core feminists who questioned their commitment to women's equality. The labor movement suffered substantial setbacks in the 1920s at the hands of the courts, the open-
shop movement, and labor's conservatism; but unionism among
women was especially weak due to particular characteristics of
industrial women and the unwillingness of labor unions to
organize them.[55]

The most effective efforts at reform resulted from the collab-
oration of trade union women and their middle-class allies working through the numerous women's legislative councils. In the
1920s the Women's Bureau, headed by Mary Anderson, a trade
union veteran, aided in the effort. The bureau advanced the collection of information which had been left to social workers and
the Consumers' League in the previous decades, and it advocated
a set of industrial standards closely aligned with those of the
National Women's Trade Union League. This included equal
pay, six-day work week, eight-hour day, no night work for
women, minimum wage, prohibition of women from certain industries shown to be more dangerous for women than men, im-
proved working conditions, and the appointment of qualified
women to positions of authority in state departments of labor.[56]
The AFL usually endorsed labor legislation for women while
rejecting such laws for men, preferring to win gains through
union efforts rather than government action. The labor program
of the AFL lagged far behind that of the NWTUL in the 1920s.
The NWTUL called upon government to end the threat of

unemployment with an adequate employment service, social insurance against sickness, accident, industrial disease, and unemployment, public works in depressed times, and the nationalization of the mines, railroads, communications, and utilities.[57] The National Consumers' League was among the first to endorse compulsory health insurance and social security legislation. The Ohio Council of Women in Industry, a creation of the Ohio Consumers' League and LWV, headed by Amy Maher, argued for unemployment insurance in 1925.[58] When the Depression came, the council insisted on unemployment relief and public works.[59] Finally, the National League of Women Voters worked so diligently on behalf of social security legislation that Mrs. Harris Baldwin, NLWV representative, was the only nongovernmental person present at the signing of the Social Security Act in 1935.

Victorians placed woman in the home and denied that she should be found elsewhere. Traditionalists argued that women went out to work only to earn money for luxuries, "pin money." Furthermore, it was assumed that women lived on less than men or were supported by someone, hence they could afford to be paid less. Her role was marriage and motherhood, and anything else contributed to divorce, immorality, crime, and the destruction of the home, family, and state. "Woman labor is an economic element as abnormal as convict labor, and it is equally pernicious." [60]

The most enduring myth was this belief that women worked only to earn "pin money." This assumed they were not serious workers, and had other support. As a result, women received half the wage rate of men, were confined to unskilled occupations, and denied opportunities for training and advancement. Unless the "pin money" myth were destroyed, the demands for equal pay, training, and opportunity would be useless; and women would be the first fired in depressions. Mary Anderson said, "I resented this theory more than any of the other misstatements that were so often made about women in industry." [61]

The hardy perennial blossomed best in hard times. Women thought the myth was a casualty of World War I, but the post-war depression brought a "Back to the Home" cry. The justification was the same old story. A typical comment appeared in a large commercial magazine, "86 per cent of the women workers live at home or with relatives. It is immaterial in these cases whether the earnings of each measure up to the cost of living standard for a single woman living alone." [62] The Great Depression brought it out with full vigor. In the midst of mass unemployment, the idea that women, especially married women, worked for luxuries while men walked the streets in search of work was intolerable. The clamor to dismiss women from their jobs swept the country and became embodied in rulings of school boards, executives, state laws, and even federal law in 1932. One man wrote, "The employment of married women should be forbidden in every branch of the public service, city, State and national." He said that woman's place was in the home. Another wrote that the way to solve unemployment and mitigate the crime wave (caused by men out of work) was to run all women out of industry. "If such women were to step out of their jobs, they would make way for now unemployed men, men of family, some of whom have been known to resort to crime in order to feed hungry mouths at home. And if such women should refuse to step out, they should be legislated out of their jobs." He agreed that woman's place was in the home and concluded, "To me, it is not surprising that the United States, wealthiest nation in the world, has the lowest marriage and birth rate, the highest divorce rate and the greatest proportion of crime of any Aryan nation." [63]

No investigation sustained the "pin money" concept, but it would not die. A major conclusion of the extensive survey of the Department of Commerce and Labor (1907–08) was that "the girl or woman living at home and working only for pin money was scarcely found in this investigation." [64] In fact those who lived at home retained less money than those adrift. Of the women who lived at home, 70 to 90 percent contributed *all* of their earnings to the family income, while less than 5 percent retained all. Even those who were adrift supporting themselves frequently contributed to their families. Mary Anderson had the

Women's Bureau investigate the question at least six times between 1919 and 1929; in addition, every wage survey undertaken
by the bureau included a section on the home responsibilities of
women. The bureau found that nearly 100 percent of the married women contributed their entire earnings to the family income. Usually these earnings were small but vital because the
husband earned less than an adequate income. Of the single
women living at home, 67.8 percent gave up all of their earnings.[65] Another investigation revealed that 27 percent of the
working women with families had no male wage earner, and 21
percent were the sole breadwinners.[66] In short, women worked
because they must.

The presence of women in industry had long since passed the
theoretical state, and their number increased every decade. In the
third decade the number of wage-earning women rose from
8,500,000 to 10,700,000.[67] The men's trade unions, owing to their
preconceptions of "woman's place" as well as the economic fact
that female labor depressed wages, resisted the invasion of
women. Men believed they hurt the labor movement, and many
unions barred women even when they were in the same trades;
for example, the Carpenters and Joiners, the Journeyman Barbers, and the International Molders' Union refused admission despite the fact that women were working in furniture factories,
as hairdressers, and in foundries. The Journeyman Barbers'
Union rescinded its non-woman clause in 1924 as the ranks of
women hairdressers multiplied in the burgeoning beauty parlor
industry. At each convention the NWTUL urged that women
be admitted to all unions, but the AFL put aside these efforts
with meaningless resolutions. The AFL Executive Council engaged ten women organizers in 1918 to carry on a campaign
among the women, but little resulted. A second drive was made
in 1926, but this one was feeble and accomplished practically
nothing. The AFL did not attempt to reach the unskilled workers and most women fell into that category. In addition, the
psychology of the female worker hindered unionization since she
usually viewed her employment as a temporary situation before
marriage. The average industrial woman was single and younger

than the average male worker; however, the percentage of married women increased each year more rapidly than overall increases. Most of them felt little responsibility to improve the status of all women. Except for the factor of race, no class of adult worker was more exploited or more vulnerable to exploitation than the women.

These special problems produced special solutions: the creation of the National Consumers' League, the National Women's Trade Union League, the U.S. Women's Bureau, and protective legislation. The NCL resulted in 1899 from the union of various consumers' leagues which had grown up in the 1890s out of the concern of middle-class men and women (mostly women) for the working conditions of women and children. They attempted to change conditions through consumer pressure and governmental activity. The burning spirit of the NCL from 1899 to 1932 was Florence Kelley.[68] The NWTUL was another example of concerned middle-class women trying to help industrial women. It began in 1903 largely through the efforts of social workers and came under full trade union leadership in the 1920s. The NWTUL wanted to help industrial women help themselves through the trade union movement.[69] While it sought to organize women, it was in no sense a competitor to the AFL; in fact, it did the hard work of organizing and then turned its unions over to the AFL as rapidly as possible. (This program contributed mightily to the ultimate weakness of the NWTUL, since it gave away its mass membership and had to rely on middle-class allies.) In addition to trade unionism, the NWTUL attempted to educate women to their responsibility and advocated state and federal legislation to protect unorganized women. Margaret Dreier Robins said of the NWTUL, "We are really the woman's movement within the labor movement. All the handicap that belongs to women . . . is emphasized in the ranks of the trade union women."[70]

Protective legislation has become a target of the new wave of feminism and Women's Liberation today, but the original proponents and social feminism saw this legislation as a liberating and saving agency. Certainly it was not the work of misguided individuals who sought to block the advancement of women. Instead, often, these laws resulted from hardheaded efforts to take advantage of Victorian sentimentality in order to win some protection for some class of workers in a legal and political climate which was hostile to the labor movement. To appreciate how the effort was conducted, one needs only to compare the more than 100 pages of social and economic data in the brief of Louis Brandeis in the hours case in 1908 with the sort of language used by Justice David Brewer in rendering the unanimous decision of the Supreme Court. Brewer said that women's "physical structure and a proper discharge of her maternal functions—having in view not merely her own health but the well-being of the race—justify legislation to protect her from the greed as well as the passion of men." [71] Protective legislation was not written for women alone, but court decisions struck down laws protecting men. The state and federal courts gradually reinterpreted the Constitution after 1890 to embody the conservative concepts of laissez-faire and rights of property. "Liberty of contract" was construed to benefit management in nearly every case. The exceptions pertained to the protection of women. By rejecting an hours law for men (*Lochner* v. *New York*, 1905) while sustaining an hours law for women (*Muller* v. *Oregon*, 1908), the U.S. Supreme Court made clear that laws limiting "liberty of contract" were for women only.[72] Consequently, the Consumers' League, Women's Trade Union League, YWCA, League of Women Voters, and U.S. Women's Bureau continually worked to broaden protection for women while asking that the same be extended to men. Protective legislation included minimum wage, hours, seating, night-work prohibition, and restriction on certain dangerous occupations. The period of rapid progress was 1911 to 1921, but the 1920s saw continuous efforts with diminished success. The increasingly effective opposition included industrial and manufacturers' associations, vengeful anti-feminists, reactionary organizations like the Sentinels of the Republic, some business and professional women, and extreme feminists of the National Woman's Party. The courts also laid a withering hand on women's protective legislation. The minimum-wage movement advanced until 1923, when, in the name of "liberty of contract," it was nearly struck dead—and the National Woman's Party hailed the defeat as a victory for equal rights.[73] In 1923 seventeen states and the District of Columbia had minimum-wage laws for women; by 1930, after a series of court reversals, only six remained in varying degrees of unenforcement and ineffectiveness. Yet even in this atmosphere some progress was made; and the court contributed by sustaining the anti–night work laws of New York in 1924. Modest advances marked the progress of other protective laws. For example, in 1921 thirteen states had night-work prohibitions, while in 1931 there were sixteen. In 1921 only five states and the District of Columbia met the standard of the forty-eight-hour week, while one had a fifty-hour week and fourteen more allowed a fifty-four-hour week. In 1931 nine states and the District had a forty-eight-hour week, two allowed fifty hours, and fourteen permitted fifty-four. Even by 1931, Indiana, Iowa, West Virginia, Alabama, and Florida had no limit. The eight-hour day was well entrenched and widespread by 1921 for public employees, but only nine states and the District had it for private employees. One state permitted eight and a half hours, and thirteen had the nine-hour law. In 1931 ten states and the District now had the eight-hour day, two had eight and a half, and eighteen permitted nine hours. The same five states had no laws governing the number of hours per day that could be required.[74] Clearly the speed of advance was greatly slowed, but this was not due to any lack of effort by social feminists, who continually fought the conservative tendencies of state legislatures across the nation.

Led by social workers, the Progressive Movement tried to eliminate the curse of child labor in America. Walter Trattner argued that the organized child labor movement was an integral part of progressivism.[75] The National Child Labor Committee (NCLC), begun in 1904, helped secure a federal child labor law in 1916. In a 5-4 decision the U.S. Supreme Court declared the law unconstitutional in 1918. NCLC spurred Congress to pass another law by February, 1919, to take effect in April, 1919. While these laws stood, the NCLC broadened its program to encompass the whole scope of child welfare. The keynote of the child labor forces in 1919 was the "conservation of the child," a concept which included education, society, family, and the child's need to play. They realized that child labor resulted from the problems of ignorance, poverty, lack of opportunity, and inadequate and inappropriate education.[76]

For 1918 the Children's Bureau received a special appropriation for its "Children's Year," and it involved most women's organizations in its efforts to upgrade state requirements in infancy and maternity hygiene, child care, and mothers' pensions. The effort was significant if measured only by official state action. In 1917 only eight states had child welfare divisions, but by 1920 thirty-five had a child hygiene or child welfare division. Thirty-eight states, the District of Columbia, and Hawaii established committees to cooperate with the federal government.[77] This apparatus became the basic machinery through which the Sheppard-Towner Act was to operate later. Incidentally, these new bureaus and committees opened a new block of positions for women physicians. It was not by chance that the women's organizations lined up behind the Sheppard-Towner bill and the child labor amendment in the 1920s, or that women physicians endorsed these measures when the AMA denounced them as socialism and state medicine. Riding on a tide of concern for children, the American Child Hygiene Association, NCLC, National Consumers' League, Women's Trade Union League, and League of Women Voters were successful from 1918 to 1924 in persuading individual states to elevate standards in child welfare. The women's legislative lobbies in many states worked to have children's codes drawn up and adopted. Such codes ranged over child welfare including work, guardianship, age of consent, juvenile delinquency, care of handicapped and mentally retarded, child support, and school attendance. By 1921 seventeen states had commissions drafting a children's code, and 1924 found twenty-nine states and the District of Columbia with children's code commissions.[78]

The U.S. Supreme Court derailed the broad view of 1922 by declaring the federal child labor law unconstitutional in

Bailey v. *Drexel Furniture Company*. Not until near the end of the decade did the crusaders return to the comprehensive approach. The setback in 1922 caused proponents of federal action to quarrel over the question of what to do next. Almost immediately various men introduced a constitutional amendment, but both its wording and the method caused much disagreement. The majority led by Florence Kelley wanted an amendment to enable Congress to legislate; but a minority led by Julia Lathrop felt the times were inauspicious. "I have been astonished to find the popular distaste for governmental activity." [79] Kelley impatiently drove for an amendment. Feeling that the NCLC dragged its feet, she relied upon the Consumers' League and the women's groups. She worked primarily through the WJCC to generate support; and the women did not disappoint her. Finally the proponents agreed on the wording and the new amendment was introduced. Backed by twenty organizations, mostly women's, it passed Congress in June, 1924, by comfortable margins.

This rapid passage was a sweet victory. At a time when the progressive impulse was weakening, it gave hope. In 1925 the reform groups favoring the amendment formed a coordinating committee called Organizations Associated for Ratification of the Child Labor Amendment. The centrality of women to this effort was demonstrated by the fact that Mrs. Arthur Watkins (PTA) was chairman, Julia Lathrop was vice-chairman, Marguerite Owen (NLWV) was secretary-treasurer, and the steering committee consisted of Rose Schneiderman and Nelle Swartz (NWTUL), Florence Kelley (NCL), Irene Osgood Andrews (American Association for Labor Legislation), and two men, Owen Lovejoy and Wiley Swift (NCLC). Julia Lathrop was correct: the times were wrong. Their hopes were dashed by a resounding defeat in an "advisory referendum" in Massachusetts and a nearly complete rejection of the amendment by state legislatures. Of the forty-two state legislatures which met in 1924 and 1925, only four ratified, and by 1930 the total was only six. A cascade of propaganda against the amendment caused internal dissension in women's organizations. The General Federation of Women's Clubs overcame its problems and continued its endorsement but withdrew from the Women's Joint Congressional Committee. The National Federation of Business and Professional Women's Clubs put it on the study program for a year before re-endorsing it weakly in 1927. The Medical Women's National Association, League of Women Voters, and Women's Trade Union League remained steadfast. The NCLC became quite cautious after 1926, making the NLWV bitter and causing the despairing Florence Kelley to ask, "Why, why did I ever help to start the National Child Labor Committee?" [80]

The general protection of women and children had to wait for the New Deal. The child labor amendment was revived for another ratification attempt in 1933 but made only modest progress —fourteen more states approved. However, the NRA and later New Deal acts, such as the Sugar Stabilization Act (1934), Beet Sugar Act (1937), Walsh-Healy Act (1936) establishing minimum labor standards for government contracts, and the Fair Labor Standards Act (1938) greatly reduced the need for an amendment as they eliminated the blight of child labor in many areas.[81] The number of industrial women increased substantially in the 1930s, and they benefited from the labor reforms: hours, wages, right of collective bargaining, and social security legislation. Some protective legislation, such as minimum wage, now included men. The depression crisis supplied the conditions for the passage and fulfillment of many measures for which substantial numbers of social feminists had fought in the twenties. They sustained and promoted various causes in a conservative time until a more favorable climate for reform developed. One measure in particular was the special passion of social feminists and it was revived by the New Deal—maternity and infancy protection. The Maternity- and Infancy-Protection Act of 1921 had lapsed before the end of the decade only to be reborn in the Social Security Act of 1935.

NOTES

1. "Women Voters Demand Industrial Justice," *Life and Labor*, X (Mar., 1920), 77–78.
2. "National League of Women Voters," *Ohio Council on Women and Children in Industry* (Dec., 1922), unpaginated.

3. "Constructive Legislation," *Woman Citizen*, V (Nov. 20, 1920), 66; "How the National League Works through the States," *ibid.* (Jan. 1, 1921), 848–851; "Missouri Women's Conference," *ibid.* (Jan. 15, 1921), 896; "Righting Old Wrongs," *ibid.* (March 19, 1921), 1088–89; "Progress in Delaware," *ibid.* (Apr. 9, 1921), 1155; "We Are Coming Hundreds of Thousands Strong," *ibid.*, 1158–71; "Women Voters and State Legislatures," *ibid.*, VI (June 4, 1921), 24–25; "Report of the Executive Secretary to the Annual Convention of the Minnesota League of Women Voters," Oct. 18, 1921, NLWV Papers, Ser. II, box 1, Minnesota file, LC; Marion Weston Cottle, "Government Efficiency," *Women Lawyers' Journal*, XI (May, 1922), 24; "The Organized Work of Women in One State," *Journal of Social Forces*, I (Sept., 1923), 613–615; Mary O. Cowper, "The North Carolina League of Women Voters," *ibid.*, II (Mar., 1924), 424; Julia Margaret Hicks, "League Life—on the Bill Side," *Woman Citizen*, XII (Sept., 1927), 28–29; see also Anne F. Scott, "After Suffrage: The Southern Woman in the Twenties," *Journal of Southern History*, XXX (Aug., 1964), 298–318; Scott, *The Southern Lady*, 186–211.

4. Cornelia Bryce Pinchot to Senator Joseph I. France, Feb. 24, 1920, C. B. Pinchot MSS, box 12, LC.

5. Cornelia Bryce Pinchot to Viscountess Astor, Apr. 24, 1922, *ibid.*, box 20.

6. Cornelia Bryce Pinchot to Mrs. John O. Miller, Jan. 26, 1920, *ibid.*, box 13. Carrie Chapman Catt later said the same thing in her charge to the 1920 NLWV convention.

7. Cornelia Bryce Pinchot to Maud Wood Park, Apr. 22, 1920; telegram, Park to Pinchot, Apr. 24, 1920, *ibid.*

8. Cornelia Bryce Pinchot to Miss [Martha] Thomas, Feb. 28, 1921, *ibid.*, box 17.

9. Talk by Cornelia Bryce Pinchot to the Joint Legislative Committee of the Consumers' League of Eastern Pennsylvania, the Philadelphia WTUL, and the YWCA East Central Field Committee, Mar. 8, 1921, *ibid.*, box 16.

10. Report of NLWV organizer Gladys Pyle, Sept. 28–Oct. 1, 1921, NLWV Papers, Ser. II, box 1, Kansas file, LC.

11. Laura W. Mathison to Mrs. James Paige, Nov. 10, 1922; Lila Rose to Marie Stuart Edwards, Nov. 15, 1922; Emma Ingalls to Paige, Dec. 24, 1922, *ibid.*, Montana file.

12. Laura E. Mathison to Mrs. James Paige, Nov. 10, 1922, *ibid.*

13. Marie Stuart Edwards to Mrs. W. Z. Stuart, Sept. 13, 1922; Mrs. William G. Hibbard to Edwards, Sept. 8, 1922, *ibid.*, box 2, Wisconsin file.

14. For a fuller discussion see O'Neill, *Everyone Was Brave*, 231–249.

15. NWTUL *Proceedings* (1929), 34; O'Neill, "The Woman Movement and the First World War," 11.

16. Schneiderman and Goldthwaite, *All for One*, 164–174, 252–259.

17. Lucretta C. Chase, "The Social Program of the General Federation of Women's Clubs," *Journal of Social Forces*, I (May, 1923), 465–469.

18. Quoted in Breckinridge, *Women in the Twentieth Century*, 51.

19. "Lobbyism and the Ladies," *Outlook*, CXLIX (June 13, 1928), 247; O'Neill, "The Woman Movement and the First World War," 12–13; O'Neill, *Everyone Was Brave*, 256–262.

20. Lucile Evelyn LaGanke, "The National Society of the Daughters of the American Revolution: Its History, Policies, and Influences, 1890–1949" (Ph.D. thesis, Western Reserve University, 1951), 114–130, 210, 215–224, 294–308.

21. Otis A. Pease, "The Success of Progressivism" (paper read for the Organization of American Historians, Cincinnati, 1966), 14.

22. Harold A. Stone *et al.*, *City Manager Government in the United States: A Review after Twenty-five Years* (vol. VII, *Studies in Administration*, Chicago: Social Science Research Council, Committee on Public Administration, 1940), 30.

23. Abbott, *History of Woman Suffrage in Cuyahoga County*, 106–119; "Five Years of City Manager Government in Cleveland," *National Municipal Review*, Supp., XVIII (Mar., 1929), 203–220; William Ganson Rose, *Cleveland: The Making of a City* (Cleveland: World Publishing, 1950), 777–780; Lorin Wescott Peterson, *Day of the Mugwump* (New York: Random House, 1961), 121; "The League in the Cities," *Woman Citizen*, XI (Aug., 1926), 30.

24. Charles P. Taft, *City Management: The Cincinnati Experiment* (New York: Farrar & Rinehart, 1933).

25. Blake McKelvey, *Rochester: An Emerging Metropolis, 1925–1961* (Rochester: Christopher Press, 1961), 21–23; Jean Carter, "Wanted (and Won): A City Manager," *Woman Citizen*, XII (Nov., 1927), 22–23.

26. McKelvey, *Rochester*, 22.

27. NWTUL, *Proceedings* (1924), 50; Johnson, "Organized Women and National Legislation," 356.

28. George D. Strayer, "Making Good the Promise of Democracy," *Good Housekeeping*, LXXII (Feb., 1921), 28–29.

29. Arthur W. Dunn, "The Department of Public Welfare: Interview with General Charles E. Sawyer, White House Physician," *Good Housekeeping*, LXXIII (July, 1921), 34.

30. "President Harding and His Department of Public Welfare," *Official Bulletin of the Chicago Medical Society* (Nov., 1921), 19–21, Harding MSS, box 223, folder 312-3, OHS; Mary C. Wiggins, Executive Secretary, Massachusetts Consumers' League, to Harding, Apr. 27, 1921, *ibid.*, folder 312-1; Mrs. William Lowell Putnam, Woman's Municipal League of Boston, to Harding, Apr. 23, 1921, *ibid.;* "A Powerful Army against Corrupt Politics," *Woman Citizen*, VI (July 2, 1921), 9; NWTUL, *Proceedings* (1922), 97; Ethel M. Smith, "A New Force in American Politics," *Life and Labor*, XI (May, 1921), 148.

31. Carrie Chapman Catt, "Wanted: A New Department," *Woman Citizen*, V (Jan. 8, 1921), 861–862; editorial, *ibid.* (Jan. 15, 1921), 885. The magazine included a coupon to clip and mail to the President.

32. Charles E. Sawyer to George B. Christian, Feb. 24, 1922, Harding MSS, box 223, folder 312-3, OHS.

33. Johnson, "Women's Organizations and National Legislation," 362–363.

34. Ada L. Comstock, "An Interpretation of the National Educational Program," AAUW, *Proceedings* (1927), 17–21.

35. Carrie Chapman Catt to Minnie Fisher Cunningham, Aug. 22, 1921, NLWV Papers, Ser. II, box 3, Catt folder, LC; "Your Business in Washington," *Woman Citizen*, VI (Aug. 13, 1921), 7.

36. Mrs. Edward P. Costigan, "The Price You Pay," *Woman Citizen*, V (June 5, 1920), 10–14; NLWV, *Proceedings* (1921), 61.

37. NLWV, *Proceedings* (1921), 60; *Woman Citizen*, V (Apr. 23, 1921), 1186.

38. Speech by Dorothy Kirchwey Brown, 1942, Brown MSS, box 1, folder 23, SL.

39. Transcript of interview with Mrs. Harris Baldwin. *ibid.*, folder 25.

40. Ann Dennis Bursch, "Living Costs," *Woman Voters' Bulletin: Legislative Edition*, V (June 5, 1925), 4.

41. "Uncle Sam Needs a Yardstick!," *Woman Citizen*, XI (Dec., 1926), 33.
42. Remarks by Dorothy Kirchwey Brown in panel discussion, 1942, Brown MSS, box 1, folder 23, SL.
43. Hubbard, *Origins of the TVA*, 218; "The Excursion," Brown MSS, box 1, folder 25, SL.
44. Quoted in "No Place in Politics?," *Woman Citizen*, VI (July 2, 1921), 21; see also Smith, "A New Force in American Politics," 148; Carrie Chapman Catt, "The Direct Primary under Fire," *Woman Citizen*, V (May 7, 1921), 1210; Mary Garrett Hay, "Preserving the Primary," *ibid.*, 1221; "Legislative Report," *Forward* (Wis. LWV) (Apr., 1922), NLWV Papers, Ser. II, box 2, Wisconsin file, LC.
45. Quoted in Elizabeth J. Hauser, "The Direct Primary and the League," *Woman Citizen*, XII (Dec., 1927), 28; see also Hauser, "Save the Primary!," *ibid.*, XI (Nov., 1926), 30–31.
46. Van Riper's *History of the U. S. Civil Service* is a comprehensive study of the entire history; for reclassification and the 1920s see pp. 284–314.
47. NLWV, *Proceedings* (1921), 59–60; see also Olive Whorley, "The Influence of the National League of Women Voters in the Advancement of Federal Civil Service Reforms" (M.A. thesis, American University, 1938).
48. Samuel Gompers to Harding, July 22, 1921, Harding MSS, box 3, folder 2–6, OHS; NWTUL, *Proceedings* (1924), 48.
49. Quoted in "Your Business in Washington," *Woman Citizen*, VI (July 2, 1921), 8.
50. NWTUL, *Proceedings* (1926), 47; Van Riper, *History of the U.S. Civil Service*, 302.
51. "Women's Wages and Government Standards," *Life and Labor Bulletin*, II (Mar., 1924), 1–2; "On Guard for the Working Woman," *Woman Citizen*, V (Jan. 15, 1921), 896; "To Standardize Women's Wages," *Medical Woman's Journal*, XXVII (Feb., 1920), 61–62.
52. George E. Mowry, *The Era of Theodore Roosevelt and the Birth of Modern America, 1900–1912* (New York: Harper Torchbooks, 1958), 99–103.
53. Harry A. Stewart, "Where the 'Y' Stands Now," *Good Housekeeping*, LXX (June, 1920), 104.
54. *Ibid.*, 108.
55. For a general history of the labor movement in the 1920s, see Irving Bernstein, *The Lean Years: A History of the American Worker, 1920–1933* (Baltimore: Penguin Books, 1960).
56. NWTUL, *Proceedings* (1919), 6–7; "The League of Women Voters," *Life and Labor*, IX (May, 1919), 118; NLWV, *Proceedings* (1921), 58–59; Elizabeth Frazer, "Harnessing Industry with the Vote," *Ladies Home Journal*, XXXIX (Nov., 1922), 24.
57. "Program of the Committee on Social and Industrial Reconstruction of the National Women's Trade Union League," *Life and Labor*, IX (Mar., 1919), 51–53; NWTUL, *Proceedings*, (1919), 62; NWTUL, *Proceedings* (1922), 97–98; Fletty, "Public Services of Women's Organizations," 208.
58. "Serving as Surplus," *Ohio Council on Women in Industry* (Nov., 1925), 1.
59. For example, see "Stabilizing with Public Works," *Information Bulletin on Woman's Work* (Jan., 1929), unpaginated; "Impending Disasters Cast their Shadows Before," *ibid.* (Nov., 1930).
60. Flora McDonald Thompson, "Truth about Woman in Industry," *North American Review*, CLXXVIII (May, 1904), 756; see also Thompson, "Work of Wives," *Outlook*, XCI (Apr. 24, 1909), 994–996.

61. Anderson, *Woman at Work*, 140.

62. Quoted in *The Share of Wage-Earning Women in Family Support*, Women's Bureau, U.S. Department of Labor, *Bull. 30* (Washington Government Printing Office, 1923), 2.

63. Quoted in "Should Married Women Work," *Equal Rights*, XV (July 6, 1929), 171.

64. *Summary of the Report on Conditions of Woman and Child Wage Earners in the United States*, Bureau of Labor Statistics, U.S. Department of Labor, *Bull. 175* (Washington: Government Printing Office, 1916), 211; see also Eleanor L. Lattimore and Ray S. Trust, *Legal Recognition of Industrial Women* (New York: YWCA, War Work Council, Industrial Committee, 1919), 12–15.

65. *Share of Wage-Earning Women in Family Support*, 12–14.

66. *Family Status of Breadwinnnig Women in Four Selected Cities*, Women's Bureau, *Bull. 41* (1925), 12; see also *Family Status of Breadwinning Women*, *Bull. 23* (1922); *Women Workers and Family Support*, *Bull. 49* (1924); Agnes Peterson, *What Wage-Earning Women Contribute to Family Support*, *Bull. 75* (1929), 14.

67. U.S. Bureau of the Census, *Fifteenth Census of the United States: 1930, Population*, V (Washington: Government Printing Office, 1933), 39.

68. Josephine Goldmark, *Impatient Crusader: Florence Kelley's Life Story* (Urbana: University of Illinois Press, 1953), 51–65; Chambers, *Seedtime of Reform*, 4–5.

69. Chambers, *Seedtime of Reform*, 8–9; Allen F. Davis, "The Women's Trade Union League: Origins and Organization," *Labor History*, V (Winter, 1964), 3–17.

70. Margaret Dreier Robins to Cornelia Bryce Pinchot, Apr. 26, 1920, C. B. Pinchot MSS, box 11, LC.

71. Quoted in Bernstein, *The Lean Years*, 227.

72. The NCL used the Brandeis-type brief to reverse an 1895 decision invalidating the eight-hour day for women in Illinois (*Ritchie* v. *People*, 1910), and won hours cases in Ohio (1911)—affirmed by the Supreme Court (1914), California (1912)—affirmed (1915), and Oregon (1917)—affirmed (1917); see Richard C. Cortner, *The Wagner Act Cases* (Knoxville: University of Tennessee Press, 1964), 14–15.

73. The split which developed in feminist ranks in the 1920s still persists. In the most recent hearings on the equal rights amendment before Congress, professional women and the new-wave feminists supported the amendment, which they readily and gladly admit will end protective industrial laws. On the other hand, the National Consumers' League, trade union women, and women associated with government agencies concerned with industrial women opposed it. See "Women's Equal Rights Amendment," *Congressional Digest*, L (Jan., 1971).

74. *Night Work Laws in the United States*, Women's Bureau, *Bull. 7* (1920); *Eight Hour Day in Federal and State Legislation*, *Bull. 5* (1921); *State Laws Affecting Working Women*, *Bull. 16* (1921); *State Laws Affecting Women*, *Bull. 63* (1927); Florence P. Smith, *Chronological Development of Labor Legislation for Women in the United States*, *Bull. 66-II*, rev. (1932).

75. The most comprehensive study of the child labor movement is Walter I. Trattner, *Crusade for the Children: A History of the National Child Labor Committee and Child Labor Reform in America* (Chicago: Quadrangle Books, 1970); see also Ned Weissberg, "The Federal Child Labor Amendment: A Study in Pressure Politics (Ph.D. thesis, Cornell University, 1942).

76. For a full discussion of "The Crusade for Children" see Chambers, *Seedtime of Reform*, 12–14, 28–58.

77. "Children's Bureau Handicapped by Inadequate Appropriations," *Medical Woman's Journal*, XXVII (June, 1920), 172–173.

78. "The Carrie Chapman Catt Citizenship Course: The Work of the Children's Bureau," *Woman Citizen*, V (Jan. 22, 1921), 916–917; "Child Welfare Legislation," *Medical Woman's Journal*, XXXI (Mar., 1924), 79.

79. Quoted in Chambers, *Seedtime of Reform*, 33; see also Richard B. Sherman, "The Rejection of the Child Labor Amendment," *Mid-America*, XLV (Jan., 1963), 3–17.

80. Florence Kelley to Lillian Wald, Apr. 13, 1927; Grace Abbott to Wald, Apr. 7, 1927, Lillian Wald MSS, file 1, drawer 3, NYPL.

81. Weissberg, "The Federal Child Labor Amendment," 53–67.

SIX

The Sheppard-Towner Act:
Progressivism in the 1920s

The first venture of the federal government into social welfare legislation—the Sheppard-Towner Maternity- and Infancy-Protection Act of 1921—has been generally ignored in discussions about the persistence of progressivism in the 1920s.[1] The maternity bill was a link in a chain of ideas and actions from Roosevelt to Roosevelt, which began with the White House Conference on Child Welfare Standards in 1909 and ended with the Social Security Act of 1935. In addition, the Sheppard-Towner Act was the first major dividend of the full enfranchisement of women. Social feminists helped to force the enactment of the bill and later fought to preserve it from repeal. Although passed in the first year of the Harding administration, it was a product of progressivism.

The development of programs and instruments to protect children and infants was a natural direction for American women to travel as they moved out of the close confines of the Victorian home. Who could object that the care of children was not their "sphere"? Consequently, the movement for child and infant care had roots in the 1880s and 1890s, especially after the establishment of the settlement houses. Infant-milk stations were set up, school health programs started, infant hygiene and care taught, and nursing services established. Lillian Wald at Henry

Street Settlement in New York began the visiting nurse service and urged the city to institute a school lunch program.[2] She first suggested the creation of a federal children's bureau in 1903 and was invited to the White House to discuss the idea. The National Child Labor Committee spent 1904–06 marshaling support for the plan and drafting a bill with Florence Kelley and Julia Lathrop as chief architects. One of the significant results of the White House Conference on Child Welfare Standards, called by Roosevelt in 1909, was a special message from the President to Congress calling for a children's bureau. It was finally created in 1912 with Julia Lathrop as chief.[3]

The first major investigations of the bureau were into the causes of maternal and infant mortality. The studies revealed that the United States had unusually high rates. In 1916 more than 16,000 mothers died, and this increased to 23,000 in 1918. In addition more than 250,000 infants died each year, and 80 percent of expectant mothers received no advice or trained care.[4] For 1918 the United States ranked seventeenth of twenty nations in maternal and eleventh in infant mortality. The bureau found a correlation between poverty and mortality rates. For families earning less than $450 annually, one baby in six died within the first year; for the income range of $650–850 the rate was one in ten; and for those earning about $1,250 the rate was one in sixteen. Even the latter rate compared unfavorably to the average of a nation like New Zealand, which had a thorough program of care and an infant death rate of one in twenty-one.[5]

The Children's Bureau argued that the weapons against this death rate were an adequate income for the family in addition to instruction in maternal and infant hygiene. In 1917 Julia Lathrop recommended that federal aid be given to the states to provide public protection for maternity and infancy, after the manner of the Smith-Lever Act of 1914, which provided matching funds for county agricultural extension agents. Jeannette Rankin introduced Lathrop's proposal in July, 1918, calling for instruction of expectant mothers in pre- and post-natal care, in addition to federal aid to states for medical aid, hospital care, consultation centers, and visiting nurses. President Wilson gave scant encouragement, and little progress was made toward its passage until the full enfranchisement of women in 1920. The House Committee on Labor reported the bill favorably but the session ended without further action. Senator Morris Sheppard (D—Texas) and Congressman Horace Towner (R—Iowa) submitted the bill which bore their names in the Sixty-sixth Congress. They asked for an appropriation of $4,000,000 to provide matching grants to states in addition to an initial $10,000 contribution by the federal government to each state to start the program.

With the bill still pending at the time of the nominating conventions, the National League of Women Voters urged the national parties to endorse it in their platforms. The Democratic, Socialist, Prohibition, and Farmer-Labor parties approved the proposal. The Republicans ignored it, but Harding came out squarely for it in his Social Justice Day speech on October 1, 1920. When Congress reconvened for the lame-duck session in December, women expected the bill to pass.

The bill became the first goal of the newly enfranchised women and took precedence over all other efforts. One of the original subcommittees of the Women's Joint Congressional Committee was headed by Florence Kelley to work for the bill. Of this she said, "Of all the activities in which I have shared during more than forty years of striving, none is, I am convinced, of such fundamental importance as the Sheppard-Towner Act." [6] The WJCC lobbied vigorously while the constituent organizations drummed up grass-roots support through meetings, leaflets, and newsletters, causing members of Congress to receive a deluge of letters and telegrams. One senator's secretary reported, "I think every woman in my state has written to the Senator." [7] Nearby organizations dispatched delegations to lobby and present resolutions and petitions. The number of proponents testifying for the bill far outnumbered the opponents.

Because the bill lay in committee from May to December, 1920, proponents became impatient. *Good Housekeeping* declared, "Herod is not dead," and urged women to besiege Congress with telegrams and letters. It rounded up endorsements of thirty-four governors.[8] Testifying for the bill, Florence Kelley invoked King Herod also. She recalled that Herod condemned an unknown number of children and has been infamous for 2,000 years. Yet daily, 680 children, 20,000 per month, died of largely preventable causes. "Six times as many children on an average have died every day, on Sundays and holidays and Christmas, every day, as there are men in the United States Senate. . . . Will Congress let Christmas come and go and New Year's come and go. . . . ?" She noted that a legislative biennial had passed since the House held its first hearings on the subject in January, 1919. "What answer can be given to the women in a myriad of organizations, who are marveling and asking, 'Why does Congress wish women and children to die?' " [9]

The Senate passed its version on December 18, 1920, with President-elect Harding favoring it. After holding hearings the last week in December, the House Committee on Interstate and Foreign Commerce cut the appropriation to $1,000,000 and sent it to the Rules Committee, where it died in the Sixty-sixth Congress. The Boston League of Women Voters urged its members to telegraph P. P. Campbell, chairman of the Rules Committee, to release the measure. He opposed it but excused himself, saying that the calendar was already crowded with appropriations bills.[10] Women wanted Harding to intervene; instead he replied, "I think I can say to you safely, however, that the bill will become a law no later than the middle of April, in case the present Congress fails to act." [11]

Harding called a special session to begin the Sixty-seventh Congress, but reformers feared that the Sheppard-Towner bill might be ignored in the press to deal with tariff and budget matters. They urged the President to single out the bill for passage in his message to Congress; Harding responded with a one-sentence endorsement, "I assume the maternity bill, already strongly approved, will be enacted promptly, thus adding to our manifestation of human interest." [12]

Sheppard and Towner resubmitted the bill in April, and it passed the Senate on July 22, 1921, by a vote of 63-7.[13] But it seemed destined to perish in the House Committee on Interstate and Foreign Commerce, whose chairman, Samuel Winslow, was an ardent anti-suffragist. For months he refused even to hold hearings, so women put the heat on Harding to dislodge the bill. Harriet Taylor Upton, vice-chairman of the Republican National Committee, warned that the delay was alienating women.[14] Harding finally prodded Winslow into beginning hearings on July 12. However, Winslow still hoped to kill it. As opposition witnesses paraded by, repeating themselves and protracting the hearings, Upton again urged Harding to "put the skids" under the bill. He assured her that he was concerned.[15]

Winslow had become an enemy of Julia Lathrop and opposed her efforts in the Children's Bureau and the measure at hand. She had wanted to retire for several months, having brought the matter this far, but held back until August to be certain that Grace Abbott would succeed her. Now she felt that her resignation would help the maternity bill, giving Winslow some reason to surrender to the mounting pressure.[16] Others looked for exits also. Actual sentiment among congressmen probably opposed the bill, but the threat of "20,000,000 organized women" was too much to ignore. They looked to Harding as President and party leader for the signal which way to vote. Individual congressmen and senators evaded protests from the newly aroused medical profession, saying, "I am an organization republican and await instructions."[17] An Illinois congressman wrote Harding that he felt the bill invaded states' rights, but he would vote the way he was instructed. The President's secretary replied that Harding had repeatedly spoken in favor and had not changed his position.[18] When it came to a vote, the bill passed easily, 279-39. Ironically, the only woman in Congress, the anti-suffragist Alice Robertson, voted against it. Harding signed the measure on November 23, 1921.

The principal force moving Congress was fear of being punished at the polls. The women's vote was an unknown quantity at the time. For years suffragists had promised to clean house when they got the vote, and they claimed that women would be issue-oriented rather than party-oriented. Politicians feared that women voters would cast a bloc vote or remain aloof from the regular parties. Opponents of Sheppard-Towner tried to break this illusion. Alice Robertson declared that the vast majority of women knew nothing of the bill and would oppose it if they did. She felt the measure incorporated "German paternalism," intended to loot the Treasury, and was pushed by unconscionable propaganda by the Children's Bureau. She denounced the appeals which spoke of the deaths of hundreds of children daily as "sob-stuff." [19] One woman wrote Samuel Winslow that organized women constituted only a minority of all women, and even at that only the leadership, not the membership, was behind the bill. Of the National League of Women Voters she wrote, "As a medium of expression of a corporate opinion on living questions, it is valueless, for it is a fertile field for pandemic psychosis, that is the formation of mass opinion by contagion, it is not a former for the creation of sound, informed, responsible opinion." [20] Mrs. G. M. Kenyon, a director of the American Medical Liberty League and a member of the Minnesota LWV, wrote Harding to suggest that he had been falsely convinced by the National League of Women Voters that all the women wanted the bill. She argued that even the NLWV was badly divided.[21] However, the best evidence suggests that in 1921 the women's organizations were not divided on the issue. Every member of the Women's Joint Congressional Committee joined the Sheppard-Towner subcommittee and numerous other women's groups endorsed the bill too.[22] If a woman read any of the mass circulation women's magazines —*Good Housekeeping, Pictorial Review, McCall's, Woman's Home Companion,* or *Delineator,* as well as *McClure's* and *Atlantic Monthly*—she was exposed to many articles which favored the Sheppard-Towner bill.

In retrospect, this pioneering bill seems pitifully small. The act authorized an appropriation of $1,480,000 for fiscal 1921–22 and $1,240,000 for the next five years ending June 30, 1927. Of this sum, $5,000 would go to each state outright; $5,000 more to each state if matching funds were provided; and the rest would be allocated on a population percentage and matching basis. The cost of administering the program could not exceed

$50,000, and the money was channeled by the Children's Bureau through the state child welfare or health divisions. Before a federal grant could be made, a state had to pass enabling legislation, provide a satisfactory plan for implementing the program, and vote matching funds. Both the state and the individual retained the right to reject aid. The law expressly denied agents or representatives of either state or federal government the power to enter a home uninvited or take charge of a child without legal consent. The law provided for instruction in the hygiene of maternity and infancy through public-health nurses, visiting nurses, consultation centers, child-care conferences, and literature distribution.

An early problem was Harding's attempt to cut the appropriation from $1,240,000 to $800,000 after the first year because it was estimated that only $800,000 would actually be used. He hoped to reap the rewards of apparent economy, but Harriet Taylor Upton objected that the outward cut would have a negative political effect among women. She pointed out that the full authorization was needed because the grants to each state were proportional to the total appropriation. If the authorization were reduced, each state's quota would be reduced proportionally. Even though only $800,000 was expected to be spent, the money not used by one state could not be diverted to another state to equal the quota allowed under a $1,240,000 appropriation. Although Harding was not pleased, the appropriation remained at $1,240,000.[23]

Although the Children's Bureau had revealed high maternal and infant death rates and despite the modest character of the Sheppard-Towner bill, the measure was assailed as a threat to the very institutions of the nation. Some objected for fiscal reasons. Because suffragists favored the bill, anti-suffragists opposed it. Extreme conservatives condemned the plan as part of a Bolshevist conspiracy against America. States' rights advocates alleged that it threatened the integrity of the states. Finally the bill was caught in the crossfire between the American Medical Association and a collection of quack medical cultists. Sheppard-Towner was one of the first pieces of federal legislation to catch the brunt of the AMA's new fear of state medicine. The arguments advanced by the opponents at the time of the original debate and passage of the measure were repeated when the proposal came up for renewal in 1926 and in 1929.

Senator William E. Borah objected to the bill on fiscal grounds. He declared that the country was in a financial crisis and that no new government expenses should be undertaken until taxes could be cut.[24] Senator Francis E. Warren opposed, saying, "We shall have to put an end to these new fad appropriations. . . ." Senator James Reed tried everything including slander and ridicule to stop the bill, even proposing an amendment to entitle it "A Bill to authorize a board of spinsters to control maternity and teach the mothers of the United States how to rear babies."[25] He charged that it was communist-inspired and that the standards drawn up by the Children's Bureau were done by crackpots.[26]

The principal advocates of the theory that the Sheppard-Towner bill was a communist invention were the National Association Opposed to Woman Suffrage and its legacy, the Woman Patriots. For years they had maintained that feminism and woman suffrage were the same as socialism and communism. Mary Kilbreth, NAOWS president, wrote Harding a six-page letter which condemned his signing of the bill. She argued that he had violated the Constitution, the 1920 Republican platform, and his own acceptance speech. She declared that the 1920 election was a mandate against feminism, and that Sheppard-Towner was part of the feminist platform. "It is not brought forward by the combined wisdom of all Americans, but by the propaganda of a self-interested bureau associated with the Feminist Bloc." Kilbreth warned, "There are many loyal American men and women who believe that this bill, inspired by foreign experiments in Communism, and backed by the radical forces in the country, strikes at the heart of our American civilization. . . ."[27] The Woman's Municipal League of Boston, the Constitutional Liberty League of Massachusetts, the Massachusetts Civic Alliance, and the Massachusetts Public Interests League agreed. (Their agreement stemmed from the fact that all had begun as anti-feminist organizations and had extensively overlapping memberships.)

Certain "medical liberty" organizations (they opposed any state regulation of medicine: vaccination, quarantine, the Wasserman test, licensing of doctors, hospitals, and medical schools) viewed the Sheppard-Towner Act as another step in the campaign of the regular physicians to use state power to eliminate all but orthodox practices. The Citizens Medical Reference Bureau, a small organization of approximately 400 members, argued that the bill would create a centralized medical bureaucracy which would create unrest in the nation by forcing acceptance of certain medical ideas. The American Drugless Association said that the bill was a ploy by the "medical machine"—the regular physicians—to gain more power. The American Medical Liberty League declared that "medical liberty is just as important as religious liberty." [28] The Drugless Association, having about 1,000 members, tried to generate pressure on Harding by urging all delegates to the 1920 Republican national convention to support medical freedom. One woman wrote Harding saying, "I object to being looked after by the M.D.'s. . . . I am heart and bone for Medical freedom and personal liberty." The president of the Washington Humane and Anti-Vivisection Society declared, "Medical freedom is the voice of the people." [29]

The Citizens Medical Reference Bureau attempted to stir opposition among state governors under the guise of soliciting their views. The letters asked their opinion, but included extracts from the *Journal of the American Medical Association* and the *Illinois Medical Journal* attacking the bill. The response was disappointing. Only three governors indicated their opposition; most were non-committal, and others like Lynn Frazier of North Dakota said, "I am strongly in favor of the measure." Governor Everett Lake of Connecticut said that while he did not want to encourage further erosion of the state's position, he would stand by the vote of the Connecticut congressional delegation. Governor Lee Russell of Mississippi favored aid if the states matched it. [30]

Thirty-five of the governors had already expressed their approval in letters to *Good Housekeeping* or to the congressional committees.

Far more significant than the medical cultists was the opposition from physicians, who expressed themselves through the American Medical Association. The AMA marched within the broad ranks of progressivism from 1900 to World War I and vigorously campaigned for pure food and drugs, protection of the public from medical quackery, a federal department of health, and the elevation of standards of medical practice and education. However, the AMA had always been silent on other great health problems: slums and tenements, factory hazards, child labor and the exploitation of women in sweatshops, and dangerous trades.[31] Before 1920 the AMA had been a principal advocate of government intervention in the practice of medicine, which had been characterized by extreme laissez-faire. The AMA first broke away from progressivism over the issue of compulsory health insurance and became a vigorous opponent of the Sheppard-Towner Act. The irony was that the AMA found itself saying much the same as the medical quacks in opposing the bill. This reversal can be understood in light of one goal of the AMA: it has always sought to establish and maintain complete control of the supply of medical service. At first it achieved this through an alliance with government in establishing procedural safeguards: standards of medical training, licensing, and the ethics of practice. Up to 1920 government was the chief ally in setting up and enforcing the standards of medical practice; but when the government threatened to provide certain medical services, the AMA went into opposition. It opposed anything that deviated from the "fee for service" system and fought legislative attempts to establish medical services.[32]

The AMA became alarmed first at the threat of compulsory health insurance. The American Association for Labor Legislation (AALL) began studying the question of health insurance in 1907, and in 1912 they adopted the idea of *compulsory* health insurance. They drew up a model bill and presented it to various states for approval. The AMA became interested, and it created a Committee on Social Insurance in 1916 to study the question. Dr. Isaac M. Rubinow, who helped draft the model bill for AALL, was secretary of the AMA committee. While making no formal recommendations, the committee reported quite favorably on compulsory health insurance to the AMA House of Delegates in 1916 and again in 1917.

The 1917 report said it detected a rising spirit of irrational opposition to the idea of health insurance and warned the AMA not to adopt blind opposition. The *Journal of the American Medical Association*, which had agreeably publicized the insurance question, became noticeably less favorable in early 1917. The war diverted attention from the issue and no mention was made from mid-1917 to February, 1919. When the Committee on Social Insurance was reorganized, Isaac Rubinow was no longer a member. The 1919 House of Delegates took no stand, but the Reference Committee on Legislation and Political Action refused to submit for consideration a resolution of the Medical Society of the State of New York condemning medical insurance. The ax fell in New Orleans in April, 1920. The Committee on Social Insurance was disbanded, and the House of Delegates passed the New York resolution. Having condemned compulsory health insurance, the AMA came to see Sheppard-Towner as only another form of the same thing.[33]

State medical societies in Massachusetts, New York, Illinois, Ohio, and Indiana spearheaded the opposition to health insurance and the Sheppard-Towner proposal. The *Illinois Medical Journal*, official organ of the Illinois State Medical Society, declared in May, 1920, "Today Washington, D.C. is a hotbed of Bolshevism. . . ." It attacked the Sheppard-Towner bill as well as bills calling for a department of health, department of education, aid to rural sanitation, promotion of physical education, the U.S. Public Health Service, Children's Bureau, Vital Statistics Division of the Census Bureau, and the Interdepartmental Social Hygiene Board. "Where will it all end? We know where it ended in ruined Russia. . . . Can the people of America set up Bureaucratic Autocracy in Washington without a resulting industrial slavery?"[34] Physicians from Massachusetts testified against the bill in hearings. Yet on December 28, 1920, Dr. W. S. Rankin, representing the American Public Health Association and the AMA's own Council on Health and Public Instruction, wrote the committee that these organizations "are strongly in favor of this measure and want to be clearly understood as heartily endorsing the bill. . . ." [35] This was the last positive word as the AMA's opposition became implacable. The *Journal of the American Medical Association* launched its campaign against Sheppard-Towner with an editorial in the February 5, 1921, issue. It said that while the AMA would agree with the objective of reducing death rates it disagreed with the method because it infringed upon state and local responsibility, cost too much, and centralized the administration of medicine. [36] This attack was followed by other editorials and a heavy flow of opposing letters.

The 1921 AMA convention was much agitated by the Sheppard-Towner question, and several state societies offered strongly worded resolutions denouncing all such plans. The Illinois State Medical Society asked the AMA to "oppose State Medicine, Compulsory Health Insurance, Nationalization of the City, County and State Health Agencies and allied dangerous Bolsheviki schemes. . . ." [37] More physicians testified against the bill in 1921 and more letters of disapproval were submitted. The 1922 AMA convention condemned Sheppard-Towner as an "imported socialistic scheme." [38]

In the 1920s the AMA did not speak for the whole medical profession. The Mayo brothers of Mayo Clinic endorsed Sheppard-Towner, as did the Medical Women's National Association. Testifying for the measures were Dr. Josephine S. Baker, director of the Bureau of Child Hygiene of the New York City Department of Health, Dr. Ellen Potter, director of the Division of Health of the Pennsylvania Department of Health, Dr. Philip Van Ingen, professor from Cornell Clinic, and Dr. John A. Foot of Georgetown University. Dr. Ella Oppenheimer wrote the *Journal of the American Medical Association* inquiring how it was possible that the AMA could find itself on the same side as the National Association Opposed to Woman Suffrage, the American Medical Liberty League, the Citizens Medical Reference Bureau, and the American Drugless Association—composed of chiropractors, naturopaths, mechanotherapists, sanipaths, hydropaths, anti-vivisectionists, anti-vaccinationists, and other exotic medical cultists.[39] Even as the 1922 AMA House of Delegates condemned Sheppard-Towner "as a type of undesirable legislation which should be discouraged," the Section on Diseases of Children at the same convention passed a resolution giving its approval "of the principles encouraging public education in the hygiene of maternity and infancy embodied in the Sheppard-Towner Act." The American Child Health Association, headed by physicians, heartily endorsed the bill. A number of physicians organized the Sheppard-Towner Emergency Committee to support the bill. Its leadership included Dr. Royal S. Copeland, health commissioner of New York and later U.S. senator, and Dr. Richard Bolt, director of the American Child Health Association. The State and Provincial Health Officers Association approved the bill in 1920 and 1921 and reaffirmed it in their 1922 convention, pledging their aid in administering it.[40]

While the AMA opposed the Sheppard-Towner Act, the Medical Women remained a steadfast proponent of the program throughout the 1920s. The *Woman's Medical Journal* had called for a comprehensive program to reduce infant and maternal mortality in January, 1917. Dr. Kate Mead, who became Medical Women's president in 1923, reported how the Scandinavian countries had cut infant mortality rates in half in the last ten years with legislation which covered the range from housing for working people to training of midwives, hospital care, and training of new mothers in child care and hygiene.[41] Another future Medical Women's president, Esther Lovejoy, argued that the first job of reconstruction after the war would be the preservation of the health of mothers and children. Noting that one-fourth of the men drafted were physically unfit, she said that in order to have sound men in wartime you must first have fit mothers in peacetime. The high infant and maternal death rates were proof that America had a serious problem.[42] After the AMA backed away and denounced state medicine as socialism, the women physicians continued their support. "The state should be responsible for the care of prospective mothers," wrote Dr. Laura Mearns. The *Medical Woman's Journal* said, "The protection of the child must begin with the protection of the mother . . . there is little prospect of providing adequate care until the problem is recognized as a national problem, and met in a national way." It endorsed the Sheppard-Towner bill, saying, "We hope that Congress will be made to recognize the importance of this problem and that the physicians of the country will receive this assistance in their efforts to save the lives of mothers and infants." [43] In those AMA conventions which condemned health insurance and Sheppard-Towner, women physicians were not heard. No women were members of the House of Delegates.[44] While the AMA growled about the passage of the act, the women physicians spoke of the fine work being done.[45] One of the leading advocates, Dr. Josephine Baker, head of the first bureau of child hygiene in the world, was hailed by *Medical Woman's Journal* as one of the world's great citizens. Reduction of infant mortality in New York City had been her object from 1908 to 1923. When she became director, one baby in seven was dying; in 1921 it was one in fourteen. She had helped cut the rate in half and saved the lives of 82,549 babies.[46] She testified repeatedly for Sheppard-Towner. A constant ally of the National Consumers' League and the National League of Women Voters, she became president of the Medical Women's National Association in the early 1930s.

Many physicians wondered why the AMA was unable to prevent the passage of the bill. The *Journal of the American Medical Association* replied that the women's lobby for the bill was "one of the strongest lobbies that has ever been seen in Washington." Congressmen reported that they were told that if they opposed the bill, every woman in their district would vote against them in the next election. "Members of Congress of years' experience say that the lobby in favor of the bill was the most powerful and persistent that had ever invaded Washington." In addition, opposition was hampered by the fact that the Democrats endorsed the measure in their 1920 platform and President

Harding came out for it during the campaign.[47] Samuel Winslow complained that the "proposed legislation had undoubtedly stirred up more sentiment, wisely or unwisely created, than any bill which had been before Congress in 10 years. . . ." [48] In fact, while the WJCC subcommittee checked congressional pulses, the organizations beat the bushes for support. Petitions, letters, and telegrams rolled in by the thousands. Delegations trooped to Washington to see their representatives and President Harding. In the final weeks before passage the WJCC subcommittee conducted interviews with congressmen at the rate of fifty per day. The result was a handsome margin and full credit from friends and foes alike. Senator Kenyon, a strong backer of the bill, confirmed the effectiveness of the lobby: "If the members could have voted on that measure secretly in their cloak rooms it would have been killed as emphatically as it was finally passed in the open under the pressure of the Joint Congressional Committee of Women." [49]

The question of who should get credit for the passage revealed a misunderstanding between Carrie Chapman Catt and NLWV leaders. After winning suffrage, Catt rapidly became immersed in the search for peace and detached from the workings of her brainchild. Evidence of this detachment appeared in the 1921 NLWV convention in April, when Catt dramatically cast aside her prepared speech on election laws and reforms and gave an impassioned plea for women to work for peace. At that moment the principal issue in most minds was Sheppard-Towner. Except for a tiny number who knew otherwise, Catt was still considered the spokesman of the NLWV. When she wrote an article for *Woman Citizen* in January, 1922, saying the NLWV passed the bill, a storm threatened to break. While the NLWV had a major role, perhaps the key role, the bill was put through Congress by the WJCC with the cooperation of top women in the Republican and Democratic national committees. Catt's article hurt many feelings. Mrs. E. A. Yost, WCTU president, stirred resentment among the women in the Republican National Committee and the WJCC. Maud Wood Park, NLWV president, had to soothe everyone and save the WJCC from disruption. She wrote a letter to *Woman Citizen* giving equal credit to all the members of the WJCC and especially to Florence Kelley, who headed the subcommittee.[50]

Now Catt became angry. She typed a hot letter to Maud Wood Park, but never sent it. Instead she mailed copies to Marie Edwards and Belle Sherwin, first and second vice-presidents of NLWV, for their comments. Catt's trial letter accused Park of facilitating the destruction of the NLWV at the hands of certain Republican women. "These women were all in our suffrage association. They were good and loyal workers then . . . the moment the high appeal of principle was removed, they descended in to the pit of the darkest kind of narrow partisanship. . . . This enmity is subterranean, secret, maligning, lying and thoroughly dishonest in every respect." Catt argued that Park only aided these turncoats in their work. "Your greatest fault, my dear girl, is a cavity where your bump of conceit ought to be, and this time you have positively done your organization a decided wrong by belittling its work and influence." Finally, she charged that Park had made her out to be a liar.[51] Catt demanded of Marie Edwards, "If it was not the League that was the driving force which got it through, can you tell me what the League has done with the $30,000 hard cash the Leslie [Woman Suffrage Commission] gave it." Bristling with irritation, she wanted to know more about the subcommittee and Florence Kelley.[52] Catt said to Bell Sherwin, "The League was either the directing force which put the maternity bill through or it was not. . . . When the League with a fight on, admits to its attackers that it was only doing the same amount of work as the Girls Friendly Society and the Women's Home Economics [American Home Economics Association], I am almost persuaded that babies *was* the proper place to begin!" She repeated that Park's letter to the *Citizen* all but called her a liar.[53]

Both tried to pacify Catt by pointing to all the work that the NLWV had done in Washington and how hard Park worked to make the WJCC function a necessary instrument for focusing women's efforts in Washington. Edwards said, "Your letter about broke my heart because it was so evident from that that you had no real knowledge of what this child of your brain, the League, was really doing." She concluded that the letter by Park was vitally needed to keep the WJCC from flying apart over hurt feelings and to give Florence Kelley deserved credit. A recent article on the WJCC and Sheppard-Towner ignored Kelley entirely and mistakenly gave Mrs. Yost credit instead. "We are all very much distressed over the Ladies Home Journal article and the general trend, which is to shut Mrs. Kelley entirely out of recognition. She has been a gallant fighter and there is an unfair war being waged against her now. . . ." [54] Sherwin declared that others besides the NLWV had played significant roles. For example, she pointed out that the General Federation of Women's Clubs was largely responsible for the immense volume of letters and telegrams which poured into Washington. Finally, Sherwin felt that Park had not implied that Catt was a liar and that her statement was a literal statement of facts: "It is only fair as well as politic to be literally correct even to the sacrifice of deserved credit." [55] Catt shot another letter to Edwards, brimming with irritation, saying she would never defend the NLWV again and not to bother coming to New York to tell her about the league either since she was too busy writing a book. [56]

Maud Wood Park sadly wrote her former commander to say that she regretted very much that Catt did not approve of the work of the NLWV: "I cannot honestly agree with your view in most of these matters. . . ." She concluded that she did not want to be president of an organization at odds with its founder, and she asked Catt to suggest who should be the new president. [57] Catt did not reply, and Park continued to serve until 1924, when Belle Sherwin took over.

II

By and large, the Sheppard-Towner Act was well received by the state authorities. Forty-one states joined in 1922, and eventually only Connecticut, Illinois, and Massachusetts remained aloof. In New Jersey the legislature passed the enabling act over the

governor's veto in 1922. In Washington the governor was un-
alterably opposed, but a new chief executive in 1923 accepted
it. Louisiana waited until 1924 to enter the program, and Vermont joined in 1926. Unexpected opposition kept Rhode Island
out until 1925, and Maine and Kansas finally accepted in 1927.

In New York, Governor Nathan Miller, who had upset Al
Smith in the Harding sweep, announced at the opening session of
the 1922 legislature that he would veto any bill accepting Sheppard-Towner. Twenty-eight women's organizations formed the
Association for the Sheppard-Towner Act and worked to have
New York provide $75,000 for the program. The association
circulated petitions, but Miller declared that he would not be
influenced if every woman in the state signed. "The people . . .
have no business to interfere with men in office." [58] In keeping
with Miller's mood, the legislature formally rejected the Sheppard-Towner Act. While deploring the financial drain of a
maternity program, Miller signed a bill appropriating $125,000
for a hog barn for the state fairgrounds; and he approved a twin
barn for 1923. Florence Kelley remarked, "It does not improve
the outlook of a candidate for the governorship of New York to
have twenty-eight organizations of women experienced in working together know that swine shelters appeal to him more
strongly than dying mothers and babies." [59] Miller lost the next
election in November, 1922, to Al Smith, who pushed the
Sheppard-Towner plan through in 1923. Smith credited the New
York LWV and others for its passage. [60]

The law allowed a governor to accept the program until the
legislature met. Governor Lake of Connecticut accepted, but the
legislature refused. Connecticut did not need an enabling act
since a 1919 law permitted the Department of Health to accept
such funds; all that was required was a matching appropriation. [61]
The appropriations committee rejected Sheppard-Towner money
on the grounds that it infringed on the rights of the state. While
acknowledging that the state had accepted matching grants for
armories, agriculture, and highways, the committee felt that it
was time to stop this method of federal encroachment and reject
any new aid. This excuse seemed hollow to Sheppard-Towner

advocates, as the committee then voted to accept a new federal aid program for an airplane squadron.[62] Nevertheless, the legislature established a state program for maternity and infancy protection with an appropriation of $55,000. While this represented an increase of $19,000 for the Health Department, it was $12,000 less than would have been available under Sheppard-Towner. Furthermore, the appropriation was offset by a $30,720 cut in the funds for the Bureau of Child Welfare. This bureau, the major achievement of the Connecticut LWV in the 1921 legislature, was partially sacrificed to the states' rights cause.[63] The refusal of the state to accept Sheppard-Towner was a bitter pill to the social feminists, but they worked diligently throughout the decade to expand the state's program.

From the outset, Massachusetts spawned most of the organized effort against the Sheppard-Towner plan. A state proposal for maternity and infancy protection had failed to pass three consecutive years, 1919, 1920, and 1921—the last time it received only two positive votes in the legislature. The opposition of the medical profession had been particularly vigorous. One group of critics labeled the measure "The *beginning of Communism in Medicine.* A very unjust, unwise, iniquitous and socialistic bill." "Vicious, un-American, paternal." "It is one of the greatest steps toward Socialism that has yet been undertaken." "It is a step toward Sovietism." [64] When the legislature began consideration of an enabling act for Sheppard-Towner in 1922, the attorney general (an anti-suffragist who had ruled women off the ballot and out of the jury box in Massachusetts) issued an opinion that the Sheppard-Towner Act would misuse the tax money of Massachusetts and was unconstitutional because it violated the reserved rights of the states. The state filed suit with the U.S. Supreme Court on behalf of its taxpayers to enjoin the law. Fearing that a state was ineligible to file a taxpayers suit, Harriet Frothingham, president of the Woman Patriots, filed another suit in the Supreme Court of the District of Columbia. When this court dismissed her case and the U.S. Court of Appeals concurred, she appealed to the U.S. Supreme Court. U.S. Solicitor General James Beck considered the Sheppard-Towner Act to be unconstitutional and encouraged Massachusetts to pursue the case.[65]

The suits seriously threatened the whole range of federal programs which provided either direct aid or matching grants. Ironically, at the very time Massachusetts was challenging Sheppard-Towner for violating the Tenth Amendment, the state was accepting money under twenty-two other federal programs which extended from soil surveys, county agents, highway building, state militia, and the state nautical school to the eradication of white-pine rust and the European corn borer. Ten states and the Association of Land Grant Colleges filed counter briefs. On June 5, 1923, the Supreme Court dismissed both suits for want of jurisdiction and without ruling on the constitutionality of the act. The unanimous decision said that the suits were essentially political, not judicial, in character, and therefore beyond the jurisdiction of the court.[66]

Sheppard-Towner was considered a permanent law, but its appropriation was scheduled to cease automatically on June 30, 1927. Confident that the program was a success, its proponents moved in 1926 to have the authorization extended.[67] The House of Representatives quickly voted a two-year extension by the healthy margin of 218 to 44, but opposition mobilized to stop the bill in the Senate. The struggle renewed the 1921 battle with an added measure of bitterness in the opponents. The foes included the AMA, Woman Patriots, Massachusetts Public Interests League, Sentinels of the Republic, and Daughters of the American Revolution. (In 1921, as a member of the WJCC, the DAR had supported the measure, but it ceased espousing progressive causes after 1923–24.) The opposition was fresh from having recently beaten another progressive proposal—the federal child labor amendment. They echoed the usual cries: "socializing medicine," "nationalizing the children," introducing "Bolshevism."[68] Mrs. George Madden Martin attacked the Sheppard-Towner Act as embodying "the same principle of nationalized, standardized care of children" and interference as the recently defeated child labor amendment. She charged that the Children's Bureau rigged its statistics and poured out propaganda to perpetuate itself. She bragged that she had opposed the creation of the Children's Bureau in 1912 when nearly all women favored it. She declared that she was an individualist, rejecting paternalism, "but then the whole doctrine of Karl Marx is abhorrent to those Americans who prefer a democracy and believe in representative government." [69]

Senator Thomas A. Bayard of Delaware read into the *Congressional Record* a thirty-six-page petition and letter from the Woman Patriots. It purported to show the Bolshevist origins of the entire progressive program for children, which included the Sheppard-Towner Act, the Children's Bureau, child labor laws, and the child labor amendment. The petition traced an intricate web which joined the national women's organizations together in a conspiracy to Sovietize the United States. It was a feminist-socialist-communist plot under the leadership of women like Florence Kelley Wishnieweski. She was described as "the ablest legislative general communism had produced." The petition also denounced Jane Addams, Julia Lathrop, Grace Abbott, Carrie Chapman Catt, Mary Anderson, Maud Wood Park, Harriet Taylor Upton, Emily Newell Blair, Margaret Dreier Robins, Hull House, the constituent organizations of the WJCC, the Federal Council of Churches, the Children's Bureau, the Women's Bureau, and the U.S. Department of Labor.[70] Bayard mailed copies of the petition under his frank to all state officals of the DAR, after which the president general of the DAR urged the defeat of Sheppard-Towner.[71]

The bill was blocked in the Senate for nearly eight months, and despite President Coolidge's recommendation that the appropriation be extended, passage was uncertain. Eventually proponents were forced to accept a compromise which extended the appropriations for two more years but repealed the law itself automatically on June 30, 1929. Supporters of the act hoped that a more progressive political climate might exist by 1929 and that the law would be restored. Florence Kelley wrote Grace Abbott saying, "It seems inconceivable that the next Congress should be as bad as this one. I don't believe it can." [72] It was.

President Coolidge's endorsement contained a death wish. "I

am in favor of the proposed legislation extending the period of operation of this law with the understanding and hope that the administration of the funds to be provided would be with the view to the gradual withdrawal of the Federal Government from this field, leaving it to the states. . . ." [73] Social feminists were angry at his singling out Sheppard-Towner as the place to phase out federal aid. It amounted to $1,108,000 in 1926. Why not stop the $75,000,000 spent for roads, or the $5,000,000 for agricultural extension? [74] The NLWV fought the notion that Sheppard-Towner was unique as a grant-in-aid program. Opponents saw the grant-in-aid feature as a novel device, if not a Bolshevist gimmick to subvert the states. The first such program was the Forest Fire Prevention Act of 1911, introduced by John W. Weeks, the women's old opponent! Next came the Smith-Lever Act of 1914, creating the county extension agents, the Federal Good Roads Act of 1916, the Smith-Hughes Act of 1917 for vocational education, the Chamberlain-Kahn Act of 1920 for venereal disease suppression, the Federal Highway Act of 1921, the Sheppard-Towner Act of 1921, and the Clarke-McNary Act for protection of forest lands in 1924. [75]

Efforts to preserve the maternity program resumed in 1928. The WJCC and other organizations rallied behind a bill which was more liberal than Sheppard-Towner. It specified that the money would be spent in cooperation with the states, but did not require either acceptance by the state legislatures or matching funds. The federal money was to be apportioned on the basis of need, not population. The AMA, the Woman Patriots, and the Sentinels of the Republic led the opposition again. [76] By now, the politicians were less concerned about a women's voting bloc, and the conservative propensities of Congress had freer play. This time the President would not help. Herbert Hoover issued perfunctory formal statements which urged its enactment; and refusing to press the matter, he allowed the first federal social welfare law to lapse.

In reviewing the work under Sheppard-Towner, the Children's Bureau reported for the seven years that it had conducted 183,252 health conferences and established 2,978 permanent centers of prenatal care. Visiting nurses had made 3,131,996 home visits, and 22,020,489 pieces of literature had been distributed. In the final four years, more than 4,000,000 infants and expectant mothers had been reached. The infant death rate in 1921 was 75 per 1,000 live births, and the years under Sheppard-Towner saw it fall to 64 per 1,000. The maternal death rate was reduced from 67.3 per 1,000 in 1921 to 62.3 in 1927, despite the fact that the general death rate of all people had risen slightly for the same period. Obviously, much more needed to be done; New Zealand had an infant death rate of 35 per 1,000. The Medical Women's National Association noted that Great Britain's maternal death rate was 50 percent of that of the United States; and Britain spent $3,800,000 at the same time that the United States was spending only $1,240,000.[77] The Medical Women remained at odds with the AMA. While the AMA consistently fought against state medicine, the Medical Women's National Association continued its agitation for government programs like Sheppard-Towner.[78]

The end of the act did not leave a complete void: forty-five states had participated directly after 1926, and Illinois and Connecticut had their own programs. Most states had the apparatus and the awareness of the problem to continue maternity and infancy aid on their own. The removal of federal funds, however, restricted the programs. Only sixteen states appropriated enough money to exceed or equal the previous total. Although some states at first greatly increased their efforts, as the Depression deepened the plan suffered badly in the fiscal pinch. Several states dropped it altogether.[79] An attempt to revive the federal part in 1931 failed when Senators David Walsh, Millard Tydings, and Elbert Thomas filibustered against it.[80] Consideration of maternity and infancy protection was merged with the broader development of social security legislation within the New Deal. Restoration came with the Social Security Act of 1935. Protection of maternity and infancy was embodied in Title V of the comprehensive measure. Opponents were shocked at the provisions which authorized appropriations for the Children's Bureau of $5,820,000 for maternity and infancy protection, $3,870,000 for crippled children, and $24,750,000 for aid to dependent children.

The Sheppard-Towner Act was both an example of the persistence of progressivism in the 1920s and a link between the progressive era and the New Deal. Its travail demonstrated no lack of effort because social feminists secured its passage in 1921, expanded it to include Hawaii in 1924, renewed its appropriations in 1926, and obtained its acceptance in forty-five states. Despite the defenders' claim that Sheppard-Towner was like the good roads bill and others, the plan did represent an innovation for the federal government. Florence Kelley had noted in the committee hearings in 1920 that it was the first measure to provide federal funds for a social welfare purpose. Even though conservative forces were able to eliminate the particular bill on the eve of the Depression, advocates of the idea finally triumphed during the New Deal.

NOTES

1. General treatments of the 1920s fail to mention the Sheppard-Towner Act: Eric Goldman, *Rendezvous with Destiny: A History of Modern American Reform* (New York: Vintage Books, 1956); John D. Hicks, *Republican Ascendancy, 1921–1933* (New York: Harper & Row, 1960); William E. Leuchtenburg, *The Perils of Prosperity, 1914–1932* (Chicago: University of Chicago Press, 1958); Arthur M. Schlesinger, Jr., *The Crisis of the Old Order: 1919–1933* (vol. I, *The Age of Roosevelt*, Boston: Houghton Mifflin, 1957); Richard Hofstadter, *The Age of Reform: From Bryan to F.D.R.* (New York: Vintage Books, 1955); Paul A. Carter, *The Twenties in America* (New York: Thomas Y. Crowell, 1968); Harold U. Faulkner, *From Versailles to the New Deal* (vol. LI, *The Chronicles of America*, ed. Allan Nevins, New Haven: Yale University Press, 1950); Elizabeth Stevenson, *Babbitts and Bohemians* (New York: Macmillan, 1967); Jonathan Daniels, *The Time between the Wars: Armistice to Pearl Harbor* (Garden City: Doubleday, 1966); Preston W. Slosson, *The Great Crusade and After, 1914–1928* (vol. XII, *A History of American Life*, ed. Arthur M. Schlesinger and Dixon Ryan Fox, New York: Macmillan, 1931). Even a recent biography ignored it: Andrew Sinclair, *The Available Man: The Life behind the Masks of Warren Gamaliel Harding* (New York: Macmillan, 1965). More specialized studies have almost neglected the measure: Clarke Chambers, *Seedtime of Reform: American Social Service and Social Action, 1918–1933* (Minneapolis: University of Minnesota Press, 1963); Roy Lubove, *The Struggle for Social Security in America, 1900–1935* (Cambridge: Harvard University Press, 1968); Robert K. Murray, *The Harding Era: Warren G. Harding and His Administration* (Minneapolis: University of Minnesota Press, 1969), 408. The most extensive treatments are: James G. Burrow, *AMA: The Voice of American Medicine* (Baltimore: Johns Hopkins Press, 1963); Joseph B. Chepaitis, "The First Federal Social Welfare

Measure: The Sheppard-Towner Maternity and Infancy Act, 1918–1932"
(Ph.D. thesis, Georgetown University, 1968).

2. Davis, *Spearheads for Reform*, 55–56; Chambers, *Seedtime of Reform*,
16–17.

3. Goldmark, *Impatient Crusader*, 94–101; Trattner, *Crusade for the Children*, 95–98, 119–120.

4. U.S. Congress, Senate, Committee on Public Health and National Quarantine, *Protection of Maternity and Infancy*, hearings, 66th Cong., 2nd Sess., on S. 3259, May 12, 1920 (Washington: Government Printing Office, 1920), 7–8.

5. *Sixth Annual Report of the Chief, Children's Bureau*, U.S. Department of Labor (Washington: Government Printing Office, 1918), 11–12; *Eighth Annual Report of the Chief, Children's Bureau* (1920), 10; see also Sylvia Hardy, "The Children's Year," *Life and Labor*, VIII (July, 1918), 139–140; Mary Sumner Boyd, "Let's Stop, Now, the Casualties of Motherhood," *Good Housekeeping*, LXXI (Dec., 1920), 43.

6. Quoted in Goldmark, *Impatient Crusader*, 93.

7. Dorothy Kirchwey Brown, "The Sheppard-Towner Bill Lobby," *Woman Citizen*, V (Jan. 22, 1921), 907.

8. Editorial, "Herod Is Not Dead," *Good Housekeeping*, LXXI (Dec., 1920), 4; see also Anne Martin, "Every Woman's Charge to Serve Humanity," *ibid.*, LXX (Feb., 1920), 20–21; Martin, "We Couldn't Afford a Doctor," *ibid.* (Apr., 1920), 19–20; Anne Shannon Moore, "Adventuring in Motherhood," *ibid.* (May, 1920), 28–29.

9. U.S. Congress, House, Committee on Interstate and Foreign Commerce, *Public Protection of Maternity and Infancy*, hearings, 66th Cong., 3rd Sess., on H.R. 10925, Dec. 20–29, 1920 (Washington: Government Printing Office, 1921), 27–29 (hereafter cited as House Hearings, *Public Protection of Maternity*).

10. Circular letter, Boston League of Women Voters, Feb. 7, 1921, Fannie Fern Andrews MSS, box 15, SL.

11. Warren G. Harding to Harlean James, Feb. 21, 1921, Harding MSS, box 157, folder 117-1, OHS.

12. Women's Committee on Sheppard-Towner Bill to Harding, Mar. 5, 1921, *ibid.*; address to Congress, Apr. 12, 1921, *ibid.*, box 773, folder 1921.

13. The seven negative votes: Borah (Idaho), Broussard (La.), Watson (Ga.), Warren (Wyo.), Moses (N.H.), Reed (Mo.), King (Utah).

14. Harriet Taylor Upton to George B. Christian, May 31, 1921; Upton to Harding, June 18, 1921; Harlean James to Harding, May 17, 1921; James to Christian, May 30, 1921, Harding MSS, box 157, folder 117-1, OHS.

15. Upton to Harding, July 30, 1921, *ibid.*

16. Upton to Harding, Aug. 1, 1921, *ibid.*, box 33, folder 15-14.

17. *Illinois Medical Journal* (Sept., 1921), enclosed in a letter from E. Forrest Herdien, M.D., to Harding, Sept. 9, 1921, Harding MSS, box 157, folder 117-1, OHS.

18. W. J. Graham to Harding, Sept. 30, 1921; George B. Christian to Graham, Oct. 5, 1921, *ibid.*

19. "The House Discusses the 'Maternity Bill,' " *Capitol Eye*, I (Oct., 1921), 5.

20. Ida Wood to Samuel Winslow, July 15, 1921, Harding MSS, box 157, folder 117-1, OHS.

21. Mrs. G. M. Kenyon to Harding, Apr. 28, 1921, *ibid.*; see also her testimony in House Hearings, *Public Protection of Maternity*, 127.

22. Among them were the National Association of Deans of Women, National Women's Association of Commerce, Women's Press Club, League of

American Pen Women, National Organization of Public Health Nursing, National Child Welfare Association, American Child Hygiene Association, Women's Foundation for Health, and Service Star Legion.

23. Harriet Taylor Upton to Harding, Dec. 2, 1922; memo, Upton to Harding, Dec. 6, 1922; memo, Upton to Harding, Dec. 7, 1922, Harding MSS, box 157, folder 117-1, OHS.

24. "The Senate Discusses the 'Maternity Bill,' " *Capitol Eye*, I (Oct., 1921), 4.

25. Quoted in "News Notes of the Fortnight," *Woman Citizen*, VI (July 30, 1921), 6.

26. *Congressional Record, Appendix*, 67th Cong., 1st Sess., LXI, 8759–69.

27. Mary Kilbreth to Harding, Nov. 25, 1921, Harding MSS, box 157, folder 117-1, OHS; see also Kilbreth's testimony in hearings in 1921: U.S. Congress, Senate, Committee on Education and Labor, *Protection of Maternity*, hearings, 67th Cong., 1st Sess., on S. 1039, Apr. 25–May 5, 1921 (Washington: Government Printing Office, 1921) (hereafter cited as Senate Hearings, *Protection of Maternity*).

28. "The Lobby Discusses the 'Maternity Bill,' " *Capitol Eye*, I (Oct., 1921), 6–8.

29. Grace Cole to Harding, May 16, 1921; Lenora B. Simpkins to Harding, May 18, 1921, Harding MSS, box 157, folder 117-1, OHS.

30. Senate Hearings, *Protection of Maternity*, 29; "Copy of Communications by Citizens Medical Reference Bureau to the Governors of Each State," Mar. 24, 1921; "Copy of Replies from Governors to Communications by Citizens Medical Reference Bureau," [Apr., 1921], Harding MSS, box 157, folder 117-1, OHS.

31. Burrow, *AMA*, 65–67, 105, 157–158.

32. Margaret Rundell, "The American Medical Association: A Pressure Group" (M.A. thesis, Ohio State University, 1945), 5–6. For a discussion of the issue of voluntarism and compulsory insurance, see Roy Lubove, "Economic Security and Social Conflict in America: The Early Twentieth Century, Part I," *Journal of Social History*, I (Fall, 1967), 61–87.

33. Burrow, *AMA*, 134–164.

34. *Illinois Medical Journal* (May, 1920), quoted in Citizens Medical Reference Bureau, *Bull. 33* (May 30, 1920), Harding MSS, box 17, folder 117-1, OHS.

35. House Hearings, *Public Protection of Maternity*, 184.

36. *Journal of the American Medical Association* (hereafter cited as *JAMA*), LXXVI (Feb., 1921), 383.

37. Quoted in Citizens Medical Reference Bureau, *Bull. 36*, Harding MSS, box 157, folder 117-1, OHS.

38. *JAMA*, LXXVIII (June 3, 1922), 1709; see also letter from Dr. Fred H. Clark, spokesman, Medical Society of the Southwest, *Congressional Record, Appendix*, 67th Cong., 1st Sess., LXI, 8767–68.

39. Letter from Dr. Ella Oppenheimer, *JAMA*, LXXVI (May 21, 1921), 1418–19; Julia Lathrop wrote a similar letter to the editor, Dr. George H. Simmons, Aug. 23, 1921, Brown MSS, box 1, folder 29a, SL.

40. "The Medical Profession as to the Merits of the Act," NLWV Papers, Ser. II, box 7, Sheppard-Towner file, LC.

41. Kate C. Mead, "Is Infant Mortality an Index to Social Welfare? Scandinavia's Reply," *Woman's Medical Journal*, XXVII (Jan., 1917), 10–15.

42. Esther Lovejoy, "Democracy and Health," *ibid.*, XXIX (June, 1919), 116–124.

43. Letter from Laura L. Mearns, *Medical Woman's Journal*, XXVII (Feb.,

1920), 62; "The Sheppard-Towner Bill," *ibid.*, XXVIII (Jan., 1921), 13–14; editorial, *ibid.*, 22.

44. "No Medical Women in House of Delegates of A.M.A.," *ibid.* (June, 1921), 163.

45. Editorial, "What Legislators Are Doing for Mothers and Babies," *ibid.* (July, 1921), 189; Frances Sage Bradley, "The Sheppard-Towner Bill as It Is Worked Out by Arkansas Women," *ibid.*, XXIX (Aug., 1922), 196–197; Mary Riggs Noble, "Prenatal Work in Pennsylvania," *ibid.*, XXXI (Mar., 1924), 69–70; Ellen Stadtmuller, "Promotion of Maternal and Infant Welfare in California," *ibid.*, 66–67; Frances Sage Bradley, "What Is Hoped and Planned for Arkansas," *ibid.*, 67–68; William H. Peters, "Cincinnati's Participation in Sheppard-Towner Work," *ibid.*, 72–73.

46. "One of the World's Great Citizens," *ibid.*, XXIX (Aug., 1922), 180–182.

47. *JAMA*, LXXVII (Dec. 10, 1921), 1913–14; *ibid.*, LXXVIIII (Feb. 11, 1922), 434.

48. *Congressional Record*, 67th Cong., 1st Sess., LXI, 7926.

49. Quoted by Charles A. Selden, "The Most Powerful Lobby in Washington," *Ladies Home Journal*, XXXIX (Apr., 1922), 95.

50. Carrie Chapman Catt, "Who's Scared," *Woman Citizen*, VI (Jan. 28, 1922), 8–9; letter from Maud Wood Park, *ibid.* (Mar. 11, 1922), 16.

51. Copy of letter from Carrie Chapman Catt to Maud Wood Park, Feb. 18, 1922 [never sent], NLWV Papers, Ser. II, box 3, Catt folder, LC.

52. Carrie Chapman Catt to Mrs. Richard Edwards, Feb. 18, 1921, *ibid.*

53. Carrie Chapman Catt to Belle Sherwin, Feb. 18, 1921, *ibid.*

54. Mrs. Richard Edwards to Carrie Chapman Catt, Feb. 27, 1922, *ibid.* The article was Selden's "The Most Powerful Lobby in Washington."

55. Belle Sherwin to Carrie Chapman Catt, Feb. 24, 1922, *ibid.*

56. Carrie Chapman Catt to Mrs. Richard Edwards, Mar. 3, 1922, *ibid.*

57. Maud Wood Park to Carrie Chapman Catt, Apr. 14, 1922, *ibid.*

58. Quoted in Harriet W. Laidlaw to the editor, Mar. 10, 1922, Harriet W. Laidlaw MSS, folder 27, SL.

59. Florence Kelley, "The Children's Amendment," *Good Housekeeping*, LXXVI (Feb., 1923), 170.

60. Alfred E. Smith, "Safeguarding Our Assets—the Children," *Ladies Home Journal*, XLVI (Oct., 1929), 304.

61. *Woman Voter's Bulletin*, II (Feb., 1922), 1; *ibid.*, III (Jan., 1923), 4.

62. *Ibid.*, III (May 3, 1923), 2.

63. *Ibid.* (July, 1923), 1–2.

64. "Why Physicians Are Opposing Maternity Bill," sent to Harding by the Massachusetts Civic Alliance, Harding MSS, box 157, folder 117-1, OHS.

65. Harriet Taylor Upton to Harding, Dec. 2, 1922, *ibid.*; Marian Parkhurst, NLWV Congressional Secretary, to Cornelia Bryce Pinchot, Dec. 7, 1922, C. B. Pinchot MSS, box 24, LC.

66. *Eleventh Annual Report of the Chief, Children's Bureau* (1923), 5–7.

67. Katherine Glover, "Making America Safe for Mothers," *Good Housekeeping*, LXXXII (May, 1926), 98.

68. *JAMA*, LXXXVI (Feb. 6, 1926), 421; *ibid.*, LXXXVII (Nov. 27, 1926), 1833–34; "Sentinels Appeal for Rejection of Maternity Act," *Woman Patriot*, X (Feb. 15, 1926), 32; William C. Woodward, "Further Fallacies of Sheppard-Towner Act," *ibid.* (Dec. 1, 1926), 178.

69. Mrs. George Madden Martin, "Dangers in the Maternity Bill," *Woman Citizen*, XI (Dec., 1926), 17.

70. *Congressional Record*, 69th Cong., 1st Sess., LXVII, 12918–52.

71. *Ibid.*, 69th Cong., 2nd Sess., LXVIII, 1280–81.

72. Quoted in Chambers, *Seedtime of Reform,* 51.

73. Quoted in "Congress Opens," *Woman Citizen,* XI (Jan., 1927), 31; see also *Congressional Record,* 69th Cong., 2nd Sess., LXVII, 79.

74. Editorial, "Why Begin on the Babies?," *Woman's Journal,* XIII (Jan., 1928), 23.

75. Dorothy Kirchwey Brown, "Uncle Sam's Helping Hand," *Woman Citizen,* XI (Feb., 1927), 14–16; "Federal Aid to the States," NLWV pamphlet, 1926, Brown MSS, box 1, folder 5, SL.

76. *JAMA,* XCI (Dec. 1, 1928), 1723; *ibid.,* (Dec. 22, 1927), 1999; *ibid.,* XCII (May 4, 1929), 1525–26.

77. *The Promotion of the Welfare and Hygiene of Maternity and Infancy,* Children's Bureau, U.S. Department of Labor, Pub. 203 (Washington: Government Printing Office, 1931), 28–34; Dorothy Kirchwey Brown, speech at Chicago Forum, [Winter, 1928–29], Brown MSS, box 1, folder 27, SL; Rosina Wistein, "Maternal Mortality: A Comparative Study," *Medical Woman's Journal,* XXXIX (Feb., 1932), 28–32.

78. Editorial, "Maternity-Infant Mortality Figures," *Medical Woman's Journal,* XXXVII (Feb., 1930), 51; Lydia Allen DeVilbiss, "Reducing the Maternal Mortality Rate," *ibid.,* XXXVIII (Aug., 1931), 202–203; editorial, "Maternal Mortality," *ibid.,* XXXIX (Mar., 1932), 66; editorial, "Maternal Mortality," *ibid.* (Apr., 1932), 98.

79. *The Promotion of the Welfare and Hygiene of Maternity and Infancy,* 38; Katherine F. Lenroot to Carrie Chapman Catt, Aug. 1, 1932, Catt MSS, box 1, NYPL.

80. "Maternity and Infancy Bill Lost," *Woman's Journal,* XVI (Apr., 1931), 24; for AMA opposition see *JAMA,* XCIV (Apr. 19, 1930), 1240; *ibid.* (Jan. 24, 1931), 274.

SEVEN

"feminists against Feminists"

Social feminism experienced its time of triumph in the period 1920–25. The defeat of the child labor amendment signaled the waning of this era. From then until the New Deal, social feminism entered a period of defense, frustration, and fragmentation. A number of factors combined to weaken the movement, such as attacks from extreme conservatives and adverse judicial decisions. Especially disruptive and distracting was the persistent struggle between social and hard-core feminists. Hard-core feminists had carried the fight for woman suffrage to a dead end until the growing numbers of social feminists had taken up the issue. Social feminists wanted the vote as a matter of justice, surely; but they wanted it most of all for the good they could do with it.[1] Even in the latter days of the suffrage crusade—a single issue upon which all feminists agreed—the gulf between militant and social feminists was evident in the newsworthy antics of the Woman's Party and the cool efficiency of the National American Woman Suffrage Association. Once the vote was won, the militants temporarily pondered what to do next while the social feminists immediately went to work for the Sheppard-Towner Act, consumer legislation, good government, independent citizenship for women, jury service, conservation, and a host of other measures across the nation. Finding that equality was not won with enfranchisement, the hard-core feminists concentrated their considerable energy and talent on promoting a new constitutional amendment, the equal rights amendment. The implications of this amendment were not lost on social feminists struggling to preserve and advance laws to protect women in industry, and quickly the social and hard-core feminists were again arrayed against each other. The National Woman's Party was quite alone in 1923 with its amendment, but began picking up support in the late twenties, especially among business and professional women. After the buffeting which social feminism took over the child labor amendment and as professional concerns increased among women, a growing number turned from social issues to questions of personal interest. The equal rights amendment provided a pole toward which business and professional women gradually moved in the 1920s; and the 1930s saw a substantial number of the business and professional women's associations endorse the Woman's Party's amendment.

The National Woman's Party originally grew out of militant impatience with the slow, state-by-state approach to which NAWSA, under the leadership of Anna Howard Shaw, was committed. Alice Paul and Lucy Burns arrived with the militant spirit of the English suffragettes and formed the Congressional Union in 1913 as a NAWSA auxiliary. The union was devoted solely to passing a federal suffrage amendment; and it split with NAWSA in 1914 over money, tactics, and temperament. In 1915 NAWSA elected Carrie Chapman Catt president, and she increased NAWSA membership from 100,000 to over 2,000,000 in two years and reinvigorated NAWSA's congressional effort with the able lobbyist Maud Wood Park. The Congressional Union called itself the National Woman's Party in 1916 and was captained by Alice Paul and financed by the redoubtable Mrs. Oliver Hazard Perry Belmont.[2] The Woman's Party was responsible for the most memorable scenes of the suffrage fight. They practically invented the publicity stunt. On the other hand, NAWSA got the job done in the halls of Congress and in the legislatures. With suffrage won, NAWSA's offspring plunged immediately into further reform, while the Woman's Party drifted as its leadership cast about for a new role.

From its inception the National Woman's Party attracted women who were impatient with piecemeal, compromise approaches. Although never large, the NWP was composed of able, gifted women who were mostly middle-class business and professional women. The dynamo was Alice Paul, a tireless champion of single causes. Nothing could swerve her from suffrage; the same intense energy was focused on the equal rights amendment. Mrs. Belmont was born Alva Smith, the daughter of a cotton planter from Mobile, Alabama. She married William K. Vanderbilt, crashed into Mrs. Astor's high society Four Hundred and scandalized them all by divorcing Vanderbilt in 1895 and marrying O. H. P. Belmont. An ardent suffragist, she became the financial angel of the Woman's Party from 1916 until her death in 1933. She was president of the NWP from 1924 to 1933. Others who joined included Edna St. Vincent Millay, Gloria Swanson, Amelia Earhart, Pearl Mesta, Mrs. John J. Raskob (wife of the president of General Motors), Ruth Hale (wife of Heywood Broun), Dr. M. Carey Thomas (president of Bryn Mawr College), Mrs. William Randolph Hearst, Gail Laughlin (first president of the National Federation of Business and Professional Women's Clubs), Lena Madeson Phillips (president of NFBPWC 1926–35), and Emma Gillette (dean of the Washington College of Law). A few came from trade union backgrounds, but were denounced by trade union women in the 1920s for their opposition to protective industrial laws for women. The NWP women were usually well educated, highly motivated, and talented; and they infiltrated many of the professional women's organizations and percolated to the top. They kept the rest in an uproar most of the time and drained the spirit from many social feminists. They disrupted the Women's Bureau conferences in 1923 and 1926, diverted enormous time and energy to the equal rights amendment, and dominated some international aspects of the American feminist movement.

The separation of the NWP from the majority of feminists in the 1920s developed into a deep, abiding split in 1921. The Woman's Party summoned a convention in Washington in February, 1921, and invited all other women's organizations to

present their programs. The declared purpose of the convention was to decide the future of the NWP—either to disband or
reform for a new campaign. However, the National Advisory
Board of the NWP announced at the end of January that it
wanted the NWP to reform for a drive to remove all legal disabilities of women.

Their legal survey had revealed that the law books of all states
were cluttered with restrictions and discriminations against
women. Many states recognized the father as sole guardian of
children and alone entitled to their services and earnings. In
Maryland and Georgia the father could will away the custody
of his child. In the case of illegitimacy, the woman was usually
held responsible. In nearly all states the wife's services belonged
to the husband, and frequently only he could collect for the
loss of her services. In one instance a woman, long separated
and self-supporting, lost a leg in an industrial accident. She sued
the company for $10,000. While her case was being tried, her
husband showed up, settled out of court for $300, and disap-
peared with the money. The woman had no legal way to reopen
the case or even recover the $300. In some states a woman could
not enter business or sign contracts without her husband's consent. Her property rights were greatly curtailed. Divorce laws
tended to favor men, office-holding was limited in some states,
and women were barred from jury service in most states. In
1921 every state except Wisconsin had an average of six major
legal disabilities against women.[3] The list seemed endless and a
wide sweep seemed necessary to catch them all.

After hearing all of the women's programs, the NWP announced that it would adopt a single goal—complete equality.
This goal would be attained by amending specific laws, blanket
equality bills in all states, and an amendment to the Constitution
guaranteeing equal rights. The National Women's Trade Union
League and supporters of protective legislation such as Florence
Kelley and Mary Anderson recoiled immediately. Kelley had
been a member of the NWP's National Council, and a complete
sweep of discrimination appealed to her natural impatience. The
threat to industrial women restrained her. She was consulted on

the amendment and had preliminary drafts submitted to her for criticism, but she could not be satisfied that the amendment would not jeopardize protective labor legislation. As a result, she broke with the NWP and became a principal opponent. Kelley argued that a blanket equality law could not bring true equality because men and women had different problems and needs; furthermore, the courts would become jammed with endless litigation, during which time women would suffer. "The cry Equality, Equality, where Nature has created inequality, is as stupid and as deadly as the cry Peace, Peace, where there is no Peace." [4] Mary Anderson mulled the effects of the constitutional amendment for several weeks and concluded that it could not be worded to protect the labor legislation. She told Alice Paul that the amendment would do away with all special legislation. Paul shot back, "It won't do anything of the kind!," and refused to speak to her for a long time.[5]

During 1921 both sides solicited legal opinions on the effect of the amendment. The preponderate conclusion was that the amendment would either nullify or throw open to question all special legislation benefiting women. Despite the fact that the NWP, especially Alice Paul, received this opinion directly, they preferred to believe their own Lawyers Council. William Lewis Draper, dean of Pennsylvania's law school, informed Alice Paul that the amendment would endanger protective laws and said unless a reservation were inserted he would oppose it with all his power. The prominent Washington lawyer, J. H. Ralston, echoed Draper's advice to Paul.[6] In letters to various inquiring women, leading lawyers Conrad H. Syme, Clarence G. Shenton, Jesse C. Adkins, Harold Ickes, William H. Holly, James Garfield, and Senator George Wharton Pepper warned of the adverse effects.[7]

Felix Frankfurter wrote Ethel Smith that he was shocked at the NWP proposal, one to benefit a handful at the expense of the well-being—even the lives—of millions.[8] The very conservative George Sutherland, who later as a Supreme Court justice wrote the majority opinion killing minimum-wage laws for women, said that court interpretation was unpredictable. "The

Supreme Court might take the view that the amendment meant precisely what it said, and that a law which gave unequal advantage to women was as obnoxious to the amendment as one which was unequally to their disadvantage." [9] Sutherland later demonstrated that one needed only the Nineteenth Amendment to kill women's labor laws. Philadelphia lawyer Francis Fisher Kane said, "I am of the opinion that if the Woman's Party Amendment were adopted, the existing state statutes regulating the employment of women *should* be declared unconstitutional, and I am absolutely sure that the Supreme Court will so decide." [10] Roscoe Pound, dean of Harvard Law School, and Professor Ernest Freund of Chicago Law School both voiced their objections and warnings. Washington lawyer Dean Acheson wrote in September, 1921, that experiences with the courts showed that they tended to be restrictive in their interpretation. "Surely by this time we should have learned that in removing anachronisms from the law we must name them, book and page, and not furnish the courts with undefined powers for nullifying legislation." [11]

Various women's organizations wrestled with the NWP proposal and tried to work with the NWP to get suitable wording for the amendment. First drafts exempted protective legislation; but when a protective clause could not be drawn to suit everyone, the NWP said that it was not necessary anyway.

The Women's Trade Union League particularly tried to settle the question in 1921. The NWTUL and NWP had no quarrel until the equal rights issue. Maud Younger, NWP treasurer, had helped with the eight-hour law for women in California, and grateful waitresses had made her an honorary member of their union. Josephine Casey had been a union organizer before 1920, and Alice Paul had been a WTUL member before she became completely absorbed in the suffrage fight. Cornelia Bryce Pinchot, NWTUL's Finance Committee chairman, tried to induce Paul to join her committee in late 1920: "I believe that your spirit and interest and point of view would be immensely valuable to the whole Trade Union League movement." [12] Rose Schneiderman, president of the New York branch of the

WTUL, learned first of the NWP's idea from a friend in the Woman's Party. Margaret Dreier Robins, Elizabeth Christman, and Ethel Smith had a long conference with Maud Younger about the amendment, and the NWTUL participated in the final attempt at compromise on December 4, 1921. Ethel Smith (NWTUL), Florence Kelley (NCL), and Maud Wood Park (NLWV), and representatives of the General Federation of Women's Clubs and YWCA met with Alice Paul and two others for several hours, but compromise failed. Now the NWP reversed itself, admitted that the amendment would eliminate protective laws, and said that the laws were holding back women and limiting their opportunities.

One factor which helped shape the NWP's ideas about equal rights laws and constitutional amendments was the Wisconsin Equal Rights Law of 1921. Its unsolicited appearance caused the NWP to think that the time was right for a broad push for such laws. The Wisconsin law grew out of a general desire to clarify women's rights after the Nineteenth Amendment and from politicians' hopes of capturing the women's vote. Governor John J. Blair had been elected on a platform promising equality. Introduced in May, 1921, the bill granted equality in all matters and ordered the courts and executive officers to construe the state laws to include women, "unless such construction will deny to females the special protection and privileges they now enjoy for the general welfare." [13]

Nationally, the question of equal rights was in flux; in Wisconsin the bill received wide support. Mabel Putnam, chairman of the Wisconsin branch of the NWP, admitted that the Woman's Party was powerless alone to secure passage of the law, so it lined up other groups: the DAR, Polish Housewives League, Wisconsin Women's Progressive Association, Wisconsin Consumers' League, YWCA, State Association of Catholic Women's Clubs, and various elements of the Wisconsin League of Women Voters.[14] The state LWV testified for the bill, but later the president of the Milwaukee LWV wrote each legislator saying that the league wanted only jury service, none of the rest. "Our position is that jury service is closely associated with vot-

ing citizenship, while neither women nor the public generally
may be ready for the other provisions. . . ." Her statement was
disputed by the state LWV vice-president, who endorsed the
full bill.[15]

Alexander Matheson led the legislative opposition in denouncing the bill as a threat to the home. "Our civilization is tottering
and crumbling and I think we should go slow in passing this
kind of legislation. This bill will result in coarsening the fibre of
women—it takes her out of her proper sphere."[16] His prediction
of doom, however, did not stop the bill, and Governor Blaine
signed it in July, 1921. Between 1921 and 1933 the Wisconsin
Supreme Court sustained the equality of women under the law
in six test cases. Conservative lawyers repeatedly attacked the
law, predicting the shattering of the social order and serious dis-
turbances of the family relationship. The courts rejected such
contentions. "It is only when the ideal family relation has for
some reasons been disrupted that rights under the statute are
asserted."[17]

None of the women was totally satisfied with the law and all
watched it closely. The Wisconsin State Federation of Women's
Clubs created a committee to study the effect and included representatives of the Association of University Women, WCTU,
League of Women Voters, Woman's Party, Women's Trade
Union League, Consumers' League, Council of Jewish Women,
and State Conference of Social Workers. They found that the
law clearly prevented abuses; for example, in September, 1921,
when an unemployment crisis hit Milwaukee, the Civil Service
Commission proposed a rule limiting the employment of married
women by excluding them from examinations and dismissing
them from the service. The city attorney general ruled that it
was illegal. Likewise, feminists worked hard to get policewomen
on the Milwaukee force, only to be told that married women
were barred. The equal rights law eliminated those discriminations. Contrary to fears, the courts were not jammed with suits
demanding interpretation. The committee concluded that "the
law had worked for a greater degree of justice and greater

equality of women with men than they had before the passage of the law." [18]

While social feminists felt that the protective clause was the saving grace in a vague law that threatened special legislation, the NWP saw the clause as the flaw. The relationship between the NWP and the rest deteriorated in 1921 and 1922 to the point where social feminists would not accept blanket laws even with a protective clause, and the NWP rejected such clauses altogether. The Wisconsin example was not assurance enough. Finally, the Wisconsin attorney general ruled in 1923 that the equal rights law did not affect a 1905 law excluding women as legislative employees. "I base this conclusion on the fact that employment in legislative service necessitates work during very long and often unseasonable hours. . . ." [19] The Woman's Party denounced this as sabotage and cited this ruling as proof that protective legislation really protected men by excluding women or hurting their bargaining position. The passage of the Wisconsin bill encouraged the NWP to press for such bills in many states, but cooperation with social feminists ended on the question of protective legislation. The Wisconsin law was the only such blanket law ever passed in the nation.

The NWP's position on protective legislation outwardly underwent a pronounced shift from 1921 to 1923. Originally, the Women's Party argued that an amendment would not endanger such legislation or that the amendment would force the extension of the protection to men. Next the party maintained that the laws protecting women were a form of reverse discrimination. Either a law should apply to both men and women or not exist. Special laws were said to hinder women's employment opportunities, abolish jobs for women, and protect men in their positions. Rheta Childe Dorr charged that 150,000 women lost their jobs in New York alone as a result of the laws; Mary Murray scaled the figure down to 50,000 when testifying before the Senate Judiciary Committee.[20] (A Women's Bureau survey found the numbers to be 149 ticket sellers and eight printers!) When the U.S. Supreme Court handed down the *Adkins* vs. *Children's Hospital* decision in 1923, declaring the minimum wage to be unconstitutional, the NWP hailed it as a great triumph for equal rights, while all the social feminists were horrified.

Opposition to the NWP proposals became firm in most circles in 1922. In April, 1921, the NLWV voted to study the desirability of a blanket amendment, but came down against it in the 1922 convention. The NLWV tended to follow the Women's Trade Union League, partly because Margaret Dreier Robins, NWTUL president, was the NLWV Women in Industry chairman. After the conference with the NWP failed in December, 1921, the National Consumers' League voted its opposition; and in the next year the NWTUL, American Association of University Women, YWCA, General Federation of Women's Clubs, and others voted to oppose the equal rights amendment and blanket laws. The only major organization which did not forthrightly oppose was the National Federation of Business and Professional Women's Clubs. The question of protective legislation was vigorously debated in their 1920 and 1921 conventions, and they took a neutral position. They resolved to endorse neither inclusive resolutions on protective legislation nor blanket equal rights. The clubs were to deal with each proposal in light of place and circumstances. In short, the NFBPWC allowed each state federation to do what it wanted on the question; and some state federations opposed protective legislation from the beginning.

The National Women's Trade Union League took the lead in organizing opposition to the activities of the NWP. They called a conference which met in Washington on February 26, 1922. Fifty trade union women and delegates from the Consumers' League, NLWV, and American Home Economics Association discussed the question and declared, "We distinguish between 'equal rights' in theory and equal rights in fact. . . ." They maintained that all the present labor laws for women would be jeopardized and the courts would be filled with challenges and clarifications, during which time women would be deprived of legal protection. "It is impossible, lawyers tell us, to determine the far-reaching and possibly disastrous effect of the proposed amendment." The conference concluded by unanimously opposing the blanket equal rights approach, even with a safeguarding clause such as in the Wisconsin equal rights law.[21] In the meantime the NWTUL worked with the NCL and NLWV to stop equal rights laws, killing them in five states, preventing introduction in two, and securing an investigating commission in two more.[22]

Stopping blanket equal rights laws and being stopped in turn on protective legislation became a regular occurrence in the 1920s. The two sides inflicted losses by balancing each other in legislative hearings all over the country. The NWP frequently appeared as the chief supporter of the manufacturers' associations' position on labor legislation and thwarted the effort of the other groups to win new protections for working women. The NAM recognized the value of the NWP in defeating labor legislation and endorsed the equal rights amendment in 1923. Mary Anderson felt that the equal rights amendment was a time-consuming controversy which wasted efforts more profitably given to other attempts to improve women's status.[23] In fact, it was more than a waste of time, it was destructive.

The NWP announced formally in November, 1922, its intention to work for a federal amendment, a women's "Fourteenth Amendment"—to give full citizenship and full equality. The final draft was approved at Seneca Falls in July, 1923, on the seventy-fifth anniversary of the Seneca Falls Equal Rights Convention of 1848. Invoking the shades of the earlier leaders of the women's rights movement, the NWP called its amendment the "Lucretia Mott Amendment": "Men and women shall have equal rights throughout the United States and every place subject to its jurisdiction." On December 10, 1923, the nephew of Susan B. Anthony, Congressman Daniel Anthony, introduced the amendment in the House of Representatives; and three days later Senator Charles Curtis, Republican whip and later Hoover's Vice-President, submitted it to the Senate. The Women's Joint Congressional Committee girded for this event by forming a subcommittee to oppose the amendment in Congress.

In the 1920s hardly a group of women could meet for any purpose without the NWP interjecting its program. This was true at home and abroad. At the convention of the International League for Peace and Freedom in 1924 Alice Paul and Doris Stevens so successfully marshaled support that Jane Addams had to call in Mary Anderson and Alice Hamilton to state the case for protective legislation and the necessity for each nation to work out its own course of action.[24] The principal disruptions at the meetings of the Interparliamentary Union in 1925 and the Congresses of the International Suffrage Alliance in 1923 and 1926 were caused by the NWP.[25] The NWP succeeded with foreign delegations because many nations had more advanced labor legislation regulating conditions of both men and women and constitutions including declarations of equal rights. Between 1919 and 1922 seven European nations adopted such clauses in their constitutions. On the other hand, constitutional interpretation in the United States was backward and only legislation protecting women had any chance of standing. An equal rights amendment would have had unfortunate consequences not affecting the more advanced European nations, but the NWP ignored that fact in its appeal for equality.

Being past masters of publicity, the NWP grabbed the spotlight at nearly every meeting. The Women's Bureau summoned the First Conference on Women in Industry to meet in Washington January 11–13, 1923, to discuss problems of industrial women. Yet the headlines were grabbed by the principal disruption—the attempt of the NWP to use the occasion as a forum for the discussion of the equal rights amendment. The Second Conference on Women in Industry, called for January 18–21, 1926, was all but wrecked by the Woman's Party. When the invitations were sent out, Mabel Vernon, executive secretary of the NWP, asked that one session be devoted to equal rights; but Mary Anderson told her that the program had already been made up. The NWP seized the publicity initiative by holding a rally and sending a delegation to see Coolidge two days before the conference opened, conveying the impression that their activities were part of the Women's Bureau conference. News releases featured the NWP delegates, especially the two ex–trade union organizers and a union president.

The president of the National Association of Manufacturers made the principal headlines on the first day by denouncing legislative interference in industry—with only the NWP members applauding. He charged that women were dupes of the communists on the child labor amendment and that the Children's Bureau was advancing the communist work of a mysterious Soviet bureaucrat named Madame Kollontai.

The NWP threw the conference into a deliberate uproar the second day. Gail Laughlin gained the floor and moved that the third morning's session be given over to a discussion of equal rights. A tremendous tumult followed which lasted for an hour. Laughlin's motion was greeted with hisses, boos, and some shouts of disapproval. All of the dozen NWP members leaped to their feet demanding recognition, supposedly to make short seconding speeches. However, Mabel Vernon went around exhorting them to "get up and yell—you've got good lungs!" The rest of the delegates responded with more shouts and boos. Mary Anderson pounded the gavel to no avail. Rather than call the police or expel the Woman's Party delegates, which would have got them maximum publicity, she let the tumult blow itself out. Near the end Anita Pollitzer of the NWP rushed over to the press table and asked, "Have we done enough to get into the papers? If we have, we'll stop." [26] Finally a vote was taken on Laughlin's motion, and it lost by a huge, angry majority.

The following day the NWTUL proposed an extra night session to discuss the problem with strict rules of debate. The special session was chaired by Ella Boole, WCTU national chairman, and a lively debate was held. The next morning the NWP offered a resolution prohibiting the Women's Bureau from taking any position on protective legislation while the issue was pending in Congress or the state legislatures. This motion provoked a flock of counter resolutions and more angry words until the AAUW representative offered a compromise resolution calling for an investigation by the Women's Bureau into the effects of protective legislation. Yet the great majority resented even this motion, and it would have failed if Mary Anderson had not appealed for its passage from the chair. Dissatisfaction can be gauged by the fact that only one-third of those present voted.[27]

The disruptive tactics backfired on the NWP. Although they considered their efforts successful, in fact the turmoil astonished the uncommitted and solidified opposition against the equal rights amendment. Many at the conference first felt that the NWP ought to be given a hearing but were so incensed by the tactics that they emerged solid opponents. One woman wrote Mary Anderson, "If I had not seen them with my own eyes and heard them with my own ears, no one could have ever made me believe there could be such a diabolical group of women." [28]

The NWP tried to use the investigation as a propaganda vehicle but only caused a complete breakup of the Advisory Committee. On the Advisory Committee were Sara Conboy (AFL), Maud Wood Park (NLWV), Mabel Leslie (NWTUL), and three NWP women, Alice Paul, Maud Younger, and Doris Stevens. In addition the committee was assisted by a Technical Consulting Committee composed of Mary Van Kleeck of the Russell Sage Foundation, Dr. Charles P. Neill, Theodore Roosevelt's Commissioner of Labor, and Lillian Gilbreth, a well-known engineer. The NWP wanted open hearings and calling of witnesses; the rest wanted to use the standard techniques of fact-gathering and the Women's Bureau statistical methods. The Technical Consulting Committee was emphatic in arguing that hearings in advance of investigation by trained investigators would be useless. Open hearings would produce nothing but testimony against protective legislation because working women who favored protective legislation would not testify for fear of losing their jobs. In previous public hearings in New York and Illinois employers paid the way of women to testify against hours laws.

The NWP resorted to coercion by pressuring the chairmen of the House and Senate appropriation committees, other members of Congress, and the Secretary of Labor to force the Women's Bureau to hold open hearings. Mary Anderson refused to budge; and in May, 1926, the non-NWP members of the Advisory Committee reported to Anderson that they refused to meet any longer with the NWP representatives. Anderson dissolved the committee and proceeded with the investigation. It became the most expensive, extensive, and important investigation conducted by the Women's Bureau in the entire period. It used nearly the entire staff of the bureau and two years' appropriations.[29] It covered eleven states, 1,661 factories, and 665,561 women.

When the results were published in 1928 the major conclusion was that "labor legislation was not a handicap to women . . . it did not reduce their opportunities, and . . . it raised standards not only for women but for thousands of men too." [30] The wage minimum never became the maximum; on the contrary, workers covered by minimum-wage laws received higher pay than those not covered. Limiting women's hours was the one means of equalizing the position of men and women, and women were not handicapped by hours laws because men's hours were shortened also. Far from being displaced, the states with the most advanced laws seemed to have the greatest opportunities for women to work. Instead of reducing the number of jobs, the reverse seemed to be true. In the final analysis, women's job opportunities did not depend upon legal regulation of the conditions of employment, but upon the employer's idea of what were "women's jobs." Most significantly, the bureau found that the laws usually enforced upon the entire industry what the most advanced elements were already doing; in short, the laws tended to protect the most progressive tendencies in American business.

Another conclusion was that laws needed to be drafted carefully to prevent unnecessary hardships. Only in scattered instances were women dismissed as a direct result of protective laws. Most controversial were the night-work regulations, but the bureau found that while a few women lost positions, daytime opportunities greatly increased. Where the law was unfair, as in the case of the printers in New York in 1919, the law soon exempted them. The most celebrated and misunderstood instance was the dismissal of the streetcar conductors and ticket sellers in 1919. The Brooklyn Rapid Transit Company simply dismissed all women working at night and blamed the law, but the B.R.T. intended to dismiss them anyway since the war was over. These women formed the Equal Opportunity League to oppose all protective laws. The report felt that laws prohibiting women from certain occupations were unfair unless special hazards existed for women. It supported prohibition of women from the lead industries because Alice Hamilton's research indicated that women were more susceptible to lead poisoning, but the bureau opposed the barring of women from driving taxis (Ohio did so until the Ohio Supreme Court declared the law unconstitutional) or from buffing, polishing, grinding jobs, welding, and gas and electric meter reading.

The report effectively countered the NWP's factual arguments about protective legislation. All they had left was the ideological conviction that such laws promoted a sense of inferiority among women. They continued to insist that protective laws must apply to men or not exist: "Women fought for equal rights. . . . Special privileges do not plumb well with equal rights."[31] The report capped the NWP's domestic problems. Their attempts to influence either of the major parties in the decade had failed, their effort to create a women's bloc like the farm bloc had failed, their "woman for Congress" campaign got nowhere, and their amendment never got beyond committee hearings.[32] By the late 1920s the NWP had been checked domestically; therefore they attempted to change U.S. law by international treaties and conventions.

II

The Fifth Pan-American Conference, meeting in Santiago in 1923, voted to include the discussion of women's rights on the agenda of the Sixth Conference for Havana in 1928. When the Sixth Conference met, no women were in the American delegation headed by Charles Evans Hughes; and the resolution of the Fifth Conference was ignored until the NWP dispatched four women to Havana. They demanded a hearing; but the conference politely refused, saying that women had never spoken before an international congress and a precedent could not be set now. The women employed well-tested techniques and got their hearing. They focused attention on their demands by cornering delegates, holding mass rallies, presenting petitions, and giving numerous press interviews. They got several delegations to pledge support for an equal rights treaty. The women wanted the conference to negotiate a treaty declaring that "men and women shall be equal before the law." When a committee of jurists submitted a draft treaty with fifty-three articles relating to the civil status of women, the NWP denounced it as inadequate and piecemeal. Jane Norma Smith declared that an attempt not providing full equality "would leave women at the end of another century still struggling for their equal rights in every country." [33] Rather than write such a treaty, the conference unanimously voted to create the Inter-American Commission of Women to study women's conditions and make recommendations to the Seventh Pan-American Conference in 1933 at Montevideo. The NWP scored a double coup by forcing this concession and having a NWP member, Doris Stevens, appointed as chairman.[34]

The first investigation undertaken by the Inter-American Commission of Women was a study of nationality. Doris Stevens decided this because nationality was on the agenda of the First World Conference for Codification of International Law to be held at The Hague in March, 1930. The nationality committee created by the Inter-American Commission was nearly a Woman's Party affair: Alice Paul, chairman, Elizabeth Selden Rogers, Emma Wold, Muna Lee, Maud Bradbury, Laura Berrien—all NWP members, plus two women from other countries. This committee submitted a draft which read, "The contracting parties agree that from the going into effect of this treaty, there shall be no distinction based on sex in their law and practice relating to nationality." [35] The Inter-American Commission unanimously approved it on February 20, 1930. Doris Stevens presented the treaty draft to the Hague conference, which rejected it.

All American women were in agreement on independent citizenship, and equal nationality was the American position at the Hague conference. President Hoover came under heavy pressure from feminists and Congress to stand firm; consequently, the United States cast the only negative vote on the nationality convention, which passed 40–1. America's position was the most advanced; and although defeated, feminists were immensely proud. "There is something magnificent, something quite altogether overwhelming, in belonging to the only country on the planet that dared to stand up among the nations at The Hague and demand equal nationality rights for men and women." [36]

The NWP's influence extended to the Seventh Pan-American Conference in 1933. It scored another coup when the conference adopted a treaty guaranteeing equal nationality for women and recommending equal civil and political rights as soon as possible. Doris Stevens was again the leading figure in this effort. The U.S. delegation, in an apparent reversal of the stand taken at The Hague, announced that it would not sign the treaty. Congressional opinion was outraged and besieged President Roosevelt to order the signing. The NWP charged that Eleanor Roosevelt, who was a social feminist and close ally of the Women's Trade Union League and NLWV, had influenced the American stance and that President Roosevelt had put Sophonisba Breckinridge in the delegation in order to defeat equal rights. These charges were greatly oversimplified, if not completely false. Breckinridge was extremely prickly about discriminations against women, but she favored protective industrial legislation. Roosevelt ordered the delegation to sign the treaty. Breckinridge voted against the equal rights provisions, signed the document, and urged the U.S. Senate to ratify it anyway. In this position she found herself at odds with the League of Women Voters. The NLWV argued that the Montevideo treaty was a meaningless declaration. They had supported equal nationality at the Hague conference in 1930 because that treaty had the force of law, but the Montevideo treaty of 1933 was only advisory. Both Breckinridge and the NLWV agreed that fulfillment of the declarations entailed specific legislation. Breckinridge feared that U.S. rejection of the treaty would be misunderstood in the hemisphere, but the NLWV feared that acceptance of rhetoric would hinder the actual elimination of discrimination.[37] The treaty was ratified by the Senate in May, 1934; and nothing for women resulted from it.

As the equal rights amendment was mired in congressional committees, the NWP sought to win their proposal by getting it inserted in a treaty and ratified by Congress. NWP lawyers believed that such approval would have the force of law within the nation and would save them the more difficult process of amending the Constitution. While never ceasing to agitate for an amendment, the NWP pursued the treaty alternative through the basic charters of the United Nations.

III

In the latter part of the 1920s the isolation of the NWP from *all* other women's organizations began to end. The NWP and the strongly social feminist groups remained as far apart as ever, but domestic circumstances began drawing business and professional women to the equal rights amendment. From a position of early neutrality on the issue of protective legislation, business and professional women moved increasingly to oppose such laws. Class considerations entered because these women came to identify with management's view of industrial and labor questions. They saw industrial women as workers, not women. Moreover, they believed that the modest progress being made by business and professional women was being hindered by the protective laws. They came to feel in the late 1920s that their gains and position had not matched earlier expectations, and many felt threatened by legislation which sought to prevent the exploitation of industrial women.

The impact of protective legislation on business and professional women was not wholly theoretical. Unfortunately, the categories of industrial and business women overlapped, especially in "mercantile" establishments. In the view of the NCL, NWTUL, NLWV, and others, women who worked in department stores were women in industry. Exploitation of store clerks had been one of the issues which produced the Consumers' League. The business women viewed these same women as business women, potential executives, and managers. Hence, a law to limit the hours of clerks would be seen as a victory by the NCL and a hindrance by the business women. In addition, some of the prohibitions put on women were unfair, for example Ohio's rule against women driving taxis, and regulations elsewhere forbidding women from reading gas and electric meters, welding, buffing, polishing, and grinding. Finally, some of the laws were so loosely drawn as to jeopardize business and professional women. Such women usually had no need for such protection and correctly resented attempts to restrict them. However, they tended to overreact and oppose all protective legislation.

An early example of the conflict came in New York, where the main support for the Equal Opportunity League's opposition to protective laws came from a number of professional and semi-professional women's groups: Women's Press Club, Women's Medical Association, Women Lawyers' Association, New York State Federation of Women's Clubs, Women's Real Estate Association, Federation of Women Dentists. They vigorously opposed the efforts of the New York LWV, Consumers' League, and WTUL to win more protection for industrial women even though the laws did not apply to them.

A woman journalist attacked the New York WTUL for adopting the "typical anti-suffrage, anti-feminist attitude" by supporting protective legislation. "But why should you, who are self-supporting women stand back of a law which will so hobble and blindfold us that no man will give us any job that cannot be held by the cheapest of clock-watchers?" [38] Margaret Dreier Robins replied by noting that professional newspaper women were not covered by the laws. The WTUL worked for legislation because industrial women demanded and needed it. [39] Rose Schneiderman echoed the point that professional women were not included in the laws. While professional women fought for entrance to the professions, women had always worked in the factories. Their problem was exploitation, not exclusion.[40]

The issue of protective laws was a serious matter within the National Federation of Business and Professional Women's Clubs, whose membership had mixed feelings about it. The 1920 convention revealed the division. Merica Hoagland of Indiana addressed the convention and urged an end to any labor legislation which recognized a difference between sexes. The protectionists, led by Mary Stewart, chairman of the federation's Legislative Committee, rejoined vigorously, and the debate lasted three days. Stewart's committee proposed a resolution endorsing protective legislation; however, the convention adopted a substitute. It declared that the federation earnestly favored shorter hours and better conditions, but "this Federation stands for the principle of equality of rights and special opportunities for none. This Federation stands for the principle that legislation limiting the hours of labor and determining industrial conditions be framed on the basis of conditions . . . not along the lines of sex." [41] The anti-protectionists won a victory when Hoagland was appointed chairman of the federation's Industrial Relations Committee.

The 1921 NFBPWC convention wrestled with the issue again, and adopted a neutral position. The convention resolved against supporting any blanket resolution on protective legislation or equal rights. Instead, the federation would consider each proposal in the light of its time and place, and each state federation was free to do as it pleased. This compromise lasted until 1926, when the Woman's Party contingent moved to have the NFBPWC oppose all special legislation. After extended debate, the convention put the question on the study program for a year. Mary Stewart and the social feminist element of the NFBPWC were able to have the federation return to its earlier neutrality at the 1927 convention. However, after 1927 the anti-protectionist sentiment gradually overpowered the social feminist spirit, and the NFBPWC eventually endorsed the equal rights amendment in 1937. The adoption of the amendment by the National Federation brought it into harmony with the position taken by some of the state federations much earlier.

The Indiana FBPWC actively opposed industrial legislation as early as 1920. It had fought attempts, led by the Indiana League of Women Voters, to pass an hours law for the state. The Indiana FBPWC informally allied itself with the Indiana Manufacturers Association, reprinting articles and editorials from the manufacturers' organs and from the NWP's *Equal Rights*. The bill supported by the Indiana LWV in 1920 and 1921 was framed in such a way that it would apply to white-collar women in industrial and commercial establishments; therefore business women had good reason to believe that the law would interfere with them. In 1920 and 1921 the social feminist effort to secure an hours bill was led by Adah Bush, who was state secretary of the League of Women Voters and personal secretary to the state governor. She secured the governor's support for the measure, but still it died in the Indiana Assembly after passing the Senate.[42] The Indiana federation reported to the 1926 NFBPWC convention that it had helped defeat an hours bill introduced by the Indiana League of Women Voters at every session of the legislature since 1920. In 1928 the Indiana FBPWC secured a long list of business and civic groups who formally protested to the U.S. Secretary of Labor against a proposed Women's Bureau survey of Indiana industrial conditions, and again in 1930 they blocked a Women's Bureau survey which the YWCA had wanted. An Indiana federation spokesman declared, "We feel that the movement for a survey is but a fore runner of the labor department's attempt to obtain an eight-hour day for Indiana women. . . . The eight-hour day may be right for the woman who holds a position temporarily until marriage, but the businesswomen want to be treated in hours and wages on an equal footing with a man." [43] Indiana was one of only five states with no hours law in 1931.

Until 1927 most business and professional women could remain somewhat neutral toward protective legislation because it rarely applied to them. However, an attempt to require an eight-hour day for all women except nurses, housemaids, and cannery workers in California in 1927 began to stimulate opposition among business and professional women. The Women Lawyers' Association, reflecting the influence of an energetic faction of NWP members, had opposed protective legislation since 1923–24; but now it became crusadingly hostile. The editor of the *Women Lawyers' Journal* warned that "similar laws are likely to bob up wherever Legislatures meet in any one of our forty-eight states, only constant vigilance on the part of wage-earning women and organized opposition to all special labor laws for women will prevent their passage." [44]

The California eight-hour law was defeated, in large part because of the opposition of business women. To combat future attempts, the Business Woman's Legislative Council was formed in the winter of 1927–28 and held its first biennial convention in October, 1929. The president of the council was a member of the NWP and secured council endorsement of the equal rights amendment in 1931. The California FBPWC decided upon complete opposition to protective legislation in 1929, as did the Soroptimist and Zonta clubs across the state. In September, 1932, the California FBPWC took the next step and endorsed the equal rights amendment. The Pennsylvania FBPWC came out against protective laws in 1927, and in 1928 the Iowa federation passed resolutions against such laws and presented these resolutions to the Republican and Democratic national conventions. That same year the Illinois federation overwhelmingly rejected special legislation to protect women workers. In 1929 Franklin Roosevelt as governor of New York asked the legislature to pass a forty-eight-hour-week bill which included women in business offices. As a result, the New York FBPWC formed the Business and Professional Women's Legislative Council to oppose the measure and any future protective laws. Although the bill was defeated in 1929, F.D.R. saw it passed in 1931. [45]

With the protectionists trying to include business women within the scope of the special laws, business and professional women moved into opposition to such laws. Not only did an increasing number of state federations reject protective legislation, they endorsed the equal rights amendment. By 1932 the New York City and Brooklyn federations and the state federations of New York, Indiana, Iowa, Minnesota, Vermont, New Hampshire, and California had endorsed the amendment.[46] In 1937 the NFBPWC came over, becoming the first major organization to support the amendment. In the 1930s many of the smaller, more specialized associations accepted the amendment as the answer to women's problems: Osteopathic Women's National Association, Association of American Women Dentists, American Alliance of Civil Service Women, National Women's Real Estate Association, American Society of Women Certified Public Accountants, American Federation of Soroptimist Clubs, National Association of Women Lawyers, Pilot International, and Medical Women's National Association. Through the influence of its president, Mrs. Harvey Wiley, the wife of Dr. Harvey Wiley of pure food and drugs fame, the General Federation of Women's Clubs was won over gradually in the 1930s. One of the original opponents of the equal rights amendment in 1921, the GFWC endorsed the amendment in 1944.

The feminist movement divided into warring factions on the question of how best to continue women's progress after winning the vote. Given the peculiar climate of legal opinion, labor legislation generally meant laws for women to protect them from abuse in the industrial system. Social feminists preferred to pursue this line; however, the National Woman's Party wanted a constitutional amendment guaranteeing equality even though the amendment would destroy labor laws for women. The equal rights amendment became an uncompromisable issue which helped fragment the feminist movement and weaken the progressive impulse. The antagonism between industrial and business women became increasingly open in the decade as protective legislation seemed to encroach on the freedom of business and professional women. Although the NWP utterly failed to advance its amendment in the 1920s, the conflict of interests within feminism brought many new supporters for a sweeping solution in the 1930s.

NOTES

1. Aileen Kraditor has shown that the appeal by advocates of woman suffrage for the vote on the grounds of justice alone (the essential argument of the hard-core feminists) failed; and only as women argued for the vote as a social good (the essential position of the social feminist) did it succeed. See Kraditor, *Ideas of the Woman Suffrage Movement.* While it was certainly true that men had to grant the vote, the argument was mostly aimed at *women.* They had to be won first of all, and not until many women really wanted the vote was it granted. The hard-core feminists convinced precious few women and the woman suffrage movement was generally a failure. It picked up momentum and attracted the best leaders of women as its reform role became clearer. Janet Giele has argued that the reason woman suffrage began supplanting prohibition as the main concern of women at the end of the century was that suffrage arguments were socially inclined and more liberal than temperance arguments, which were individually directed and conservative. She suggested that suffrage was in tune with the progressive tendency which sought to replace the individualistic emphasis in American life with social concern. Another example of this was the Social Gospel critique of evangelical protestantism. See Janet Zollinger Giele, "Social Change in the Feminine Role: A Comparison of Woman's Suffrage and Woman's Temperance, 1870–1920" (Ph.D. thesis, Radcliffe College, 1961). If William O'Neill is correct in saying that the 1920s was a time when people turned again to individual pursuits from social concerns, then it would help explain why more and more women turned from social feminism to the cultivation of their own interests and supported the equal rights amendment as a way to advance themselves. See O'Neill, *Everyone Was Brave,* 307–308.

2. Sinclair, *The Better Half,* 300–303; see also NAWSA, *Proceedings* (1914), 23–26, 82–88; Ida Husted Harper, *History of Woman Suffrage* (New York: National American Woman Suffrage Association, 1922), V, 415–424, 453; James P. Louis, "Sue Shelton and the Woman Suffrage Movement," *Tennessee Historical Quarterly,* XXII (June, 1963), 178–181.

3. Edna Kenton, "The Ladies' Next Step: The Case for the Equal Rights Amendment," *Harper's,* CLIII (Feb., 1926), 370.

4. Florence Kelley, "The New Woman's Party," *Survey,* XLV (Mar. 5, 1921), 827; see also Goldmark, *Impatient Crusader,* 183.

5. Anderson, *Woman at Work,* 161–162.

6. William Lewis Draper to Frieda S. Miller, n.d.; J. H. Ralston to Ethel Smith, Dec. 13, 1921, C. B. Pinchot MSS, box 19, LC.

7. Conrad H. Syme to Ethel Smith, Dec. 22, 1921; Clarence G. Shenton to Frieda Miller, Dec. 19, 1921; Jesse C. Adkins to Florence Kelley, Nov. 12, 1921; Harold Ickes to Agnes Nestor, Dec. 22, 1921; William H. Holly to Nestor, Dec. 21, 1921, *ibid.;* James Garfield to Cornelia Bryce Pinchot, Feb. 6, 1922, *ibid.,* box 22; George Wharton Pepper to Pinchot, Mar. 11, 1922, *ibid.,* box 24. See also Ellerton James to Stockton Raymond, Family Welfare Society of Boston, Jan. 17, 1922; H. C. Fabyan to Family Welfare Society of Boston, Jan. 19, 1922; John R. Lazenby to Ida Mason, Jan. 10, 1922, Charity Organization Society Papers, Community Service Society Archives, New York City.

8. Felix Frankfurter to Ethel Smith, Sept. 8, 1921, NLWV Papers, Ser. II, box 4, Miscellaneous Correspondence folder, LC.

9. George Sutherland to Ethel Smith, Dec. 24, 1921, C. B. Pinchot MSS, box 19, LC.

10. Francis Fisher Kane to Ethel Smith, Jan. 19, 1922, *ibid.*

11. Quoted in Alexander E. Matheson, "The Status of Women under the Equal Rights Law: Discussion of Chapter 529 of the Wisconsin Laws of 1921," *Proceedings of the Bar Association of Wisconsin,* XIV (1922–23), 195; Ernest Freund, "Legislative Problems and Solutions," *American Bar Association Journal,* VII (1921), 658.

12. Cornelia Bryce Pinchot to Alice Paul, Oct. 7, 1920, C. B. Pinchot MSS, box 11, LC; also interview with Alice Paul, July 22, 1965.

13. "Text of Equal Rights Law, Chapter 529, Wisconsin Laws of 1921," NLWV Papers, Ser. II, box 2, Wisconsin file, LC.

14. General letter, "Greetings from Wisconsin," from Mabel R. Putnam, May 10, 1922, Mabel R. Putnam MSS, NYPL.

15. *The Capital Times* (Madison), June 10, 1921; *Milwaukee Leader,* June 14, 1921; and earlier support: *Milwaukee Journal,* May 15, 1921, Mabel R. Putnam MSS, folder 1, SL.

16. *The Capital Times* (Madison), June 10, 1921, Putnam MSS, folder 1, SL.

17. Edwin E. Witte, "History and Purpose of the Wisconsin Equal Rights Law," Dec., 1929; Howard F. Ohm, "History and Purpose of the Wisconsin Equal Rights Law," July, 1938, Putnam MSS, folder 3, SL.

18. "Report of Wisconsin Women's Committee on Study of Chapter 529, Wisconsin Laws of 1921, Women's Equal Rights Law," Sept. 23, 1922, National Women's Trade Union League Papers, box 4, folder 43, SL.

19. Leaflet, "Special Privilege for Women," n.d., Caroline Lexow Babcock MSS, box 3, folder 32, SL.

20. Rheta Childe Dorr, "Should There Be Labor Laws for Women: No," *Good Housekeeping,* LXXXI (Sept., 1925), 164; "Senate Committee Hears Arguments on 'Equal Rights' and Labor Laws," *Life and Labor Bulletin,* VII (Mar., 1929), 2–3; for the NWP position one can find dozens of articles, representative of which see Blatch and Lutz, *Challenging Years,* 278–290, 320–329; Burnita Shelton Matthews, "Special Feature: The Equal Rights Amendment," *Congressional Digest,* III (Mar., 1924), 195–196; Kenton, "The Ladies' Next Step," 370–374; Inez Haynes Irwin, "Equal Rights Amendment: Pro," *Good Housekeeping,* LXXVIII (Mar., 1924), 158–160; Alma Lutz, "Shall Woman's Work Be Regulated by Law?," *Atlantic Monthly,* CXLVI (Sept., 1930), 321–327; Anna Harbottle Whittic, "A Defense of the Blanket Amendment," *Woman Citizen,* IX (June 28, 1924), 17; "Women Ask to Be Protected from Their Friends," *Literary Digest,* LXXXVIII (Feb. 6, 1926), 12.

21. "Declaration Adopted by the Conference of Trade Union Women," Feb. 26, 1922, Harding MSS, box 311, folder 1382-1, OHS.

22. NWTUL, *Proceedings* (1922), 57.

23. Anderson, *Woman at Work,* 172; see also Chambers, *Seedtime of Reform,* 78–79. Rose Schneiderman said of the NWTUL's effort, "Of course, we had the backing of the labor movement and a number of women's civic organizations, but we did the work. There were endless debates and hearings in Congress year after year. . . . Finally we grew tired of wasting our time at these debates and refused to meet with them any more." *All for One,* 126.

24. Mary Anderson to Margaret Dreier Robins, May 8, 1924, Anderson MSS, box 2, folder 8, SL.

25. Mary Anderson to Marjorie Corbett Ashby, Oct. 15, 1925, *ibid.,* folder 17; Martha Mundt to Anderson, June 30, 1926, *ibid.,* folder 18; Anderson to Mundt, Sept. 24, 1926, *ibid.;* "Women's Congress against Women's Parties," *Ladies Home Journal,* XL (Aug., 1923), 25; "Equal Rights before the IWSA,"

Equal Rights, XII (June 12, 1926), 141; Cornelia Stratton Parker, "feminists and Feminists," *Survey,* LVI (Aug. 1, 1926), 502–505.

26. "Second Women's Industrial Conference and the Assaults upon It," *Life and Labor Bulletin,* IV (Feb., 1926), 2.

27. *Ibid.;* see also Anderson, *Woman at Work,* 165–169; Ruby A. Black, "Equal Rights at the Industrial Conference," *Equal Rights,* XXII (Jan. 30, 1926), 402–403; "Trade Union Women Challenge Woman's Party to Debate," *Life and Labor Bulletin,* IV (Feb., 1926), 3–4; O'Neill, *Everyone Was Brave,* 283–285.

28. Olive A. Colton to Mary Anderson, Jan. 23, 1926, Anderson MSS, box 2, folder 18, SL; Anderson to Margaret Dreier Robins, Feb. 4, 1926, *ibid.,* folder 17.

29. Anderson, *Woman at Work,* 169–171; "The Real Issue: A Fact-Finding Investigation, or Woman's Party Propaganda?," *Life and Labor Bulletin,* IV (June, 1926), 1–3; Mary Anderson to Margaret Dreier Robins, May 17, 1926, Anderson MSS, box 2, folder 17, SL; Anderson to Mary Van Kleeck, Jan. 26, 1926, *ibid.,* folder 18.

30. Anderson, *Woman at Work,* 171; see also *Summary: The Effects of Labor Legislation on the Employment Opportunities of Women,* Women's Bureau, U.S. Department of Labor, *Bull. 68* (Washington: Government Printing Office, 1928), 13–22. The benefits of protective legislation were documented again in the 1930s; see Pidgeon, *Women in the Economy of the U.S.A.,* 86–120.

31. Rose Falls Bres, editorial, *Women Lawyers' Journal,* XIV (Oct., 1926), 2.

32. Johnson, "Organized Women and National Legislation," chap. 5.

33. Jane Norma Smith, "For Equal Rights Treaty," *Equal Rights,* XIV (Feb. 25, 1928), 21.

34. Doris Stevens, "Feminist History Was Made at Havana," *ibid.* (Mar. 3, 1928), 29; "Equal Rights at the Pan-American Conference," *ibid.* (Jan. 28, 1928), 403; Muna Lee, "What Women Accomplished at Havana," *ibid.* (Feb. 25, 1928), 21; Lee, "Woman's Place in the Sun," *Independent Woman,* n.s., VII (Oct., 1928), 435–436.

35. Fanny Bunand-Sevastos, "What the Inter-American Commission of Women Has Accomplished," *Congressional Digest,* IX (Nov., 1930), 267.

36. "An Inevitable Corollary," *Equal Rights,* XVI (Apr. 19, 1930), 82; see also Doris Stevens, "America Takes Her Stand among Nations for Equality," *Congressional Digest,* IX (Nov., 1930), 280; Ruby A. Black, "United States Refuses to Accept Unequal Code," *Equal Rights,* XVI (Apr. 19, 1939), 83–85; Laura M. Berrien, "The Campaign of the National Association of Women Lawyers for Equal Rights," *Women Lawyers' Journal,* XVII (Apr.–Oct., 1930), 8–12.

37. Sophonisba Breckinridge to Edith Abbott, Dec. 22, 1933, Breckinridge MSS, box 5, LC; Mabel Denney to Breckinridge, Dec. 30, 1933, *ibid.,* box 16; Breckinridge to Florence Allen, Apr. 9, 1934, *ibid.,* box 4; draft of proposed radio talk, "The Mystery of Montevideo," Jan. 10, 1934, *ibid.,* box 27; see also *New York Times,* Dec. 17–19, 21, 24–25, 1933.

38. Marguerite Mooers Marshall to Editor, *Life and Labor,* X (Mar., 1920), 84.

39. Reply by Margaret Dreier Robins, *ibid.,* 84–87.

40. "Put Yourself in Her Place," *ibid.* (May, 1920), 152–153; see also the same argument in Ethel Smith, "Professional Women, Business Women, Industrial Women: The Common Cause—but Different Needs," *Life and Labor*

Bulletin, VI (Nov., 1928), 1–3, reprinted in *Independent Woman*, n.s., VIII (Feb., 1929), 75.

41. Quoted in "Report of M. E. Hoagland, Chairman, Legislative Committee, Indiana Federation of Business and Professional Women's Clubs," Mar. 26, 1921, Indiana FBPWC Papers, Indiana State Library; see also Elizabeth O. Toombs, "What Business Teaches Women," *Good Housekeeping*, LXXI (Nov., 1920), 197.

42. "Reports of M. E. Hoagland," March 26, 1921, Indiana FBPWC Papers, Indiana State Library.

43. Quoted in "Indiana Women Oppose Labor Legislation," *Equal Rights*, XVI (Apr. 12, 1930), 79.

44. Rose Falls Bres, "Shall There Be Special Restrictive Laws for Women?," *Women Lawyers' Journal*, XV (July, 1927), 4.

45. Business Women's Legislative Council of Southern California FBPWC, Nov. 26, 1928, Jane Norma Smith MSS, folder 229, SL; Jane Norma Smith to Mrs. Nelson Whittemore, Mar. 7, 1931, *ibid.*, folder 77; Smith to Sue Brobst, Mar. 23, 1931, *ibid.;* Brobst to Smith, May 16, 1931, *ibid.;* telegram, Brobst to Smith, May 23, 1931, *ibid.;* Brobst to Smith, June 10, 1931, *ibid.;* resolution of California FBPWC, Sept. 10, 1932, *ibid.*, folder 228. See also "Reporting State Conventions," *Independent Woman*, n.s., VI (July, 1927), 24; "Does Industrial Legislation Concern Business and Professional Women?," *Equal Rights*, XV (June 8, 1929), 143; "New York Defeats 'Welfare Bills,'" *ibid.*, XVI (Apr. 19, 1930), 85–86.

46. Jane Norma Smith to Ada M. Burk, June, 1931, Smith MSS, folder 77, SL.

EIGHT

The Spider Web

As for the Communists, they are
logically letting the Gold Dust Twins,
Feminism and Pacifism do their work. . . .
The pinks are all red sisters under the skin.[1]

Feminist organizations and leaders were battered by charges of being agents or dupes of a Bolshevist conspiracy to conquer the United States. Anti-feminists, extreme conservatives, open-shop advocates, anti-pacifists, and patriotic groups made such accusations against organizations as diverse as the Women's Trade Union League, League of Women Voters, American Association of University Women, YWCA, and Women's Christian Temperance Union. All were denounced as part of a "Spider Web" to promote communist objectives. These accusations originated among opponents of woman suffrage and were picked up and spread by the National Association of Manufacturers and its state affiliates and by the American Medical Association and state medical societies. The efforts of social feminists for peace, infancy and maternity protection, child labor prohibition, and industrial reform generated opponents who used the red smear to defeat the reforms and intimidate the women. Time and energy which might have been devoted to social and industrial measures were expended in rebuttal and defense. The attacks weakened the progressive impulse as distrust and confusion crept into the feminist ranks.

Attacks upon the feminist movement were not new. Before World War I, anti-suffragists had declared, "Polygamy, free love and the disruption of the home are to follow in the wake of woman suffrage. There is no difference between woman suffrage, socialism, and the present feminist movement." [2] During the war, the Anti's charged that suffrage was a pro-German plot; and when the Bolsheviks took over in Russia, suffrage became a Bolshevist device. Anti-suffragists retreated into super-patriotism, and the change of their publication from *Woman's Protest* to *Woman Patriot* in 1918 signaled the transition.

The war produced "100% Americanism" and broad attacks upon civil liberties. During the Red Scare of 1919–20, those who supported trade unionism or pacifism were held to be suspect. Jane Addams was a special target of abuse from super-patriots during the war and Red Scare because she opposed the war and defended the civil liberties of radicals. "It's high time Miss Addams that yourself and all such people were accomodating some ordinary, common, everyday horsesense," wrote one army colonel. "What every one of such malcontents need is not more liberty, but a new set of brains and I would reccommend getting the first nigar you meet to supply you. Give him a hatchet and set him to work. When he finishes the job I venture to say you will be able to reason more correctly altho you may not talk so much." [3] Addams continued to be a favorite target, and one Spider Web chart drawn up in the late 1920s put her at the center. [4]

Although the fever of the Red Scare subsided, the virus lived in the bloodstream of the nation. When the Woman Patriots or the AMA linked the Sheppard-Towner Act with Bolshevism in 1921 and 1922, social feminists considered such charges beneath refutation. But the accusations never ceased. In 1923 *Survey* laughed off the activities of the Woman Patriots, saying that they were making the reactionary position look ridiculous; however, by 1925 *Survey* concluded that red-baiting was the principal reason for the defeat of the child labor amendment. In 1925 the *Woman Citizen* ran a series of articles replying to attackers, and Carrie Chapman Catt wrote several strong articles against the red smear in 1924, 1926, and 1927. *Woman Citizen* recalled that once it was possible for a person to endorse or propose a policy without incurring the charge of subversion, but that in 1926 any liberal attitude was suspect. "The sad part of it is that the gag is accepted"; attacks intimidated people. Maud Wood Park addressed the 1927 convention of the American Association of University Women on the need to refute insinuations, and the major issue at the 1927 meeting of the National Council of Women was the attacks upon women's groups and the U.S. Children's Bureau. In November, 1928, the editor of *Woman's Journal* expressed great weariness at the constant slandering.[5]

Recoiling from the impact of war and revolution, many Americans wanted to disengage from the turmoil of the world or be prepared in case of more trouble. The specter of international communism increased the concern of military preparedness advocates because they feared that the strong urge for disarmament and peace among feminists might strip the United States of its defenses in the face of militant, revolutionary forces loosed by the Bolshevist Revolution. While American women had had substantial ties to an international feminist effort for women's rights and peace before World War I,[6] the period after the war saw these contacts multiplied. The development of international contacts alarmed anti-feminists, extreme nationalists, anti-pacifists, and preparedness proponents. The essence of the Spider Web indictment was that feminist organizations were part of an international conspiracy to promote Bolshevism and to subvert American institutions.

The year of 1919 witnessed the creation of a number of new international links. The Woman's Peace Party, emerging from the war experience, created the Women's International League for Peace and Freedom with Jane Addams as president. The Association of Collegiate Alumnae (soon to be the American Association of University Women) established the International Federation of University Women to promote contacts between college-educated women of the world. The organizational thrust of business and professional women included an international dimension. The women's service club organizations, Zonta,

Altrusa, and Quota, established themselves internationally, even if it only meant that some clubs were in Canada. The National Federation of Business and Professional Women's Clubs, itself founded in 1919, eventually established the International FBPWC. Of a more specialized character was the International Medical Women's Association, which began in December, 1919. The Women's Trade Union League sponsored a conference which created the International Federation of Working Women. However, the NWTUL withdrew in 1923 when the federation voted to affiliate with the Amsterdam-based International Federation of Trade Unions. The American Federation of Labor did not belong to the IFTU; and until it did, neither would the Women's Trade Union League. The Women's Trade Union League was a feminist organization while the IFTU was a class organization.[7] (Later the Woman Patriots charged that the NWTUL was part of the socialist Amsterdam International, "an organization so radical that it has been repeatedly denounced by the American Federation of Labor."[8])

During the 1920s other groups emerged to promote the rights of women and work for world disarmament and peace. The Pan-American Conference of Women in 1921 resulted in the creation of the Pan-American Association for the Advancement of Women with Carrie Chapman Catt as president. As noted earlier, the National Woman's Party secured the creation of the Inter-American Commission on Women at the Sixth Pan-American Conference in 1928. In addition, the Woman's Party extended its reach and founded the World Woman's Party with Mrs. O. H. P. Belmont as president. The considerable concern for peace produced the Women's International Organization, an umbrella association which many other groups joined to coordinate efforts.[9] The Woman Patriots charged that all the international aspects of feminism were actually controlled by the International Secretariat of Communist Women, which was begun by Alexandra Kollontai in Moscow in July, 1920.[10]

The Woman Patriots were the reorganized remnant of the National Association Opposed to Woman Suffrage, and to them Alexandra Kollontai was a demonic figure whose ideas and influence reached around the world and threatened the American Way of Life. The Woman Patriots were extremely concerned as social feminists pressed federal solutions to the problems of women and children. In 1922 the Woman Patriots issued a pamphlet charging that the U.S. Women's Bureau and its allies were trying to Bolshevize America by destroying the family. This destruction would be accomplished by federal legislation for mothers and children. The key people and organizations in this effort were Mary Anderson, Julia Lathrop, Margaret Dreier Robins, Jane Addams, Carrie Chapman Catt, the Women's International League for Peace and Freedom, NWTUL, NLWV, the Women's Bureau, the Children's Bureau, and the principal organ of social feminism, *Woman Citizen*. The Woman Patriots declared that the Women's Bureau had endorsed and was promoting the book and ideas on maternity-benefit systems of the Soviet communist writer Madame Alexandra Kollontai.[11] In fact, the Women's Bureau had listed Kollontai's name once in the bibliography of a 206-page pamphlet about maternity-benefit systems of fourteen nations. Kollontai's book on the Russian system was in Russian only, published in 1916 during the reign of Czar Nicholas II; and a footnote in the pamphlet stated that the book was of "historical interest only."[12] From that single thread the Woman Patriots spun a web of conspiracy.

Attacks caused some suspicion and fragmentation in women's groups even before the great controversy over the child labor amendment developed. Opposition to the Sheppard-Towner Act brought some delegates to the 1921 NLWV convention to claim that the Sheppard-Towner campaign was being supported by the Communist International. The National Council of Women, an all-embracing, loosely associated council of women's organizations, was pressured by its patriotic elements to force the resignation of the American Section of the Women's International League for Peace and Freedom. The WILPF was a particular target of anti-pacifist organizations. R. M. Whitney, a former Associated Press writer and author of *The Reds in America*, said of the 1923 meeting of the WILPF, "The entire conference was dominated by the spirit of Russian Communism, and the words of the speakers left no doubt in the minds of the hearers that Communism—the Third International . . . was the directing force back of the conference." [13]

The National Women's Trade Union League also received much abuse. It had adopted an advanced platform in 1919 which included social security, labor reform, and nationalization of the railroads, telegraph, telephone, and the mines. The Red Scare began a decline for the NWTUL from which it never recovered. Opponents continually charged that the league was part of the communist conspiracy. Documents seized by federal agents in a raid upon a Communist party meeting in Michigan in 1922 revealed that the party hoped to infiltrate and use the NWTUL. The rightist groups took this evidence and proceeded as if what the communists intended to do was already done. *Industrial Progress,* an open-shop organ, characterized the NWTUL as a communist organization in an attack upon social feminist programs for labor reform.[14] The impact of such charges on other women's groups could be seen in the 1923 convention of the National Federation of Business and Professional Women's Clubs. Some members sought to prevent the federation from entering into discussions with the NWTUL on mutual concerns because the NWTUL was supposedly a communist-run organization.[15]

The War Department, with the old anti-suffragist John W. Weeks at the helm, became alarmed at the peace movement, which commanded wide support among women; and beginning in 1921 and 1922, army officers toured the patriotic circuit denouncing disarmament, arms control, international arbitration, and the peace movement in general. They expounded upon the need for universal military training, the Army Reserve, the National Guard, and continued preparedness. Especially vocal was General Amos Fries, head of the Chemical Warfare Service in the War Department. His main target was the National Council for Prevention of War, another of those collections of groups associated to achieve some goal; and many women's organizations were members of the council. The National Civic Federation began attacking the National Council in 1922; and Ralph

Easley, NCF executive secretary, maintained contact with all the patriotic groups and helped incite General Fries.[16] Because of the attacks on the National Council, the Parent-Teachers Association, the General Federation of Women's Clubs, and the Grange withdrew their memberships in 1922.

In December, 1922, General Fries charged that the purpose of the National Council for Prevention of War was to establish communism in America. He repeated this charge in a speech to the Military Order of the World War and singled out Florence V. Watkins, PTA executive secretary, for special notice. He urged those present to work for the removal of Watkins from the PTA. She had remained on the Executive Board of the National Council for Prevention of War even after the PTA had resigned from the council. Fries hoped to remove Watkins from the PTA and eliminate peace from the PTA platform. He told the February, 1923, meeting of the Institute of Government that the council was promulgating socialist and communist doctrines; and he attacked certain organizations by name—PTA, YWCA, WCTU, and the Girls' Friendly Society.[17]

The effort to oust Watkins and eliminate peace from the PTA platform failed. Yet in 1926 a state officer of the South Dakota PTA wrote inquiring if the national PTA really understood who was behind the Sheppard-Towner Act, the child labor amendment, and the bill to create a federal department of education. She supplied the answer: Florence Kelley ("whose real ideas are *red* from start to finish"), Carrie Chapman Catt, Jane Addams ("Hull House is a meeting place for communists"), and Julia Lathrop. She said she wanted to continue PTA work, "but I cannot see my way clear to work for things un-American." [18]

In General Fries's department was Lucia Maxwell, librarian, who compiled a chart tracing an interlocking directorate of women's organizations in America. This Spider Web chart, as it was called, sought to prove that all were tied together in a vast network to disarm the nation and promote a Bolshevist takeover. Appended to the bottom of the chart was a poem entitled "Miss Bolsheviki Comes to Town," clearly spelling out this thesis. After Maxwell compiled the chart, the Chemical Warfare Service printed and distributed it. Virtually the entire web rested upon two key organizations and the person of Florence V. Watkins, who held an executive position in both. One of the two central links in the iniquitous network was the National Council for Prevention of War, with Watkins listed as an Executive Board member. The other key was the Women's Joint Congressional Committee, with Watkins cited as the PTA's representative. She was also a member of the NLWV and the AAUW. Since most of the WJCC members also belonged to the National Council for Prevention of War, the Spider Web chart easily traced the connection between feminism and the peace movement. All were part of the international communist conspiracy.

The WJCC had come under bitter attack from opponents of women's legislation, the child labor amendment, and the department of education bill. All these were said to be communist-inspired, and the WJCC supposedly was under orders from Moscow. The WJCC responded angrily when they learned of the Spider Web chart. They protested so vigorously, threatening reprisals upon the administration from 12,000,000 women, that Secretary of War Weeks ordered all the charts destroyed, including those in circulation. Weeks wrote a weak letter of apology to the WJCC, saying that he regretted that the charts contained errors. He actually approved of the general idea, but the indignation of the women caused him to retreat.[19]

Nearly all of the lines promoted by the opponents of social feminism converged in Henry Ford's *Dearborn Independent* in March, 1924: Whitney's attack on the WILPF, Fries's charges against the PTA and Florence Watkins, the *Woman Patriot's* assertion that the Women's Bureau and Mary Anderson were promoting the aims of Madame Kollontai, and the Spider Web chart of Lucia Maxwell. The *Dearborn Independent* published the Maxwell chart in addition to two articles written by "An American Citizen." This author advanced her own version of the Spider Web and indicted the National Council of Women. The first article charged that the National Council of Women was controlled by select committees under the influence of women who intended to Bolshevize the United States; namely, Florence Watkins, Carrie Chapman Catt, Mary Anderson, Margaret Dreier Robins, Cornelia Bryce Pinchot, and Lucia Ames Mead, a leader in the movement for permanent peace. She warned, "Think of the network of club machinery represented by the National Council of Women and realize that this program, through Miss Anderson's chairmanship permeates the committee work of all the clubs in the United States with this Bolshevik doctrine." The second article detailed the heroic efforts of one Haviland Lund to combat the dark menace of the communist conspiracy in the women's organizations.[20] The author of the heroic saga was later found to be Haviland Lund herself! Most feminists, especially Mary Anderson, believed the *Woman Patriot* to be the source. The editor of the *Woman Patriot*, J. S. Eichelberger, heatedly denied this and revealed that Lund was the author. He dismissed her as "a second-hand dealer in anti-radical material" with a poor memory.[21] Mary Anderson demanded a retraction by the *Dearborn Independent*, asserting that the statements about her were libelous. The editor excused it all by saying that it was unimportant and promised to be fair in the matter. Nevertheless, he printed neither a retraction nor a rebuttal, but instead ran an editorial praising the Spider Web chart.[22]

Although widely denounced by social feminists, the *Dearborn Independent* articles were reprinted in pamphlet form and spread by the Manufacturers Association of Kentucky and the Allied Industries of New York. Some feminists felt that the manufacturers did not really believe the charges but hoped to stop industrial legislation by the smear method. The various versions of the Spider Web continued to appear across the nation. As Senator Thomas A. Bayard fought the Sheppard-Towner Act in 1926, he inserted into the *Congressional Record* the thirty-six-page petition and letter from the Woman Patriots which detailed an interlocking directorate promoting Bolshevism. And he mailed it to all state officers of the DAR. An army colonel told the Sentinels of the Republic that he found women in Kansas organized in a super-organization whose top members were found throughout the country. These key members were invariably communists or socialists.[23] Lilla Day Monroe, editor of *Kansas Woman's Journal*, addressed the Associated Industries of Massachusetts in October, 1925, declaring also that an interlocking directorate of women's organizations was formed for one purpose: "to harass big business, to do the bidding of the communist knave. . . ." Monroe's choice of top spider was Jane Addams. "Miss Addams perhaps comes first, Miss Addams who had Hull House provided for her because she was working under the guise of welfare. . . . She figures in the Lusk report as one of the enemies of our government, and alien enemies were found in Hull House." Other dangerous women spreading the propaganda of Madame Kollontai were Carrie Chapman Catt, Julia Lathrop, and Grace Abbott.[24]

Industrial Progress charged that the First Conference on Women in Industry, called by the U.S. Women's Bureau for January, 1923, was under communist direction and domination. In addition to the usual list of alleged subversives (Mary Anderson, Julia Lathrop, Florence Kelley, and Margaret Dreier Robins), *Industrial Progress* named the social workers Sophonisba Breckinridge, Mary McDowell, and Mary Van Kleeck.[25] At the Second Conference on Women in Industry in January, 1926, John E. Edgerton, president of the National Association of Manufacturers, declared that the economic theories of the women's organizations were Russian in origin and subversive to the American system. He said that these ideas were spread through an interlocking directorate of women's organizations, and the dominant influence on major activities of many groups was exerted by Madame Alexandra Kollontai. Afterwards the NAM reprinted Edgerton's speech in a pamphlet entitled "Protect American Womanhood against Degrading Propaganda" and distributed it over the nation, aiming especially at women's organizations. The NLWV tried to correct the misinformation and distributed rebuttals to Edgerton.[26] In 1926 the NAM created its Woman's Bureau as a means to reach the women's clubs. The NAM had recognized the importance of getting its viewpoint across to the women and the first director of this new

Woman's Bureau concerned herself with rallying opposition to the child labor amendment.

The child labor amendment brought into prominence an extremely conservative organization called the Sentinels of the Republic. It had been organized in 1922 in the New York City home of Charles S. Fairchild, Secretary of the Treasury for Grover Cleveland and president of the American Constitutional League. Louis A. Coolidge, Assistant Secretary of the Treasury for Theodore Roosevelt and treasurer and director of the U.S. Shoe Machine Company, was its first president and named the organization. The Sentinels formed to oppose federal encroachment on states' rights, and they supported efforts to prevent any more amendments like those from the Fourteenth to the Nineteenth. Their principal efforts in the 1920s were to repeal the Sheppard-Towner Act, defeat the child labor amendment, pass the Wadsworth-Garrett amendment to end all amendments, and eliminate "useless bureaus"; namely, the Federal Trade Commission, Home Economics Bureau, Women's Bureau, and Children's Bureau. The Sentinels' greatest source of pride was the defeat of the child labor amendment, as they claimed they had led the fight in Massachusetts and across the country.[27] The Sentinels were a bridge between conservatism and super-patriotism, among them Nicholas Murray Butler (president of Columbia University), Solicitor General James Beck, Senator James Wadsworth, Major General James G. Harbord (president of RCA), Governor Albert Ritchie of Maryland, Senator Henry Cabot Lodge, Leverett Saltonstall, and Sinclair Weeks joining with J. S. Eichelberger, Harriet Frothingham, Nathalie Townsend, and Mary Kilbreth of the Woman Patriots. The Sentinels were associated with conservative and patriotic organizations in the 1920s such as the National Security League, American Constitutional League, Association against the Prohibiton Amendment, American Legion, American Defense Society, and Woman Patriots, and in the 1930s with the American Liberty League.

The failure of the child labor amendment and the plague of Spider Web charts in 1924 and 1925 made social feminists aware of how potent the red smear could be. Because the child labor amendment passed Congress handily and carried endorsements from people as varied as Robert La Follette, Herbert Hoover, Henry Cabot Lodge, and President Harding (in 1922), the proponents were unprepared for the resounding rejection from the states in 1924, 1925, and 1926.[28] The belief that the amendment was communist-inspired was one of the most important factors in its defeat, and the Spider Web charts helped supply the basis of that notion.

Passed by Congress in June, 1924, the amendment was quickly rejected by Louisiana, Georgia, and North Carolina—not unexpectedly. Then came the mortal blow in a massive referendum defeat in Massachusetts in November. The amendment already had a formidable enemy in the NAM, which made defeat a major objective in 1924. The leader in organizing rural opposition was David Clark, editor of the *Southern Textile Bulletin*, who had been instrumental in the overturning of the two federal child labor laws. He created the Farmers' States Rights League and spread editorials, propaganda, and advertisements throughout the rural press. The American Farm Bureau Federation and the Grange came out in opposition to the amendment in 1924.

In Massachusetts the opponents were led by the Associated Industries of Massachusetts, Sentinels of the Republic, Woman Patriots, Massachusetts Public Interests League, and the Constitutional Liberty League. The Associated Industries and the Public Interests League created an *ad hoc* committee called the Citizens Committee to Protect Our Homes and Children with ample financing and propaganda. They charged that the amendment was unnecessary, invaded states' rights, would create a huge centralized bureaucracy, lead to a mass of federal laws covering marriage, divorce, maternity, education, and hours and wages, and prohibit children from doing household chores. The Sentinels claimed that the amendment was the most far-reaching amendment ever proposed: "It seeks to substitute national control, directed from Washington, for local and parental control, to bring about the nationalization of the children, and to make the child the ward of the Nation. It is a highly socialistic measure —an assault against individual liberty." The Citizens Committee echoed this, saying that the purpose of the amendment was to nationalize the children and that nationalization of youth was the keystone in the communist program. An army colonel told a woman's club that the amendment was conceived in the brain of Lenin's mistress. The barrage of propaganda had a telling effect as many changed from approval to opposition.[29] The finish came from the Roman Catholic hierarchy of Massachusetts. William Cardinal O'Connell directed every priest in the archdiocese to warn against the amendment. He believed that the amendment endangered parental control and threatened the parochial school system. Consequently, Boston's Mayor James Curley, Democratic candidate for governor, switched to the opposition after having favored the amendment all summer; and Senator Walsh opposed despite having voted for the amendment in the Senate. The amendment lost at the polls three to one and never recovered.

The Spider Web charts, red-baiting, and attacks took their toll. Social feminism was definitely on the defensive as the child labor amendment was rejected. Internal dissension caused some organizations to defect from the women's coalition and induced caution into the decision-making process of others. The General Federation of Women's Clubs, the largest women's organization in the 1920s, experienced internal stress over the issue. It continued its endorsement of the child labor amendment, but withdrew from the Women's Joint Congressional Committee in 1928. This withdrawal did not satisfy the Women Patriots, who charged that the General Federation was communist-influenced and ought to have its charter revoked.

The National Federation of Business and Professional Women's Clubs found its state federations badly divided on the child labor amendment. The amendment had received an easy endorsement in the 1924 national convention; but after the red smears, re-endorsement in 1925 came only after extended debate. The 1926 convention backed away and submitted the question to the state federations for study, and the 1927 convention passed a weak endorsement which left the question of pushing for ratification of the child labor amendment to the state federations.[30] In addition the National Federation moved to prevent divisive issues from emerging on the national level. It decided that no question could be considered at the convention unless submitted by the National Legislative Committee to the full membership through *Independent Woman* six months prior to any convention. Furthermore, the NFBPWC would not accept any blanket measure, and all future endorsements required a two-thirds majority.[31] The National League of Women Voters also developed a slower process of formulating positions. Belle Sherwin introduced the "consensus method" to the league after she became president. Decision-making was stretched out and made more complex in order to assure maximum solidarity in the league on controversial issues before taking a public stand. A proposal required several trips between national and local levels, taking several years, before it could be adopted as a legislative objective of the NLWV.[32]

Other more specialized professional groups responded in a mixed fashion. The Medical Women's National Association remained steadfast in its support of social legislation for mothers and children. The Medical Women, the American Nurses Association, and the Women's Homeopathic Medical Fraternity joined the Women's Joint Congressional Committee in 1924 and 1925 and worked for the amendment. On the other hand, the National Association of Bank Women simply stopped discussing social issues. From the National Women Lawyers' Association came only exceedingly hostile opinion in the *Women Lawyers' Journal*. Mrs. Charles Martin, past president of the Kansas Women Lawyers' Association and assistant attorney general of Kansas, wrote that every communist and socialist in the nation was behind the child labor amendment; and the current president, Mabel Foltz, declared that the amendment was the antithesis of Americanism. The amendment "ended where it begins, in political jobbery, paternalism and Bolshevism." Lilla Day Monroe, president emeritus of the Kansas Women Lawyers' Association and a member of the Sentinels of the Republic, said that the amendment would nullify the Bill of Rights and change the form of government.[33]

The most extreme case of the loss of a reformist impulse was the Daughters of the American Revolution. The DAR had supported progressive legislation like the Sheppard-Towner Act and endorsed the League of Nations. After 1923 new leadership moved the DAR sharply to the right, opposed the child labor amendment in 1924, repudiated the Sheppard-Towner Act in 1926, undertook a purge of moderates and liberals from the organization, and blacklisted anyone holding a contrary opinion. The DAR circulated a pamphlet entitled "The Common Enemy," which expanded Lucia Maxwell's 1924 Spider Web chart to include ninety organizations allegedly "interlocked with radical groups." Included on the list were the YWCA, YMCA, WCTU, National Association for the Advancement of Colored People, Federal Council of Churches, and U.S. Department of Labor. The leaders of nearly all such organizations were barred from addressing DAR societies. While the DAR did not actually draw up the blacklists (that was done by other groups and individuals), the state and local societies circulated them. Blacklisted individuals included Roscoe Pound, Felix Frankfurter, W. E. B. Du Bois, William Allen White, David Starr Jordan, Rabbi Stephen Wise, Clarence Darrow, Mary Anderson, Jane Addams (who saw her honorary membership in the DAR withdrawn), Julia Lathrop, and Mary E. Woolsey, president of Mount Holyoke College.[34]

William Allen White ridiculed the blacklisting: "The D.A.R. is all right, just foolish leadership and a taste for idle, apoplectic old gentlemen in red flannels who escape boredom of their rich wives by sitting in club windows in Washington and bemoaning the decadence of a growing world." [35] Harry Emerson Fosdick, another blacklisted speaker, called the list an honor roll; and a group of them began the "Nation's Blacklist Committee" and threw a big party in New York. Carrie Chapman Catt did not think it all so funny and unleashed a slashing attack against the DAR and super-patriots. She especially defended the main targets of the DAR: Jane Addams, Florence Kelley, Rose Schneiderman (whom Captain Darte had denounced at the 1927 DAR congress as "the Red Rose of Anarchy"), the Women's

International League for Peace and Freedom, the Children's Bureau, the Sheppard-Towner Act, and the child labor amendment. She charged that the super-patriots were unable to find any Bolshevists; therefore, they turned their fear and hatred on other citizens, charging that those interested in reform were "in reality an army secretly allied to the dread Bolsheviki." These red-hunters, she said, were "irredentist anti-suffragists, groups of the D.A.R. and other patriotic societies, some elderly army and navy men," those opposed to all proposals for peaceful settlements of international disputes, opponents of the child labor amendment and the Sheppard-Towner Act.[36]

Hermine Schwed, field secretary for the National Association for Constitutional Government, shot back at Catt with a pamphlet called "The Strange Case of Mrs. Carrie Chapman Catt." It purported to show that Catt was actually a communist. Schwed asserted that socialism and communism were the same thing; the child labor amendment, the Sheppard-Towner Act, and the education department bill were all of socialist origin, and Catt supported them all. She said that Florence Kelley was the chief promoter of communism in the United States, Jane Addams was aiding the communist cause, and Catt admired them both. Schwed printed parallel columns of communist pronouncements and Catt's writings on a variety of issues showing the likeness. She concluded that while Catt might not belong to the Socialist or Communist party, any fair-minded student could see from the evidence of her associations, ideas, and philosophy that "Mrs. Catt . . . intentionally or otherwise . . . has been a broadcaster for the Communists." [37]

By 1927 and 1928 the social feminist movement had been considerably weakened. With much of its energy being sapped by the endless wrestling with the hard-core feminists and combatting retrogressive court decisions on social legislation, social feminism found itself unable to prevent an erosion of support caused by persistent allegations that their program was communist-inspired and threatened the fabric of the nation and its form of government. While an important source of rightist opposition to social feminism stemmed from the international ties to the peace movement, the attacks were more general. States' rights groups, industrial, commercial, and medical associations joined and used the cry of Bolshevism to discredit and defeat social and labor legislation. The rejection of the child labor amendment was a cardinal example of the effect; and after that setback, the progressive-minded women were on the defensive. The child labor amendment was never ratified, the pace of legislation for working women slowed to a crawl or retreated, and the Sheppard-Towner Act was repealed and lapsed in 1929. While social feminism faced a number of difficulties in the late 1920s, one of the most emotion-charged and persistent problems was its entanglement in the Spider Web controversy.

NOTES

1. "Both Pacifists and Reds: There Is a Bit of Red in Every Pink," *Woman Patriot*, XI (Jan. 15, 1927), 1.

2. Florence Goff Schwarz, "Whom the Gods Would Destroy They First Make Mad," *Woman's Protest*, V (May, 1914), 5.

3. Colonel Charles Mosher to Jane Addams, Feb. 24, 1920, Addams MSS, microfilm reel 5, Swarthmore College Peace Collection.

4. "The Spider-Web," compiled and printed by Charles Norman Fay, [1927], *ibid.*, microfilm reel 8.

5. *Survey*, L (Apr. 15, 1923), 68–69; William L. Chenery, "Child Labor—the New Alignment," *ibid.*, LIII (Jan. 1, 1925), 379–382; "Suspicions and Courage," *Woman Citizen*, X (May, 1926), 21; AAUW, *Proceedings* (1927), 99; "National Council of Women," *Woman's Journal*, XIII (Jan., 1928), 28; "More Red Alarms," *ibid.* (Nov., 1928), 27.

6. The YWCA had been international in scope since 1873, but the American branch of the YWCA was established only in 1906. The International Council of Women was begun by Elizabeth Cady Stanton and Susan B. Anthony in 1888, and its greatest achievement seems to have been the World Congress of Women, which met at the Columbian Exposition in Chicago in 1893. The International Woman Suffrage Alliance was organized in 1905 with Carrie Chapman Catt as president. The Woman's Peace Party participated in the International Congress of Women at The Hague in 1915, where the idea of continuous mediation between the belligerents was advanced.

7. See Boone, *Women's Trade Union League*, 126–132; O'Neill, *Everyone Was Brave*, 242–244.

8. Quoted in Boone, *Women's Trade Union League*, 135.

9. Constituents included the International Alliance of Women for Suffrage and Equal Citizenship, YWCA, WCTU, Women's International League for Peace and Freedom, International Council of Women, International Federation of University Women, and Carrie Chapman Catt's National Conference for the Cause and Cure of War—itself a coalition which contained forty-one organizations by 1934.

10. "Organizing Women for Class and Sex War," *Woman Patriot*, VII

(Apr. 15, 1923), 2-7; see also "The Woman's Party and Communism," *ibid.*, VI (Oct. 1, 1922), 12-13; "The Interlocking Lobby Dictatorship," *ibid.* (Dec. 1, 1922), 1-6.

11. "Organizing Revolution Through Women and Children," pamphlet, 1922, Anderson MSS, box 1, folder 6, SL.

12. Ann Dennis Bursch, "Who Is Madame Kollontai," *Woman Voter's Bulletin*, VI (May, 1926), 5-7; see reprint in Anderson MSS, box 1, folder 6, SL.

13. R. M. Whitney, "Peace at Any Old Price," pamphlet, 1923, 3, Anderson MSS, box 1, folder 6, SL; see also Eva Perry Moore to Hannah Clothier Hull, Dec. 6, 1924, Addams MSS, microfilm reel 9, Swarthmore College Peace Collection; Hull to Moore, Dec. 16, 1924, *ibid.*; Abbott, *History of Woman Suffrage in Cuyahoga County*, 90.

14. "What Is Behind the 'Women's Conference on Industrial Problems'?," *Industrial Progress*, V (Jan., 1923), 43-44; "The Camouflaged Conference of the National Women's Trade Union League," *ibid.*, 44-48.

15. Helen Havener, "The Business Woman Awake," *Independent Woman*, n.s., VII (Mar., 1928), 136.

16. See letters between Ralph Easley and Frederick J. Libby, in addition to numerous letters to Easley about the National Council for Prevention of War, National Civic Federation Papers, box 60, NYPL.

17. *Kansas City Star*, Dec. 17, 1922; *Washington Post*, Feb. 21, 1923; unsigned letter marked "confidential" to Elizabeth H. Tilton, n.d.; Mrs. Arthur C. Watkins to Tilton, Feb. 16, 1923, Tilton MSS, folder 22, SL. Mrs. Fries was part of her husband's problem. At a meeting of the Pen Woman's Club in Washington, a woman gave a talk on the development of music, giving examples of Greek, Roman, German, French, Italian, and closing with some fine selections of Russian music. At the end of the lecture Mrs. Fries rose and said that she was extremely sorry to have been in charge of a meeting "where such Bolshevistic, communistic propaganda had been introduced"; see Watkins to Tilton, Apr. 4, 1923, *ibid.*

18. Letter from Mrs. A. Hoy to National PTA, Dec. 12, 1926, *ibid.*, folder 24.

19. Letter from WJCC to John W. Weeks, Apr. 2, 1924; Weeks to WJCC, Apr. 10, 1924; Maud Wood Park to Weeks, Apr. 22, 1924; Weeks to Park, May 2, 1924, NLWV Papers, Ser. II, box 9, LC.

20. An American Citizen [Haviland Lund], "Are Women's Clubs 'Used' by Bolshevists?," *Dearborn Independent*, XXIV (Mar. 15, 1924), 2; Citizen, "Why Don't Women Investigate Propaganda?," *ibid.* (Mar. 22, 1924), 10; the Spider Web chart was on p. 11.

21. J. S. Eichelberger to Mary Anderson, Apr. 24, 1924; copy of letter from Eichelberger to W. J. Cameron, editor, *Dearborn Independent*, n.d., Anderson MSS, box 1, folder 6, SL.

22. Mary Anderson to W. J. Cameron, Apr. 4, 1924; Cameron to Mrs. Philip North Moore, May 27, 1924; Anderson to Moore, June 13, 1924, Anderson MSS, box 1, folder 6, SL; "The Women—Bless Them," *Dearborn Independent*, XXIV (May 10, 1924), 8.

23. *Congressional Record*, 69th Cong., 1st Sess., LXVII, 12918-52.

24. Lilla Day Monroe, "Big Business—the Great Magician," *Industry* [Associated Industries of Massachusetts], XVI (Oct. 24, 1925), 1-7.

25. "What Is Behind the 'Women's Conference on Industrial Problems'?," *Industrial Progress*, V (Jan., 1923), 43-44; "The Camouflaged Conference of the National Women's Trade Union League," *ibid.*, 44-48.

26. "Propaganda against Our Women's Organizations," *Woman Voter's Bulletin*, VI (May, 1926), 5.

27. Alexander Lincoln to Samuel B. Fisher, Feb. 6, 1929, Alexander Lincoln MSS, folder 3, SL; see also William Whitehead, "The Story of the Sentinels of the Republic," pamphlet, 1936, *ibid.*, folder 5.

28. Richard B. Sherman, "The Rejection of the Child Labor Amendment," *Mid-America*, XLV (Jan., 1963), 3–17; Chambers, *Seedtime of Reform*, 37–43; Trattner, *Crusade for the Children*, 163–180.

29. "The Shame of Massachusetts," *Life and Labor Bulletin*, III (Dec., 1924), 1–2; William L. Chenery, "Child Labor—the New Alignment," *Survey*, LIII (Jan. 1, 1925), 379–382; Catherine Waugh McCullough to Mary McDowell, June 15, 1927, Catherine Waugh McCullough MSS, Dillon Collection, folder 16, SL; Alexander Lincoln to Mr. Gilke, Sept. 12, 1924, Brown MSS, box 3, folder 65, SL; Charles R. Gow to Dr. and Mrs. Day, Oct. 8, 1924, *ibid.*, box 2, folder 55; Michael H. Sullivan to Dorothy Kirchwey Brown, Sept. 3, 1924; F. B. Towne to Brown, Sept. 2, 1924; Professor Bliss Perry to Brown, Sept. 9, 1924; Austin F. Riggs to Caroline E. Wilson, Oct. 16, 1927, *ibid.*, box 3, folder 63.

30. Helen Havener, "The Business Woman Awake," *Independent Woman*, n.s., VII (Apr., 1928), 179–180; (May, 1928), 206–207; (June, 1928), 286–287; (July, 1928), 326.

31. *Ibid.* (July, 1928), 326.

32 See description of the method in *Woman Voter's Bulletin*, VIII (Mar., 1928), 1.

33. "The Child Labor Question," *Women Lawyers' Journal*, XIV (Jan., 1925), 12–17.

34. La Ganke, "National Society of the Daughters of the American Revolution," 167–195, 277–278; *Evening Star* (Washington), Apr. 2, 1928, Anderson MSS, box 1, folder 7, SL; "Blacklists," *Woman's Journal*, XIII (Apr., 1928), 22–23; "Wanted—Another Blacklist," *ibid.* (May, 1928), 22.

35. *Washington Post*, Apr. 3, 1928, Anderson MSS, box 1, folder 7, SL.

36. Carrie Chapman Catt, "An Open Letter to the D.A.R.," *Woman Citizen*, XII (July, 1927), 10–12; Catt, "Lies at Large," *ibid.* (June, 1927), 10–11.

37. Hermine Schwed, "The Strange Case of Mrs. Carrie Chapman Catt," pamphlet, 1927, Catt MSS, biographical file, SL.

NINE

The Ebb Tide of Social Feminism, 1925-33

The rejection of the child labor amendment signaled the end of the flush times of social feminism and the beginning of famine years. From then until the coming of the New Deal, social feminists entered a defensive stage. Instead of being able to count the number of reforms won, they often had to be satisfied with preventing mischief. Because the great promises of the suffrage crusade seemed unfulfilled, the tenth anniversary of enfranchisement found some questioning the utility of the ballot and others urging a new female solidarity. Results had not matched expectations. In spite of harassment from hard-core feminists, discouraging judicial decisions, legislative conservatism, and continued attacks from rightists, many kept the faith and continued to work for political, social, economic, and industrial reform. They helped develop the issues and proposals from which the New Deal would grow.

Anna Howard Shaw predicted in 1919 that the toughest time lay ahead for feminism: "We suffragists have had the easier end of it. More and more women will go into business and as they become individually successful they will forget or become uninterested in the fight for woman's equality as a class." [1] She was partially correct, because business and professional women increasingly became absorbed in a struggle for equality for their particular class. As has been noted earlier, this effort brought these women to oppose the interests of industrial women and their allies. While articles continued to report women's advancement, many women asked, "Why aren't we doing better?" The American Association of University Women and the NFBPWC undertook studies of their membership to learn their status, and the University of Michigan investigated the earnings of business and professional women. The *Annals of the American Academy of Political and Social Science* devoted an entire issue to the condition of women in 1929, and a statistical study of women in "Who's Who" was conducted for *Social Forces*. All the studies revealed gains, but a major conclusion was that women's advance was hampered by continued discrimination.[2]

The *Independent Woman*, the official journal of the NFB-PWC, conducted a debate in its pages from 1927 to 1930 on the issue of who was at fault for the limitation of women's achievement in business. Progress had been made since World War I, but less than expected. Mary Margaret McBride, noted writer and journalist, declared that women were not even viewed as competition by men: "So far the advance of women in business looks so unimportant to man that it wouldn't occur to the average of his species to regard her as a rival. The business world is still a man's realm and his attitude toward the woman who enters it is one of entirely absentminded, usually courteous endurance."[3] Some blamed women. A common refrain was that women do not make good executives, and often women would confess their reluctance to work for another woman. Nevertheless, the great obstacle was discrimination. Women were paid less, had fewer important jobs, and faced discrimination in appointments and promotion. They had to be better prepared and have more unusual qualifications than men to secure the same opportunities. A typical complaint ran, "It's actually necessary for a woman to do half again as much work to attain recognition as a man would have to do to attain the same recognition. Even then she'll earn the same title, but draw only half the salary."[4]

A survey of professions revealed the limitations. Although

women composed the preponderate majority of all teachers, they held subordinate ranks. The higher the position, the fewer the women. In elementary education 80 percent were women, but they held only 4 percent of college professorships. A woman architect declared, "There is no hindrance in the way of a woman's career in architecture." Yet she was the *only* woman architect in the entire city of New York. In 1920 there had been forty-one female engineers; 1930 found 113. Nearly all medical schools now admitted women students, but many hospitals still refused to accept women interns. The *Medical Woman's Journal* in 1929 reflected on the treatment of women physicians since the Great War: "Truth compels us to state that only in isolated instances are individual women doctors being accorded such recognition as this splendid record deserves." The 1930 census revealed what women physicians, surgeons, and dentists had feared: their number declined since 1920, the number of dentists falling nearly 30 percent. The Institute of Women's Professional Relations discounted prejudice as a significant factor in the decline of dentists and concluded that women in the 1920s preferred the easier rewards of business than the difficulties of a profession. In government women received a growing number of appointments, but the vast majority were clerical.[5]

The advent of the Great Depression intensified prejudice against working women, especially married women. While the attack was centered on married women, there was always the lurking presumption that every woman worked for "pin money" and kept a family man out of a job. The effort to remove married women had been constant but low-keyed until the Depression, when it developed considerable force. Assemblyman William Breitenback of New York introduced a bill to tax heavily the income of married women in industrial and professional pursuits. He admitted that the bill was not a revenue measure, but one to drive women from jobs. "This will tend to eliminate unemployment by stopping married women from seeking employment. . . ." The Iowa Federation of Labor in 1930 sought to remove married women from jobs on the grounds they were keeping men from employment. The Baltimore and Ohio Railroad began personnel cutbacks at the expense of married women first; and attempts to pass laws removing married women were made in Massachusetts and Vermont. In Indiana the goal for discharging all married women from public employment was January 1, 1933. Married women were asked to resign from the University of Wyoming. In Cincinnati and Columbus, Ohio, the Depression brought a systematic removal of married women teachers. The National Education Association disclosed that as of January, 1937, of 291 cities investigated 76 percent would not employ married women and 45 percent required their dismissal.[6]

The federal government joined the attack on the right of women to work in passing the Economy Act of 1932. Section 213 required personnel reductions to be made at the expense of persons whose spouses were employed by the government. This procedure was the same as proposed by Senator McCumber in 1921. While the law read "persons," the intent was clear as it was originally worded "married women"; but the House committee changed it. The House passed the section without protest or recorded vote. The Senate objected and twice struck it out, but each time the House conferees reinserted it. Finally, to save the large and important legislative appropriations bill of which it was a part, the Senate agreed. Hoover protested section 213 but signed the measure. When dismissals were made, women left in nearly every case. Since they almost always worked from necessity, these women were forced to search for employment in lower and more crowded occupations. Feminists bitterly protested section 213, and Congressman Emmanuel Celler of New York led the repeal effort to its eventual success in 1937.[7]

The National Recovery Administration of the New Deal permitted lower minimum wages for women in some occupations in about one-fourth of the NRA codes.[8] While feminists fought against this discrimination, many recognized the NRA codes as a step forward in the fight for equal pay since three-quarters of them stipulated equal pay for industrial women. In spite of the attacks on the right of women to work, the number of working

women increased in the 1930s by 2,500,000. Part of this increase
may be attributed to the fact that women usually worked for
lower wages, and the 1940 census reflected growing defense
production. The difficulties helped persuade a growing number
of women to endorse the equal rights amendment as an answer.
Many professional groups, including the NFBPWC, adopted it
in the decade, and even the General Federation of Women's
Clubs, one of the original opponents, endorsed it in 1944.

The sense that expectations had been unmet, the persistent discrimination, and the active attack on the right of women to
work caused various women to urge a new female solidarity.
Anne W. Armstrong, personnel director of the Eastman Kodak
Company, charged that the disloyalty of women to others
hindered women's advancement in the business world. She urged
women to support each other, to help others climb the business
ladder. A crucial problem of professional women was the difficulty of getting clients and establishing a practice. Women were
reluctant to consult a woman physician or lawyer. A leading
woman lawyer attacked this attitude and said that women must
join together to overcome obstacles: "Loyalty to our women
leaders will carry our banner to victory, a victory that will mean
an equal opportunity before the law for both sexes." The new
advocates of feminine solidarity demanded: "Women, Let Us
Be Loyal to Women!" The president of the NFBPWC, Lena
Madeson Phillips, addressing the national convention in 1929,
agreed that women had to unite. In fact, they had to discriminate
in favor of women. "To the detail, the drudgery, the unre-
munerative we are fairly welcome. But the mark of the slave
chain is still in our path." The feminist movement had reached
an impasse. A deadline stretched across every area of life and
only the exceptional could cross it. Feminine unity would help
break the chain and remove the deadline. Inez Philbrick, a
physician in Nebraska, declared that women were superior to
men and that female unity was needed for the sake of progress
and civilization: "Civilization has advanced and will advance just
in proportion as the qualities engendered in women . . . will
be incorporated in human institutions. . . ." She urged bloc

voting and total feminine solidarity in business and the professions. Emily Newell Blair, vice-chairman of the Democratic Committee until 1928, agreed in part with the idea of a woman's political bloc. She felt that the feminist movement had bogged down because it lacked focus and appropriate symbols. She urged that women develop a renewed consciousness of being women. She called for the end of submission and cooperation with male politicians and the beginning of a woman's bloc within each political party. Women must support women before they could have real power.[9]

Blair's concern about the political power of women was part of a general questioning of the impact and worth of woman suffrage. The tenth anniversary of the Nineteenth Amendment focused attention on its effect. Had it really made any difference? Most replied that in terms of leaders and officers it "must be set down as wholly unexciting and largely disappointing." [10] This disappointment stemmed in large part from the fact that advocates had come to invest too much significance and promise in the ballot. Suffrage leaders had argued that it would be an instrument of good. One overly sanguine proponent believed that woman suffrage would eliminate prejudice, bigotry, injustice, and oppression and support freedom of thought, opinion, and speech.[11] Opponents predicted the disruption of the family and the ruin of the nation and civilization. Suffragists had once argued for the franchise as a matter of justice, but this argument won them few converts and contests. Near the end of the century, they began to stress the utility of the vote and the reforms that women could bring with it. In doing this, they overcommitted the suffrage movement. They promised too much in arguing that the country needed woman suffrage.[12]

While the social feminists promoted progressive reform after suffrage, none of the disasters and only some of the good came to pass in the first decade. When a substantial segment of the women failed to vote, the opponents and skeptics concluded that woman suffrage was a failure. *Ladies Home Journal*, in 1923, said that women were being absorbed by the political organizations, which robbed women of their will to serve and reform. Politics was neither better nor worse than before. Another observer said that women sank into the parties without a ripple.[13] As a result, the question arose: "Is woman suffrage a failure?"

Jane Addams answered with a question: "Why don't you ask if suffrage in general is failing?" Alice Paul demanded: "Why not ask if this country is better off because men have voted for the last four years, the last forty years or a hundred years?" Ethel Smith felt that no justification was needed; the vote was a matter of justice. Carrie Chapman Catt rejected the idea that suffrage was failing, arguing that the defects were not in women but of the total society. She felt that no adequate appraisal could be made on the basis of just ten years. Men had been voting for more than a hundred years and the verdict was still not in. The most that could be said in 1930 was that an increasing number of women were voting now and no movement had appeared for repeal of the Nineteenth Amendment such as faced the Eighteenth Amendment. Catt believed that women's influence had increased even though no women's bloc had appeared. "We can not expect miracles. The first ten years have been immensely educational." *Survey* agreed that a firm foundation had been made: "The first decade has been one of primary education; in the next ten years woman may be expected to enter the graduate school." [14]

In a fundamental way, questioning the success of suffrage was a bogus issue. Because feminists directed their efforts at so many problems on so many levels, the contrast with the dramatic single-issue crusade for the vote has caused observers then and now to conclude that social feminism failed and died. Such a view distorts the fact that the concentration and the unity regarding suffrage was abnormal. Social feminism had developed decades before out of local and state issues and always had its principal focus there. Long before masses of women were deeply concerned with suffrage, they were working to make their communities more "homelike." When the great diversion—the suffrage crusade—ended, social feminism tended to resume its previous interests and multiple purposes. No single issue emerged to preserve the false unity of the suffrage question. Because the equal rights amendment threatened to harm a substantial portion of working women, social feminists could not support it. Instead they turned to work for many objectives. Success would have to be measured by hundreds and thousands of little items from 1920 onward.[15]

II

One feminist issue which was resolved in those lean years was the goal of equality of citizenship, but it required a bit of drama to fix the attention of Congress on the defects of the 1922 Cable Act. The Woman's Party and the League of Women Voters called for the elimination of the remaining discriminations, but Congress did not act until the celebrated case of Ruth Bryan Owen, the daughter of William Jennings Bryan. She had married an English officer in 1910 and remained overseas until 1919, when they came to live in Florida. Circumstances prevented her from petitioning for repatriation under the 1922 Cable Act until January, 1925, after which she was naturalized in ninety days. She ran for Congress in 1928 and trounced her Republican opponent William C. Lawson by a 2 to 1 margin. Lawson challenged her right to the seat on the grounds that she had not been a citizen of the United States for seven years prior to her election, as required by the Constitution.

The House Committee on Elections investigated the matter and Ruth Owen appeared in her own behalf. She cast herself in the role of the injured woman and advanced the argument for perfecting the Cable Act. She condemned the unfairness of the 1907 law which took away her citizenship in the first place. She contended that she had lost her American citizenship not because she married an alien, but because she was a woman. No such penalty attended a man if he married an alien. He could lose his citizenship only by swearing allegiance to another government; and she declared, "I have never taken an oath of allegiance to any foreign government." She maintained that the Cable Act restored her status to that of a woman who had never lost her citizenship, but she explained that her delay in petitioning for repatriation was the crux of her objections to the Cable Act itself. The law had made it difficult for her to be naturalized. She had had to care for and support her husband, whose health had been shattered in World War I, provide for her three children, and bear a fourth child. She had made her living by lecturing for the University of Miami extension school and on the Chautauqua circuit. In order to make the necessary declaration of intent, the law required that she appear in U.S. Federal Court for the Southern District of Florida on the specific day when the immigration commissioner was there. She was likely to be in Minnesota or North Dakota on that particular day. "Having taken away my citizenship," she continued, "the Government had placed upon the regaining of my citizenship restrictions which made it impossible, without neglecting the duty of supporting my children, to present myself on the specified date at the courthouse."[16] With a case made of motherhood, dutiful wifehood, patriotism, and indignation, Owen won the unanimous support of the Committee on Elections; and the entire House concurred on June 6, 1930, without discussion or dissent.

With the citizenship issue revived, feminists moved on two fronts to eliminate the last discriminations. First were perfecting amendments to the Cable Act, and second were changes by international treaty. Congressman Cable introduced the new amendments on February 1, 1930; and the various women's groups paraded before the House committee on March 5 to support them.[17] On the other front, the League of Nations called to The Hague a conference to codify international law to meet on March 13, 1930. Women saw this conference as an opportunity to change nationality laws of the signatory nations in a sweep.

Women's groups in the United States bombarded Hoover with resolutions supporting equal citizenship.[18] Hoover responded by appointing Ruth B. Shipley, head of the Passport Division of the Department of State, as one of the five delegates, making her the first woman to be sent as an official delegate to an international conference. Dr. Emma Wold, NWP nationality expert, was one of the five technical advisors to the American delegation. At The Hague women lobbied so vigorously with the delegations that the president of the conference ordered the Dutch police to bar them. Since heavy majorities on preliminary ballots favored unequal clauses, feminists pressured the American delegation and Hoover to remain firm for equal nationality. Before the final vote was taken in The Hague, women lined up at least twenty-five Senators in Washington, including William E. Borah, chairman of the Senate Foreign Relations Committee, to oppose ratification of an unequal convention. When this sort of pressure had no effect in The Hague, feminists urged Hoover to withdraw the American delegation. They stayed, cast the only negative vote, and refused to sign the convention.

Failing abroad, women turned to the Cable amendments still pending in Congress. After some delay these passed and Hoover signed them on July 3, 1930. This action corrected certain defects in the 1922 law. The native American woman who married an alien and resided abroad was no longer subject to the presumptive loss of citizenship. Furthermore, a woman who had lost her citizenship under the 1907 law could return as a non-quota immigrant without proof of residence in the United States. The waiting period of a year was eliminated. She had only to return, file a petition for repatriation, take the oath of allegiance, and resume citizenship immediately. Then she could leave without losing it again. Had these 1930 amendments been in effect when Ruth Bryan Owen returned in 1919, the question of her seating in Congress would not have occurred. The provision in the 1922 law which stripped the citizenship of a woman marrying an ineligible alien was not repealed until March, 1931. Certain loose ends continued to bother the National Association of Women Lawyers until 1936, but these dealt with procedural questions, rectifying abuses caused by the 1907 law, and settling the citizenship of children born to parents of mixed nationalities.[19]

III

Many of the aggravations which piled up in the last half of the 1920s had begun earlier. The National Woman's Party formally presented its equal rights amendment in 1923. Extreme conservatives had assailed feminism during the suffrage crusade, but the charges of Bolshevism became really effective in the debate over the Sheppard-Towner Act and the child labor amendment. Although first proposed in 1921, the Wadsworth-Garrett amendment to end further amendments to the Constitution emerged from hiding in 1925. The U.S. Supreme Court had struck down federal child labor laws in 1918 and 1922 and declared the minimum wage to be unconstitutional in 1923.

A source of considerable disappointment and frustration was the fate of the minimum-wage movement. While other protective industrial legislation inched forward in the 1920s, the minimum-wage effort was broken and rolled back. In 1923 fifteen states and territories had minimum-wage laws; by 1930 only six remained in force to varying degrees. From its inception, the minimum wage had been challenged by opponents; but the courts had sustained it in at least seven cases, including the U.S. Supreme Court decision upholding Oregon's law in 1917. However, the Supreme Court reversed itself in 1923 and ruled the District of Columbia minimum-wage law to be unconstitutional.[20]

The National Women's Trade Union League and the National Consumers' League had won a significant victory in 1918 when Congress established the minimum wage for the District of Columbia; and the Minimum Wage Board had set a wage of $16.50 per week, the highest in the nation.[21] Congressional conservatives attempted to destroy the effectiveness of the law in 1921 by cutting out the funds for the Minimum Wage Board, but the women prevented this. At that point in time, legislators feared an antagonistic women's bloc, but the judiciary had no such concern. The District of Columbia law was challenged, but upheld by the D.C. Supreme Court in 1920. The

U.S. Court of Appeals concurred in 1921, but reversed itself in a rehearing in 1922. Justice Van Orsdel, rendering the new majority decision, said that the law infringed liberty of contract. "It should be remembered that of the three fundamental principles which underlie government, and for which government exists—life, liberty, and property—the chief of these is property." Furthermore, he felt that the Nineteenth Amendment recognized no inequality between men and women and voided laws which applied unequally.[22] The U.S. Supreme Court affirmed this decision and its reasoning in 1923. Harding's appointee, George Sutherland, rendered the majority decision in *Adkins* vs. *Children's Hospital*, which said that the minimum wage violated liberty of contract. Like Van Orsdel, Sutherland said that the *Muller* vs. *Oregon* precedent of 1908 no longer applied because the tremendous changes in the status of women had rendered the premises of the earlier case obsolete. He concluded that the Nineteenth Amendment was final proof of the equality of women; women no longer needed "restrictions upon their liberty of contract" which did not apply to men. Oliver Wendell Holmes dissented, saying, "It would need more than the Nineteenth Amendment to convince me that there are no differences between men and women, or that legislation can not take those differences into account." Chief Justice William Howard Taft, in his last pro-labor opinion, also dissented, arguing that the question of women's physical strength was not changed by the suffrage amendment.[23] Amid the general gloom of feminists, only the Woman's Party celebrated the decision as a victory for equal rights.

The immediate effect of the ruling was a 50 percent wage reduction for women workers in the District of Columbia. The long-run effect was the demolition of the minimum-wage movement in the 1920s. Proponents met fruitlessly in New York and then in Washington, D.C., at the call of the National Women's Trade Union League. The Washington conference was a study in frustration. Representatives from twenty-seven organizations met, condemned the Supreme Court's decision, debated what to do, and concluded by appointing a committee to study ways to curb the power of the court. Advocates were unable to agree on any single course of action, but sought to defend minimum-wage laws. The effort revived during the New Deal, and the Supreme Court reversed the *Adkins* ruling in 1937.[24]

The young, liberal lawyer Dean Acheson warned the Washington gathering that all but the Massachusetts minimum-wage law, which was non-compulsory, were in danger of being voided; but he urged contesting each case all the way. Indeed, the challenges came and the laws fell except in special circumstances. The laws of Arizona, Arkansas, Kansas, Puerto Rico, and Wisconsin were ruled unconstitutional between 1923 and 1928. Even Massachusetts's law was contested, but the courts ruled out only the mandatory exposure of those failing to comply with the request of the minimum-wage commission. Wisconsin passed a completely new, weak measure. Minnesota's attorney general saved the Minnesota law by ruling that it applied only to minors. The law in Utah had been inoperative since its passage in 1913, and the state repealed it altogether in 1928. A growing minimum-wage movement in Ohio dwindled away. The laws of California, Washington, Oregon, and North Dakota survived because the manufacturers supported them. For example, the Oregon Manufacturers and Merchants Association appealed to employers to support the minimum-wage law; and the association resolved to defend it, using "every effort to discourage anyone from testing the validity of the law in the courts" and to prevent repeal by the legislature. A business woman challenged the California law in 1924, but the California Supreme Court upheld it despite the *Adkins* decision. By then she was persuaded to drop the case. Most employer groups supported the law because they felt it had stabilized the conditions of female labor while working no hardship on the employers. The California Industrial Commission, charged with enforcing the law, had to bear in mind the tenuous nature of its mandate.[25]

Among the suggestions to overcome the role of the U.S. Supreme Court in voiding industrial and social legislation were proposals to amend the Constitution to allow Congress to regulate women's wages, to grant power to cover all working conditions, to require a two-thirds majority of the Supreme Court to void a law, or to permit Congress to override court decisions. However, the times favored another sort of amendment.

Conservatives had opposed that string of constitutional amendments after 1912. A number of individuals and organizations appeared around the time of World War I and after to oppose amendments which they felt were destroying the decentralized, representative aspects of the American political system. While relatively unorganized in opposition to the income tax and direct election of senators amendments, the prohibition and woman suffrage amendments brought them into organized resistance. Unable to stop the passage and ratification of these last two, they grew in strength and influence to the point where they stopped the child labor amendment and played a significant role in the repeal of the prohibition amendment.[26] Such organizations as the American Constitutional League, National Association for Constitutional Government, Woman Patriots, Sentinels of the Republic, *Constitutional Review*, Constitutional Liberty League, and various state defense leagues supported a proposed constitutional amendment which would have made further amendment nearly impossible. The immediate stimulus to this proposal was the rejection by the courts of all challenges to the validity of the Nineteenth Amendment in early 1921. In April, 1921, Senator James W. Wadsworth, Jr., of New York and Congressman Finis J. Garrett of Tennessee introduced this new amendment to end amendments. While not altering the role of Congress, the amendment greatly complicated the ratification procedures and provided for the defeat of proposed amendments. It included devices which anti-suffragists had tried to use against the Nineteenth Amendment. First, a legislature could not consider a proposed amendment until after an election had been held in which the amendment was an issue. Anti's had sought to block ratification in Tennessee on those grounds, but the courts ruled it unconstitutional. Second, the plan provided that an amendment must be approved by a majority vote of *both* houses of three-fourths of the states *and win referendums in as many states as might provide that ratification be subject to a referendum.* The referendum idea was one which the Anti's had usually found to be effective. They had sought a referendum on the Nineteenth Amendment in Ohio only to have the courts disallow it. Opposition forces found that they often had the advantage of inertia and propaganda in referendums. Dramatic proof of the conservative uses of the referendum came in Massachusetts in the "advisory" referendum which annihilated the child labor amendment in 1924. Ironically, supporters of the Wadsworth-Garrett amendment generally exhibited great fear of "democracy," but they dubbed their amendment the "Back-to-the-People Amendment" and incorporated the Populist device, the referendum.[27] Finally, the defeat of amendments was provided. A majority vote of *either* house of thirteen states or a referendum defeat in thirteen states killed it; and until the required three-fourths had approved, a state could reconsider and vote no.[28]

Carrie Chapman Catt warned in 1921 that the Wadsworth-Garrett proposal should be carefully watched.[29] Like the nymph of a cicada, the amendment lay buried, unnoticed, for several years and suddenly emerged in secret. The prohibition amendment had fallen into considerable disfavor by 1925 and the child labor amendment received a thorough mauling in November, 1924. As a result, the time seemed right for the amendment to end amendments. In the lame-duck session in 1925 supporters suddenly attempted to rush it through in the closing hours before adjournment.

Democratic minority leader Garrett was a sponsor; House Speaker Nicholas Longworth wanted the amendment, as did the chairman of the House Judiciary Committee. The House Rules Committee promised a special speedy rule. Marguerite Owen of the National League of Women Voters learned that the House Judiciary Committee had quietly taken up the amendment in a closed session. She rushed to the legislative representative of the AFL and to Maud Wood Park. They spread the alarm and the League of Women Voters, Women's Trade Union League, AFL, and the railroad brotherhoods protested the procedure and demanded open hearings. Consequently the amendment was sidetracked in committee.[30] Until the coming of the New Deal, opposition to the Wadsworth-Garrett amendment took its place beside the equal rights amendment. The Women's Joint Congressional Committee formed subcommittees to oppose both amendments.

The defensive character of the late 1920s was illustrated not only by the WJCC's having to form preventive committees, but also by the struggle against budget cuts for the Women's and Children's bureaus. After having seen increased funding for these bureaus every year, the women were unable to prevent their budgets from being reduced in two consecutive years, 1925 and 1926. With difficulty they prevented further cuts until Hoover became President, and he increased appropriations until 1932. As indicated earlier, the women were unable to prevent the termination of the Sheppard-Towner Act in 1929. (The woman's program got only little support from the women in Congress, excepting Ruth Bryan Owen and Edith Nourse Rogers.) Feminists did see home economics educational aid put on a par with vocational aid, and a compulsory school attendance measure was passed for the District of Columbia. Social feminists persisted in trying to pass a progressive program, but they had to wait for the New Deal for much of it. After 1926 the League of Women Voters widely propagandized Senator Norris's plan for the Tennessee Valley and saw it pass twice before victory in 1933. Advocates of public housing and social insurance debated and promoted the case for federal programs. The Women's Trade Union League, National Consumers' League, and NLWV urged further efforts to combat the threat of unemployment. Attempts to win the child labor amendment did not end even though passage was impossible, and social feminists worked to revive infancy and maternity protection after the federal program lapsed. The time from 1925 to the New Deal was characterized by defense of programs in existence and the exposition of others that became realities in the 1930s. In reviewing only the efforts of social feminists, one must agree

with Josephine Goldmark: "The truth is that New Deal legislation did not spring full blown. Its roots lie in the preceding
thirty years or more. . . ." [31]

NOTES

1. Quoted in "The Business Woman and the Vote: A Symposium," *Independent Woman*, n.s., VII (June, 1928), 244.

2. Chase Going Woodhouse, "The Occupation of the American Association
of University Women," *Fifteenth Yearbook* (Washington: National Associa-
tion of Deans of Women, 1928), 204–207; Persis M. Cope, "The Women in
'Who's Who,' a Statistical Study," *Social Forces*, VII (Dec., 1928), 212–223;
Martha Tracy, "Women Graduates in Medicine," *Bulletin, Association of
American Medical Colleges*, II (Jan., 1927), 21–28; Margaret Elliot and
Grace E. Manson, "Earnings of Women in Business and the Professions,"
Michigan Business Studies, III (Sept., 1930); "Women in the Modern World,"
Annals of the American Academy of Political and Social Science, CXLIII
(May, 1929).

3. Mary Margaret McBride, "That Woman Question," *Independent Woman*,
n.s., VIII (Feb., 1929), 50–51; Ethel M. Colson Brazelton, "Are You a Mar-
tinet?," *ibid.*, VII (Nov., 1928), 487–488; Ruth Hahn, "But I Won't Work for
a Woman!," *ibid.*, VI (Nov., 1927), 9; Anne W. Armstrong, "Is Your Boss a
Woman?," *ibid.* (Oct., 1927), 4–5; M. L. McGlothlin, "Do Women Executives
Nag?," *ibid.*, IX (Dec., 1930), 505; see also Dorothy Dunbar Bromley, "Are
Women a Success in Business?," *Harper's*, CLVI (Feb., 1928), 299–307.

4. Ruth Hahn, "When the Boss Has a Grudge against Women in Business,"
Independent Woman, n.s., VI (Mar., 1927), 7; see also Anne W. Armstrong,
"Are Business Women Getting a Square Deal?," *ibid.*, VII (Jan., 1928), 4–5;
Lorine Pruette, "Up from Dilettantism," *ibid.*, VI (June, 1927), 4–5; Edna
Rowe, "How High Can a Woman Climb?," *Nation's Business*, XVII (Apr.,
1929), 41–45; Lillian Symes, "Still a Man's Game," *Harper's*, CLVIII (May,
1929), 678; Symes, "The New Masculinism," *ibid.*, CLXI (June, 1930), 98–107.

5. Carol Harding, "This Question of Discrimination," *Independent Woman*,
n.s., IX (July, 1930), 268–270; Doris E. Fleischman, "Women in Business,"
Ladies Home Journal, XLVII (Jan., 1930), 16–17; (Mar., 1930), 24–25; "Dentistry as a Profession" (Institute of Women's Professional Relations, 1934),
10–12; Winifred Mallon, "Uncle Sam and the Ladies," *Independent Woman*,
n.s., IX (Sept., 1930), 355; "Armistice Day Reflections," *Medical Woman's
Journal*, XXXVI (Nov., 1929), 298.

6. "A New Way to Fight Women," *Equal Rights*, XVI (Feb. 18, 1930), 12;
"Penalizing Marriage," *ibid.* (Nov. 8, 1930), 317; "The Facts in the B. & O.
Case," *ibid.*, XVIII (May 7, 1932), 111; Gladys Oaks, "Should Married Women
Work?," *ibid.*, XVI (Jan. 24, 1931), 405–406; Alice Stone Blackwell, "May
Women Earn?," *Woman's Journal*, XVI (Jan., 1931), 26–27; editorial, "Shall
Wealthy Men Work?," *ibid.* (Feb., 1931), 22; Florence Thacker, "The Mar-
ried Woman Worker," *Women Lawyers' Journal*, XIX (Aug., 1932), 32–33;
Mary L. Bridwell, "Married Women in Business," *A.B.W. News*, XI (Jan.,
1934), 4; "The National Woman's Party," pamphlet, 1935, Babcock MSS, box
3, folder 32, SL; "Can Working Women Marry?," *Equal Rights*, XXIV (Sept.
1, 1938), 325.

7. "The History of Section 213," pamphlet, 1935, Babcock MSS, box 3, folder 32, SL.

8. Mary Anderson, "Sex Differentials in Minimum Wage Rates under N.R.A. Codes," *Women Lawyers' Journal*, XX (Nov., 1934), 29; Elisabeth Christman to General Hugh S. Johnson (mimeo.), Feb. 29, 1934, Breckinridge MSS, box 16, LC.

9. Mary Carroll, "Wanted—a New Feminism: An Interview of Emily Newell Blair," *Independent Woman*, n.s., IX (Dec., 1930), 499; Emily Newell Blair, "Why I Am Disappointed about Women in Politics," *Woman's Journal*, XVI (Jan., 1931), 20–21; Blair, "Putting Women into Politics," *ibid.*, (Mar., 1931), 14–15; see also Inez C. Philbrick, "Women, Let Us Be Loyal to Women!," *Medical Woman's Journal*, XXXVI (Feb., 1929), 39–42; Lena Madeson Phillips, "A Challenge to the Business Woman," *Independent Woman*, n.s., VIII (Aug., 1929), 342–344; Anne W. Armstrong, "Is Your Boss a Woman?," *ibid.*, VI (Oct., 1927), 4–5; "Do You, Too, Shun the Woman Doctor?," *ibid.* (Dec., 1927), 21; editorial, "Are English Women More Loyal to Sex Than American Women?," *Medical Woman's Journal*, XXXVI (Dec., 1929), 353–354; Rosalind Goodrich Bates, "Loyalty and the Woman Lawyer," *Women Lawyers' Journal*, XIX (Aug., 1932), 29–30; "Resume of Speech Given by Miss Josephine G. Seaman," *A.B.W. News*, VII (Nov., 1929), 1.

10. Frederick L. Collins, "The New Woman: What She Wanted and What She Got," *Woman's Home Companion*, LVI (June, 1929), 12; Maud Wood Park, "Ten Years of Suffrage," *Independent Woman*, n.s., IX (Aug., 1930), 316–317; Olive McKee, Jr., "Ten Years of Woman Suffrage," *Commonweal*, XII (July 16, 1930), 298–300; "Ten Years of Suffrage," *Survey*, LXIII (Jan. 15, 1930), 454; Katherine Ludington, "On March 26th: Unforeseen in 1920," *Bulletin of the Pennsylvania League of Women Voters*, X (Apr., 1930), 11; "On March 26th: The Hope of the Founders," *ibid.*, 10–11, Catt MSS, box 5, NYPL; Sarah Schuyler Butler, "After Ten Years," *Woman's Journal*, XIV (Apr., 1929), 10–11; Carrie Chapman Catt, "Woman Suffrage: The First Ten Years," *New York Times Magazine* (Aug. 24, 1920), 3, 16; Loring A. Schuler, "Ten Years of Suffrage," *Ladies Home Journal*, XLVII (Aug., 1930), 22; Josephine McGowan, "A Decade of Equal Rights," *Commonweal*, XIII (Feb. 11, 1931), 401–403; Sarah Schuyler Butler, "Why I Am Not Disappointed in Women in Politics," *Woman's Journal*, XVI (Apr., 1931), 14; "Ten Years of Woman Suffrage," *Literary Digest*, CV (Apr. 26, 1930), 11.

11. Rev. James Groton to Jane Addams, Feb. 23, 1920, Addams MSS, microfilm reel 5, Swarthmore College Peace Collection.

12. Frank R. Kent, "Women's Faults in Politics," *Woman Citizen*, XI (Mar., 1927), 23; Kraditor, *Ideas of the Woman Suffrage Movement*, 43–74; O'Neill, *Everyone Was Brave*, 264–274.

13. "Fooling Women in Politics," *Ladies Home Journal*, XL (Sept., 1923), 29; "Ascent of Women's Suffrage," n.d., C. B. Pinchot MSS, box 19, LC; Winifred Starr Dobyns, "The Lady and the Tiger," *Woman Citizen*, XI (Jan., 1927), 20–21.

14. "Is Woman Suffrage Failing—a Symposium," *Woman Citizen*, VIII (Apr. 19, 1924), 15; Charles A. Selden, "Four Years of the Nineteenth Amendment," *Ladies Home Journal*, XLI (June, 1924), 27; Carrie Chapman Catt to Joan London, Oct. 18, 1928, Catt MSS, box 1, NYPL; Catt, "Woman Suffrage: The First Ten Years," *New York Times Magazine* (Aug. 24, 1930), 3; Catt quoted in "Ten Years of Woman Suffrage," *Literary Digest*, CV (Apr. 26, 1930), 11; "Ten Years of Suffrage," *Survey*, LXIII (Jan. 15, 1930), 454.

15. See the list of 425 measures backed and passed by the League of Women Voters alone between 1920 and 1925 in *Ladies Home Journal*, XLII (Nov., 1925), 38.

16. Ruby A. Black, "The Case of Ruth Bryan Owen," *Equal Rights*, XVI (Apr. 5, 1930), 67–69.

17. This group included Ruth Bryan Owen, Sophonisba P. Breckinridge, chairman of NLWV's committee on the legal status of women, NWP, AAUW, NFBPWC, YWCA, WCTU, AFL, National Council of Jewish Women, American Home Economics Association, International Alliance of Women for Suffrage and Equal Citizenship; see *Equal Rights*, XVI (Mar. 15, 1930), 48.

18. For a sample of the widespread and numerous resolutions see *Equal Rights*, XVI (Feb. 8, 1930), 7; (Feb. 14, 1930), 15, 16; (Feb. 22, 1930), 19; (Mar. 1, 1930), 30–31, 32; (Mar. 8, 1930), 35; (Mar. 15, 1930), 46; (Mar. 29, 1930), 59.

19. Marion Gold Lewis, "Minutes of the National Association of Women Lawyers, Atlantic City," *Women Lawyers' Journal*, XIX (Fall, 1931), 13; "Report of International Relations Committee," *National Women Lawyers' Journal*, XXIII (Dec., 1936), 30–31.

20. *The Development of the Minimum-Wage Laws in the United States, 1912–1927*, Women's Bureau, U.S. Department of Labor, *Bull. 61* (Washington: Government Printing Office, 1928).

1912—Massachusetts (mandatory exposure section struck out, 1924)
1913—California (sustained by state superior court, 1924)
1913—Colorado (never in effect, no appropriations)
1913—Minnesota (attorney general ruled for minors only, 1925)
1913—Nebraska (never put into effect, repealed 1919)
1913—Oregon (sustained by U.S. Supreme Court, 1917—tie vote)
1913—Utah (never in operation, repealed 1928)
1913—Washington (sustained by state supreme court, 1919)
1913—Wisconsin (unconstitutional by U.S. Supreme Court, 1924; whole new, weak law passed)
1915—Arkansas (unconstitutional by U.S. Supreme Court, 1927)
1915—Kansas (unconstitutional by state supreme court, 1925)
1917—Arizona (unconstitutional by U.S. Supreme Court, 1925)
1918—District of Columbia (unconstitutional by U.S. Supreme Court, 1923)
1919—Puerto Rico (unconstitutional by P.R. supreme court, 1924)
1919—North Dakota (enjoined 1920, reactivated 1921)
1919—Texas (never in operation, repealed 1921)
1923—South Dakota (unenforced)

21. Ethel M. Smith, "Raising the Pay of Washington Women Workers," *Life and Labor*, IX (Aug., 1919), 191–193; NWTUL, *Proceedings* (1919), 50.

22. "Minimum Wage Legislation in the Courts," *Life and Labor Bulletin*, I (Jan., 1923), 2.

23. *Development of the Minimum Wage Laws*, 324–325; "Excerpts from Brief in Support of the Equal Rights for Women Amendment" (NWP mimeo. statement, 1941), 3. For a fuller discussion see Bernstein, *The Lean Years*, 225–232.

24. Chambers, *Seedtime of Reform*, 66–76; "Conference on Minimum Wage Legislation and the Supreme Court Decision," *Life and Labor Bulletin*, I (June, 1923), 2; "The Washington Conference on Minimum Wage," *Ohio Council on Women in Industry* (June, 1923), unpaginated.

25. Rudolf Broda, *Minimum Wage Legislation in Various Countries*, Bureau

of Labor Statistics, U.S. Department of Labor, *Bull.* 467 (Washington: Government Printing Office, 1928), 41–42; "Oregon Employers and Minimum Wage," *Ohio Council on Women in Industry* (Oct., 1923); "Experience With Minimum Wage in California," *ibid.* (Apr., 1924).

26. For the history of one such organization, see David Edward Kyvig, "In Revolt against Prohibition: The Association against the Prohibition Amendment and the Movement for Repeal, 1919–1933" (Ph.D. thesis, Northwestern University, 1971).

27. Thomas F. Cadwalader [Maryland League for State Defense], "The Wadsworth-Garrett Back-to-the-People Amendment," *Woman Patriot*, VII (Dec. 15, 1923), 2–3; "Senator Wadsworth Introduces 'Back-to-the-People Amendment,'" *ibid.*, V (Apr. 16, 1921), 1–2.

28. The Constitution is silent on the question of how an amendment is defeated or if states can change their minds once they have rejected or ratified. Opponents of the child labor amendment attempted to get it declared dead by the courts after its rejection by the states. When proponents revived the amendment for another attempt at ratification in 1933, opponents went into the courts. However, the U.S. Supreme Court ruled that the amendment was still open for ratification and that a state could switch from negative to positive, but that ratification by a state could not be rescinded.

29. Carrie Chapman Catt, editorial, *Woman Citizen*, V (Apr. 23, 1921), 1189.

30. Maud Wood Park, "National League of Women Voters, My Work after 1924, Supplementary Notes on Wadsworth-Garrett Amendment," May, 1943, Stantial MSS, Dillon Collection, folder 27, SL; Esther Dunshee, speech, Richmond convention, 1925, Brown MSS, box 4, folder 78, SL; "Setting Up Minority Control," *Life and Labor Bulletin*, III (Mar., 1925), 1–2.

31. Goldmark, *Impatient Crusader*, 205.

Essay on Sources

Abbreviations used in footnotes:

LC   Manuscript Division, Library of Congress
NYPL   Manuscript Division, New York Public Library
OHS   Manuscript Division, Ohio Historical Society
SL   Arthur and Elizabeth Schlesinger Library on the History of Women in America, Radcliffe College
SSC   Sophia Smith Collection, Smith College

As the footnotes should indicate, the backbone of this study is the manuscript collections and periodicals. The number of books used was relatively limited and provided hints and added interpretation. Books on the women's rights movement for the period before the Nineteenth Amendment far exceed those on the subsequent period, but the raw material for various studies is present in the manuscripts, memoirs, periodicals, government publications, reports and congressional hearings, and polemical writings of the 1920s.

Personal Papers

The Schlesinger Library (formerly Women's Archives) at Radcliffe afforded the richest and most varied sources. A listing can barely give the proper impression of the diversity: Corrine Marie Allen (Utah Congress of Mothers and PTA, anti-polygamy, civil liberties); Florence E. Allen (first woman state supreme court justice, U.S. Circuit Court, professional women, peace); Esther Myers Andrews (first woman on Massachusetts Governor's Council, minimum-wage board, 1915–35); Fannie Fern Andrews (Boston LWV, Boston branch—AAUW, peace); Lucy Anthony (personal secretary to Anna Howard Shaw); Caroline Lexow Babcock (NWP, equal rights amendment); Elizabeth L. Clarke (professional women in agriculture); Ada Lorine Comstock (president of Radcliffe, AAUW, National Commission on Law Observation and Enforcement, 1929–33); Mary Dewson (NCL, opposition to equal rights amendment); Mary Dingham (YWCA, industrial women); Euphemia

Drysdale (NWP, women ministers); Elizabeth Glendower Evans (minimum wage, child labor, peace); Frances Freeman Tuckerman (equal pay); Edna Fischel Gellhorn (NLWV, suffrage); Alice Hamilton (radical right attacks, opposition to equal rights amendment); Grace H. Harte (jury service); Jessie Donaldson Hodder (superintendent of Massachusetts Reformatory for Women, 1911–31, equal rights); Carrie Johnson (suffrage); Ethel M. Johnson (assistant commissioner of Massachusetts Department of Labor and Industries, 1919–32, Council of Women and Children); Florence L. Kitchelt (anti-Weeks campaign of 1918, suffrage, Connecticut LWV, equal rights); Margaret Noyes Kleinert (women physicians); Emily Kneubuhl (LWV, reminiscence); Harriet W. Laidlaw (child labor, New York LWV); Mary Lee (women journalists); Alexander Lincoln (Sentinels of the Republic); Alma Lutz (NWP, equal rights amendment); A. Winifred McLaughlin (women lawyers); Catherine Waugh McCullough (women lawyers, legal status of women); Maud Nathan (NCL); Helen Brewster Owens (women statisticians); Harriet Reid (labor arbiter, 1920–37); Grace Richardson (suffrage); Margaret S. Roberts (women in politics); Agnes Ryan (equal rights, peace); Belle Sherwin (suffrage, NLWV); Hilda Worthington Smith (industrial women); Jane Norman Smith (NWP, internecine warfare); Nellie Nugent Somerville (women in politics); Lucy Somerville-Howorth (women lawyers, politics); Doris Stevens (NWP, birth control); Anna Churchill Tillinghast (women ministers, commissioner of immigration, Massachusetts, 1929–33); Elizabeth H. Tilton (slightly hysterical autobiography, PTA and lobbying activities); Miriam Van Waters (social work, superintendent of Framington Reformatory for Women, 1931–57); Agnes E. Wells (NWP); Marguerite M. Wells (NLWV, Minnesota LWV); Helen Hunt West (NWP); Sue S. White (suffrage, NWP, women in politics).

The Mary Anderson papers (Radcliffe) contain correspondence with Margaret Dreier Robins, Katharine Philips Edson, Mary Van Kleeck, and Elisabeth Christman. Of special interest were the folders dealing with the equal rights amendment and attacks by the radical right.

The Dorothy Kirchwey Brown papers (Radcliffe) contain invaluable information on the early activities of the NLWV, including reminiscences and interviews with leaders. Especially helpful was a typescript copy of a NLWV program called "The Excursion." Brown was NLWV chairman of child welfare and in the thick of work for Sheppard-Towner and the child labor amendment.

The Edna Lamprey Stantial papers in the Dillon Collection (Radcliffe) contain significant manuscripts of Maud Wood Park and Belle Sherwin concerning NLWV work. Also there is information on the Cable Act and the Wadsworth-Garrett amendment.

Carrie Chapman Catt's papers are scattered; some are at Radcliffe, Smith College, and the New York Public Library. The latter offer a number of Catt's speeches and letters evaluating the effect of woman suffrage. The papers at Radcliffe contain more evaluations and material on the peace movement.

The Mabel Raef Putnam papers are also at Radcliffe and the New York Public Library, and both collections are concerned with her part in the passage of the Wisconsin equal rights law.

Jane Addams's papers (Swarthmore College Peace Collection) were useful to me only insofar as they told of the difficulties of the American branch of the WILPF with the National Council of Women. Also they contain examples of the most vicious sort of crank letters in the period of the Red Scare, 1919–20, a copy of a Spider Web chart from 1927, and important information on the child labor amendment.

The Sophonisba Preston Breckinridge papers (Library of Congress) have very little from the 1920s, but contain reports of her investigations for the Council of National Defense in World War I, her appointment to the Seventh Pan-American Conference in 1933, and efforts to get women appointed to the bench in Chicago. Her papers reveal an extreme sensitivity to discrimination against professional women.

The Warren G. Harding collection at the Ohio Historical Society consists of nearly 775 boxes of papers covering his presidential and pre-presidential years. I made very selective use, skimming for information about Sheppard-Towner, Department of Social Welfare, Department of Education, support for women in government, and correspondence with Harriet Taylor Upton, Helen Gardener, Mary Anderson, and Julia Lathrop.

The Cornelia Bryce Pinchot papers (Library of Congress) consist of nearly 500 boxes spanning the period 1918–37. Besides a healthy dose of politics, her papers provide an insight into liberalism in the 1920s and the travail of the NWTUL. She served as NWTUL finance chairman for several years and was a constant ally. The collection is rather chaotic, moisture-damaged, and full of extraneous things like swatches of material for drapes, designs for earrings, landscaping plans, and rat droppings. The papers of her husband (Gifford Pinchot) fill more than 2,000 boxes and I used them sparingly, only to check his attitude on women in government and the effect of women on his campaign in 1922.

The Mary Church Terrell papers (Library of Congress) gave an insight into the doubly discriminated group—the Negro woman. Terrell was a member of the NWP, a veteran of the picket lines, and supporter of the equal rights amendment. While she was a staunch Republican, her letters tell of her daughter's going to work for a Harlem politician, Adam Clayton Powell, in the 1930s.

Senator Thomas J. Walsh's papers (Library of Congress) contain a batch of letters pertaining to the equal rights amendment. He opposed it, but proponents tried to make him support it.

In the Indiana State Library I examined several small collections including the papers of William Dudley Foulke, once president of the National Municipal League and National Civil Service League, and president for several years of the old American Woman Suffrage Association. While the papers have many interesting letters from notables in the progressive period, there is little for the 1920s. Also in the library are a few letters of Lucius C. Embree and T. H. Marshall, both opponents of

woman suffrage who feared for the future of civilization. Very helpful in discussing the internecine warfare between business and industrial
women was the small collection of reports and letters of the Indiana
Federation of Business and Professional Women.

The New York Public Library has the papers of Everett P. Wheeler,
chairman of the Man Suffrage Association Opposed to Woman Suffrage
and the American Constitutional League. Also there are the papers of
Helen Kendrick Johnson of the New York Association Opposed to
Woman Suffrage. On the other side are the papers of Lillian Wald; these
were valuable mainly for the correspondence with Grace Abbott and
Florence Kelley about the child labor amendment and women in government.

The Historical Society of Pennsylvania is very strong on colonial
materials and very weak on the twentieth century. I examined the papers
of Caroline Katzenstein, but they consisted of little more than newspaper
clippings and bits and pieces used in her reminiscence entitled *Lifting
the Curtain: The State and National Woman Suffrage Campaigns as I
Saw Them* (Philadelphia: Dorrance, 1955). More useful were the Mary
A. Stillwell papers about pioneer women in dentistry and the American
Women's Hospitals in World War I.

Organizational Archives

Remnants of the papers of the National American Woman Suffrage
Association are in the Manuscript Division of the New York Public
Library. I found them quite useful for the activities of suffragists during
World War I.

The National Civic Federation papers are at the New York Public
Library also. Actually, a more accurate description would make them
the papers of Ralph Easley, executive secretary of the NCF. While the
NCF was mildly progressive before World War I, in the 1920s it was a
red-hunting, anti-radical vigilante, a vehement opponent of American
recognition of the Soviet Union, and a constant antagonist of the American Civil Liberties Union.

The National Association of Bank Women in New York permitted
me to examine what little remained of their files of the 1920s. Unfortunately, thinking that the old papers were of no further use, the
NABW threw away most of their papers after allowing Genevieve N.
Gildersleeve to research for her book, *Women in Banking: A History of
the National Association of Bank Women* (Washington: Public Affairs
Press, 1959).

The Library of Congress is the official depository of the papers of the
National League of Women Voters (now League of Women Voters of
the United States). The collection is rich in material on social feminism,
and I found it very helpful for the discussion of early problems of the
NLWV. Special folders contain correspondence of Carrie Chapman
Catt. The library also has the papers of the Women's Joint Congressional
Committee, but I was unaware of them when I researched this study.

The National Woman's Party has loaned to the Library of Congress the papers for 1913–21; the rest are retained at party headquarters at Belmont House in Washington. Those at the Library of Congress were of little use since they focused solely on suffrage.

In the Schlesinger Library at Radcliffe were various collections of papers of which I made limited use: the National Women's Trade Union League, Massachusetts Trade Union League, National Consumers' League, Connecticut Consumers' League, American Association of University Women, and the Boston branch of the AAUW.

Periodical Material

Substantial material for this study came from a survey of a number of periodicals. The dates in parentheses indicate the inclusive years for each magazine surveyed.

Except for an occasional editorial and stray article, *Better Homes and Gardens* (1924–31) stuck to its title. Much more useful was *Good Housekeeping* (1918–32), one of the six major women's magazines in the 1920s. It saw itself as a crusader for women and children, and it supported Sheppard-Towner, the Cable Act, the child labor amendment, women's labor laws, and women's rights. In contrast, *Ladies Home Journal* (1917–33) tended to go off on quixotic campaigns against jazz music, "jazz dancing," cigarette smoking among women, the disappearance of the corset, and "dirty" movies and books. While supporting some progressive measures, its pages also contained pleas for censorship of books, movies, and teachers. The third of the big six, *Woman's Home Companion* (1925–29), editorialized for Sheppard-Towner and the child labor amendment. Of the remaining three of the six major magazines, *Pictorial Review, Delineator,* and *McCall's,* I could obtain only scattered issues; but these tended to support the *Good Housekeeping* positions, if they said anything at all. A run of a year of *Delineator* in the late 1920s revealed little more than fashion and food articles and insipid fiction.

For an understanding of the business and professional women one needs to look into their little magazines. These practically rank in the "fugitive" status because they are difficult to find and were published irregularly. The National Association of Bank Women did not save a complete set of their own publication, the *A.B.W. News* (1928–34), and I was able to begin only with volume VI. By 1928 the NABW had ignored all but banking questions, so the value of the magazine was limited. The official magazine of the Medical Women's National Association (American Medical Women's Association after 1937) was the *Woman's Medical Journal* (1917–19), renamed *Medical Woman's Journal* (1920–32). It maintained a constant stream of denunciation of discrimination, allowing one to understand why the MWNA became one of the first professional groups to endorse the equal rights amendment in the 1930s. The National Federation of Business and Professional Women's Clubs published *Independent Woman* (1926–31), which was an invaluable source for learning the general attitudes of business and professional women. The *Women Lawyers' Journal* (1917–36), published by the National Women Lawyers' Association, revealed a pronounced shift from protectionism to advocacy of the equal rights amendment. The position changed most markedly in the early 1920s, when a member of the NWP became the editor of the magazine.

The publications of the National Women's Trade Union League provided the main source of information about industrial women. The physical appearance of the NWTUL's official publication reflected its altered fortunes in the 1920s. From a regular, full magazine called *Life and Labor* (1916–21), publication was suspended in the winter of 1921–22 because of financial difficulties, and resumed in 1922 with the *Life and Labor Bulletin* (1923–32), a smaller, more limited, irregular newsletter. In the 1930s the *Bulletin* became little more than a single mimeographed sheet.

The *Woman Citizen* (1914–23, 1926–27) was an extremely significant source for political and reform news. Until 1921 it served as the official organ of NAWSA and NLWV. Although the magazine became independent in 1921, the NLWV continued to buy several pages for news and opinion. It was retitled *Woman's Journal* (1928–31) in an effort to broaden appeal, but ceased publication in mid-1931. The publication of the National Woman's Party, *Equal Rights* (1923–32), provided help in understanding the equal rights amendment issue. Given its bias, the magazine was a fertile source of factual information. The *Woman Voter's Bulletin* (1921–37) of the Connecticut League of Women Voters provided a fine example of state-level league activity. I used it particularly for the section on jury service.

The *Woman's Protest* (1914–18), the official organ of the National Association Opposed to Woman Suffrage, was the main source of anti-suffrage attitudes. Its successor, the *Woman Patriot* (1918–26), moved to the extreme right and was one of the chief promoters of the Spider Web interpretation. The pamphlets of the Illinois Association Opposed to Woman Suffrage, numbers 1–20, supplied additional examples of rabid anti-suffragism.

The Ohio Council on Women and Children in Industry published a little newsletter by the same name (1922), renamed *Ohio Council on Women in Industry* (1923–26) and *Information Bureau on Women's Work* (1927–32), which supported minimum wage, child labor laws, unemployment compensation, public works, and social security in the period.

The *Journal of the American Medical Association* was scanned from 1919 to 1931 for its position on federal infancy and maternity protection. In addition I used occasional articles from the *American Bar Association Journal, American Federationist, Atlantic Monthly, Century Magazine, Commonweal, Congressional Digest, Harper's, House and Garden, Journal of Social Forces, Nation, New Republic, New York Times Magazine, North American Review, Outlook, Proceedings of the Academy of*

Political Science, and *Survey.* The May, 1929, issue of the *Annals of the American Academy of Political and Social Science* was entitled "Women in the Modern World."

Official Proceedings

The official proceedings of the American Association of University Women (1927), National Education Association (1918–27), National Association of Deans of Women (1924–32), National League of Women Voters (1920, 1922–24), National Women's Trade Union League (1913–36) helped interpret the positions and intentions of those organizations. Especially useful to me were the *Proceedings* of the NWTUL.

The bulletins of the U.S. Women's Bureau supplied important raw material and interpretation. Under Mary Anderson the Women's Bureau was a sturdy advocate of women's rights and protection of industrial women. Also used were scattered publications of the Children's Bureau, Bureau of Labor Statistics, and congressional hearings on Sheppard-Towner and the Cable Act.

Articles and Unpublished Manuscripts

Most dissertations and studies of the Woman Movement stop with the winning of suffrage, but Anne F. Scott, "After Suffrage: The Southern Woman in the Twenties," *Journal of Southern History,* XXX (Aug., 1964), 298–318, is the best yet done in a brief space to indicate the persistence of women's reform efforts in the 1920s. She has incorporated this material in an excellent little book, *The Southern Woman: From Pedestal to Politics, 1830–1930* (Chicago: University of Chicago Press, 1970). Some doctoral theses have assayed the 1920s: Dorothy E. Johnson, "Organized Women and National Legislation, 1920–1941" (Ph.D. thesis, Western Reserve University, 1960), deals with the legislative programs of five major organizations; Valborg E. Fletty, "Public Services of Women's Organizations" (Ph.D. thesis, Syracuse University, 1952), is a veritable catalog of important and trivial information about the public activities of women's groups. I found her interpretation that the period 1919–21 was a watershed to be stimulating. Joseph B. Chepaitis has written "The First Social Welfare Measure: The Sheppard-Towner Maternity and Infancy Act, 1918–1932" (Ph.D. thesis, Georgetown University, 1968), which provides more detail on Sheppard-Towner; and except for a more favorable view of Harding's role, it corroborates my findings. Other theses partially deal with the 1920s while investigating other topics: William Theodore Doyle, "Charlotte Perkins Gilman and the Cycle of Feminist Reform" (Ph.D. thesis, University of California, Berkeley, 1960), reaches into the 1920s to consider why Gilman's leadership was shunned after World War I; Sister Jean Marie Daly, "Mary Anderson: Pioneer Labor Leader" (Ph.D. thesis, Georgetown University, 1968), gives the most complete biography of Anderson, but adds little to what is known of her activities in the 1920s; Lucille Evelyn

LaGanke, "The National Society of the Daughters of the American Revolution: Its History, Policies, and Influences, 1890–1949" (Ph.D. thesis, Western Reserve University, 1951), was the source of my understanding of the pronounced shift to the right in the DAR in the 1920s and its earlier mild progressivism. While not having actually read Paul Taylor's thesis, "Women in Party Politics, 1920–1940" (Ph.D. thesis, Harvard University, 1966), several discussions with the author about it have shaped my interpretation of the political activity of women in the parties in the 1920s.

Randolph C. Downes kindly allowed me to examine his book manuscript, "The Rise of Warren Gamaliel Harding, 1865–1920," which helped pinpoint Harding's attitude and tactics with respect to political women and women in government. Additional articles which were suggestive or aided in setting my study in context included: William L. O'Neill, "The Woman Movement and the First World War" (paper read for the Organization of American Historians, Cincinnati, 1966), which was incorporated in his stimulating book, *Everyone Was Brave: The Rise and Fall of Feminism in America* (Chicago: Quadrangle Books, 1969); Allen F. Davis, "Welfare, Reform and World War I," *American Quarterly*, XIX (Fall, 1967), 516–533; Davis, "The Women's Trade Union League: Origins and Organization," *Labor History*, V (Winter, 1964), 3–17; Otis A. Pease, "The Success of Progressivism" (paper read for the Organization of American Historians, Cincinnati, 1966).

For the defeat of the child labor amendment see Richard B. Sherman, "The Rejection of the Child Labor Amendment," *Mid-America*, XLV (Jan., 1963), 2–17, and the old doctoral thesis by Ned Weissberg, "The Federal Child Labor Amendment: A Study in Pressure Politics (Ph.D. thesis, Cornell University, 1942). Arthur S. Link, "What Happened to the Progressive Movement in the 1920's?," *American Historical Review*, LXIV (July, 1959), 833–851, is a suggestive discussion of the question of the persistence of progressivism. Mary Alice Johnson, "The Ohio League of Women Voters" (M.A. thesis, Ohio State University, 1930), provided a state study of the operations of the LWV. A thorough summary of the arguments over protective legislation by a defender is found in Helen Louise Stitt, "A Study of the Woman's Party Position on Special Labor Laws for Women" (M.A. thesis, Ohio State University, 1925).

Biographical Material

The struggle for professional advancement, women's rights, and social reform caused some women to want to record their experiences. Harriot Stanton Blatch, the founder of the Women's Political Union, a militant suffragist, socialist, and peace advocate, told her story to Alma Lutz in *Challenging Years: The Memoirs of Harriot Stanton Blatch* (New York: G. P. Putnam's Sons, 1940). Agnes Nestor, *Woman's Labor Leader: An Autobiography* (Rockford, Ill.: Bellevue Books, 1954) is weak on the 1920s, but Mary Anderson, *Woman at Work: The Autobiography of Mary Anderson as Told to Mary N. Winslow* (Minneapolis: University of Minnesota Press, 1951), was very good in discussing the equal rights amendment controversy and the efforts for women's labor laws. She was chairman at that uproarious Second Conference of Women in Industry. Rose Schneiderman's autobiography (written with Lucy Goldthwaite), *All for One* (New York: Paul S. Eriksson, 1967), was very interesting for the period before 1920, but began to run thin when she became more important. She was an organizer for the White Goods Workers Union and the ILGWU and became the president of the New York Women's Trade Union League (1917–41) and the NWTUL (1926–47). Other autobiographies bearing on industrial women included Alice Hamilton, *Exploring the Dangerous Trades: The Autobiography of Alice Hamilton* (Boston: Little, Brown, 1943), and Maud Nathan, *The Story of an Epoch-Making Movement* (Garden City: Doubleday, 1926). The efforts of professional women to win recognition are told in Rheta Childe Dorr, *A Woman of Fifty* (New York: Funk & Wagnalls, 1924); Helen Woodward, *Through Many Windows* (New York: Hayne & Brothers, 1926); Charlotte Perkins Gilman, *The Living of Charlotte Perkins Gilman: An Autobiography* (New York: D. Appleton-Century, 1935); Bertha Van Hoosen, *Petticoat Surgeon* (Chicago: Pelligrini & Cudahy, 1947); Florence Ellinwood Allen, *To Do Justly* (Cleveland: Western Reserve University Press, 1965).

The biography of Florence Kelley by her friend Josephine Goldmark, *Impatient Crusader: Florence Kelley's Life Story* (Urbana: University of Illinois Press, 1953), helped to develop my interpretation of the 1920s. Not so useful was the poorly written biography by Mary E. Dreier, *Margaret Dreier Robins: Her Life, Letters, and Work* (New York: Island Press Cooperative, 1950). Mary Grey Peck wrote an admiring biography, *Carrie Chapman Catt: A Biography* (New York: H. W. Wilson, 1944), which described the beginnings of the NLWV as a "progressive-liberal organization."

Other Secondary Works

Surveys of twentieth-century reform and the political and social history of the 1920s include: John D. Hicks, *A Republican Ascendancy, 1921–1933* (New York: Harper & Row, 1960); Eric Goldman, *Rendezvous with Destiny: A History of Modern American Reform* (New York: Vintage Books, 1956); Robert W. Wiebe, *The Search for Order, 1877–1920* (New York: Hill & Wang, 1967); Robert K. Murray, *The Harding Era: Warren G. Harding and His Administration* (Minneapolis: University of Minnesota Press, 1969); William E. Leuchtenburg, *The Perils of Prosperity, 1914–1932* (Chicago: University of Chicago Press, 1958). The latter noted the persistent elements of progressivism in the 1920s. Other works which emphasize the continuity include: Arthur M. Schlesinger, Jr., *The Crisis of the Old Order, 1919–1933* (Boston: Houghton Mifflin, 1957); Frank Freidel, *Franklin D. Roosevelt: The Ordeal* (Boston: Little, Brown, 1954); Richard S. Kirkendall, "The Great Depression: Another Watershed in American History?," in

Change and Continuity in Twentieth-Century America, ed. John
Braeman, Robert H. Bremner, and Everett Walters (Columbus: Ohio
State University Press, 1964); Preston J. Hubbard, *Origins of the
TVA: The Muscle Shoals Controversy, 1920–1932* (Nashville: Vander-
bilt University Press, 1961); Howard Zinn, *LaGuardia in Congress*
(Ithaca: Cornell University Press for the American Historical Associa-
tion, 1959). Most important to me was Clarke Chambers, *Seedtime of
Reform: American Social Service and Social Action, 1918–1933* (Min-
neapolis: University of Minnesota Press, 1963). A study indicating that
the lines from progressivism to the New Deal have no necessity is Otis
L. Graham, Jr., *An Encore for Reform: The Old Progressives and the
New Deal* (New York: Oxford University Press, 1967). Richard Hofstadter, *The Age of Reform: From Bryan to FD.R.* (New York: Vintage Books, 1955), emphasizes the discontinuity.

For the history of the Woman Movement before 1920, and especially
the woman suffrage crusade, one should see Eleanor Flexner, *Century
of Struggle: The Woman's Rights Movement in the United States*
(Cambridge, Mass.: Belknap Press, 1959); Carrie Chapman Catt and
Nettie Rogers Shuler, *Woman Suffrage and Politics: The Inner Story of
the Suffrage Movement* (New York: Charles Scribner's Sons, 1923);
Maud Wood Park, *Front Door Lobby*, ed. Edna Lamprey Stantial
(Boston: Beacon Press, 1960). An excellent study in intellectual history
is Aileen Kraditor's *Ideas of the Woman Suffrage Movement, 1890–
1920* (New York: Columbia University Press, 1965). Broader in scope
than just suffrage are Andrew Sinclair's witty survey *The Better Half:
The Emancipation of the American Woman* (New York: Harper &
Row, 1965); Anne F. Scott's fine study, *The Southern Lady: From
Pedestal to Politics, 1830–1930* (Chicago: University of Chicago Press,
1970); and Page Smith's impressionistic, disjointed *Daughters of the
Promised Land: Women in American History* (Boston: Little, Brown,
1970). Lively, stimulating, well written, but marred by a socialist bias is
William O'Neill's *Everyone Was Brave*, which brought the story up to
1969. Other accounts of the Woman Movement include Robert Reigel,
American Feminists (Lawrence: University of Kansas Press, 1963), and
a poorly written catalog by Inez Haynes Irwin, *Angels and Amazons:
A Hundred Years of American Women* (Garden City: Doubleday,
1933). Extremely significant but encyclopedic was Sophonisba P.
Breckinridge's *Women in the Twentieth Century* (Recent Social Trends
Monograph, New York: McGraw-Hill, 1933). Histories of women's
rights written before 1920 tended to be polemical tracts; for example
Beatrice Forbes-Robertson Hale, *What Women Want: An Interpretation of the Feminist Movement* (New York: Frederick A. Stokes, 1914),
and Rheta Childe Dorr, *What Eight Million Women Want* (Boston:
Small, Maynard, 1910).

While the discussion of the efforts to win legislation for working
women depended principally on manuscripts and periodicals, certain
books aided with factual information and interpretative leads: Alice
Henry, *Women and the Labor Movement* (New York: Doran, 1923);

Edith Abbott, *Women in Industry* (New York: D. Appleton & Co., 1919); Gladys Boone, *The Women's Trade Union League in Great Britain and the United States of America* (Columbia University Studies in History, Economics and Public Law, no. 489, New York: Columbia University Press, 1942); Elizabeth F. Baker, *Protective Labor Legislation: With Special Reference to Women in the State of New York* (Columbia University Studies in History, Economics and Public Law, no. 116, New York: Columbia University Press, 1925); Mary Anderson, *Woman at Work*, and the bulletins of the Women's Bureau under her direction.

Additional works concerning professional women which I found suggestive included: Lorine Pruette, *Women and Leisure: A Study in Social Waste* (New York: Dutton, 1924); Samuel D. Schmalhausen and V. F. Calverton, eds., *Woman's Coming of Age: A Symposium* (New York: Horace Liveright, 1931); Ishbel Ross, *Ladies of the Press: The Story of Women in Journalism by an Insider* (New York: Harper & Brothers, 1936); Madeline B. Stern, *We the People: Career Firsts of Nineteenth Century America* (New York: Schulte, 1963); Alice C. Goff, *Women Can Be Engineers* (Youngstown, Ohio: privately published, 1946).

Index

AAUW. *See* American Association of University Women

Abbott, Edith, 28

Abbott, Grace: Children's Bureau, 74; women in politics, quoted, 110; passed over by Hoover, 110; rightist attacks, 218; mentioned, 157, 173

Acheson, Dean, 186, 240

ACL. *See* American Constitutional League

Adams, Annette, 73, 76

Addams, Jane: and peace, 4, 49; calls NLWV to social justice, 50-51; supports La Follette, 122; rightist attacks, 210, 213, 215, 218; DAR blacklist, 223; defends suffrage, 234; mentioned, 80, 117, 173, 192, 211

Allen, Florence E.: and peace, 4, 49; defeated for Senate, 104-105

Altrusa Clubs, 43, 212

AMA. *See* American Medical Association

American Association for Labor Legislation, 162-163

American Association of University Women (AAUW): supports Abbott for Secretary of Labor, 110; progressivism in 1920s, 124; opposes equal rights amendment, 190; rightist attacks, 209; mentioned, 118, 130, 135, 211, 216, 229

American Child Health Association, 165

American Constitutional League (ACL): origins, 12; platform, 12; fights Nineteenth Amendment, 14; opposes department of education, 129; mentioned, 219, 241

American Defense Society, 219

American Drugless Association, 161, 165

American Federation of Labor (AFL): supports investigation of working conditions, 26; opposes women's division, 27; scant effort to unionize women, 141; mentioned, 136, 138, 212, 242

American Legion, 129, 219

American Liberty League, 219

American Medical Association (AMA): favors recognition of women in Army Medical Corps, 19; progressivism, 42, 162; opposes Sheppard-Towner Act, 159-160, 162-167, 172-174, 210; attacks feminists, 209; mentioned, 43, 145

American Medical Liberty League, 158, 165

American Women's Hospitals, 9-10, 19

Anderson, Mary: U.S. Women's Bureau, 31, 74; women's economic rights, 31; "pin money" myth, 139-141; opposes equal rights amendment, 184-185, 191, 192; Conference on Women in Industry (1926), 192-194; effect of protective legislation, 194; rightist attacks, 213, 217, 218; DAR blacklist, 223; mentioned, 29, 138, 173, 216